W9-DDJ-819

Love Slaves

Table of Contents

Chapter One
The Well

On this hot midday afternoon, Kora looked out into the pasture she had looked on so many times before. As she looked, she observed Samuel, the field slave, hard at work on the area of the acre closest to the house. Kora looked up several times a day and observed Samuel hard at work. Now, she found herself glancing at Samuel more frequently than ever before.

Kora was the illegitimate daughter of Tom Johnson, a Delaware slave owner. Her father made her the house slave, despite his wife's silent disapproval, when Kora's African slave mother died of pneumonia. One of Kora's jobs was to provide the field slaves with water several times a day. Kora hated this chore because she had to pump buckets full of well water, then she had to carry the heavy pails to the musty workers. She also felt animosity toward her amongst the field hands.

Kora didn't look like the other slaves and it was obvious she was the master's bi-racial child. Kora lived in the Big House while the other field hands lived in slave quarter shacks built by the slaves that occupied them. Kora's life was not as harsh as a field slave's, yet she couldn't forget she was a slave. She was reminded of her eternal indentured servitude every day.

Kora also didn't talk like the other slaves. The field hands spoke broken English or, "slave talk." Kora spoke proper English. She hadn't always spoken properly. Her white half sister Anna taught Kora to speak proper English. Anna and Kora were the same age. Anna was the white child master Tom acknowledged. Anna and Kora played together every day after school. Anna and Kora were very close. Anna taught Kora reading, writing and arithmetic. Even as a child, Anna knew that if it was known she was educating Kora, the lessons could be deadly for Kora. Anna and Kora agreed to keep her privet tutoring lessons their secret. To keep her master from becoming suspicious, Kora spoke "slave talk" to him and proper English to Anna.

2

As Kora prepared her buckets of water, she glanced up and noticed Samuel hard at work. She studied his beautiful jet-black body as his sweat-covered figure moved in a smooth, efficient motion. Kora quickly caught herself in her daze and continued preparing the water.

Kora started carrying the field water when she was only ten years old. She has had the same task for the last six years. Three times a day, Kora had to carry two ten gallon buckets filled with water through the field. Kora toted the buckets on a piece of wood that was curved in the middle to fit over her back. She had to learn to walk and balance the water. Kora stopped at each slaves work acre and bent her knees in a squatting position. When she put her water down the workers would drink from the spoon in the bucket. When Kora first started this physically challenging task, she spilled several gallons of water. Master Tom, her father, beat her and told her if she could not complete her assignments she could not live in the Big House. Kora never dropped another ounce of water.

As Kora started on her daily journey, she found herself staring at Samuel again. While she approached him in her daydreaming state Samuel looked up and their eyes met. Kora put her buckets down and felt warm and aroused as Samuel drank his water. Each worker was allowed two spoonfuls of water. Samuel finished his water and Kora bent down, secured the buckets and straightened up to continue walking. No words passed between the two because Kora was not allowed to talk to the workers. As Kora walked in the direction of the other slaves, Samuel turned around and watched her.

Samuel was a plow slave. His job was to turn over the soil so it could be cultivated. Tom's farm was small. He only had ten slaves. All the slaves worked in the fields except Kora. Samuel plowed all over the field and often worked alone. Samuel came to the plantation six years ago. He was only twelve. He was separated from his family because their master could not afford to keep all his slaves and had to sell several to pay off his debts. A year ago, Samuel had married another field hand named Maggie.

3

Samuel was a tall, dark-skinned man. His work in the fields made him a magnificent specimen to look at. The sun turned his skin a smooth, chocolate brown. The sun also caused Samuel to sweat so much he had no body fat. As the sun reflected off Samuel's muscles it made him appear as if someone waxed and polished his entire physique.

Kora has quenched Samuel's thirst for six years. In all that time, he never said one word to her. He certainly never looked back and stared at the master's child. He knew that if he were caught looking at Kora in a lustful manner it could mean a painful punishment. Yet this time he could not resist his urge to turn around, observed Kora and admire her hourglass form. Once again, a slave's duties had created an admirable individual to look at. Years of squats gave Kora very strong defined legs and robust, firm hips. The weight of the water made her back very defined. Kora also had long brown curly hair that ended just above her waist.

When Samuel returned to his plow, he had a small exterior grin and a very large interior smile. Unlike Kora, who was younger and did not understand her new feelings, Samuel knew how he felt about her. He understood and accepted his forbidden attraction to her.

On Kora's third water trip, Samuel and Kora met one more time. Both expressed admiration for each other through body language. Unknown to Kora, Samuel caught her rotating her eyes up and down his massive physic. As Samuel lifted the spoon to his lips for his last drink of field water, he stared intensely into Kora's eyes. This caused Kora to blush and confirmed Samuel's suspicions of her lustful, admiring feelings.

The night came over the Wilmington farm and peacefulness took over. The workers relaxed after another dinner and a hard day's work on the countryside. The moon was full and a cool summer breeze was moving through the land. Kora made her last trip to the well for the evening. Her last duty for the night was to clean up the kitchen after she

4

prepared and served supper for Tom and his family. As Kora bent down and pumped the water into another bucket, she noticed a figure moving closer in the moonlight. She stopped pumping and stood up. As the object moved closer, the night revealed to her eyes that it was the man she had been dreaming about all day.

Chapter Two

A Virgin's Love

Samuel approached Kora and she looked up at him without saying a word. She did not need to. The two of them shared an unspoken infatuation that had grown over time. They had watched each other grow up and had developed a way of communicating through body language. Samuel stood directly in front of Kora. This was the first time Kora was face to chest with Samuel. Usually he would be on her left side consuming his water. Not this evening. This night Samuel's chest was about three inches from the object of his newfound fondness. Kora started to quiver and shake. Samuel gently put his hand on her arms to comfort her. Kora stopped shaking and looked into Samuel's eyes to silently let him know she wanted him just as much as he desired her. Samuel bent down and kissed Kora's lips, and then he moved lower and kissed her neck. He tightened his hold on Kora and licked her neck. This caused Kora to quietly let out a passionate moan. Samuel's hands moved from Kora's arms to her waist as he pulled her closer and held her tightly. Kora embraced her feeling of warmth and sexual excitement. She had never felt this way before. She also knew her feelings for Samuel were taboo and could have severe consequences. Yet this didn't stop Kora from wrapping her arms around Samuel's head and submitting to him.

The two of them held each other in their own world. Oblivious to everything around them, they vigorously explored each other's bodies. Samuel held Kora around her hips while he squatted down to lift Kora's body up and onto the top of the well wall. Kora was impressed by Samuel's strength. Once on the well wall, Samuel unbuttoned Kora's blouse. Kora's beautiful firm virgin breasts were exposed to another man for the first time. As Samuel massaged Kora's chest her legs opened and she leaned back, ready to accept him.

Samuel pulled the rope from around his waist and his pants fell to the ground. Kora became even more aroused as she looked at her lover under the night's moonlight. As he stood with his shirt open and pants down, Kora studied him for a moment because

6

she had never witnessed anything so beautiful. Samuel's muscular chest was enhanced by the nights radiance. Kora moved her eyes just below Samuel's chest and admired his firm abdominal muscles. Each muscle formed a firm cage around Samuel's lower torso. Kora continued to look down and she fixated her eyes on the son of an African slave's manhood. Kora's eyes widened when she observed Samuel's long thick slightly erect black penis. She had viewed the prints of slave's genitals under their trousers but she had never witnessed any man naked. Kora also never imagined Samuel's print reflecting a penis this large.

Samuel was an experienced lover. He knew he had to be gentle with Kora. He also knew he could not let her scream with pleasure or pain. With one hand on Kora's hip and the other on his erect penis he moved further inside of her thighs. Kora put her hands on Samuel's chest and for a moment she observed their skins contrasting for the first time. Kora loved the way her small tan hand looked against his big dark brawny chest. Samuel placing the tip of his erection against Kora's vaginal lips quickly interrupted her admiration.

Samuel proceeded inside Kora and she tensed up in pain. She opened her mouth and inhaled deeply as her lover moved further inside her. Samuel was exploring areas of Kora's body that had never been explored before. He sensed her pain and started to move in a gentle rotating motion. Kora felt herself getting moist from his movement. As her body secretions lubricated her vagina, Kora became less tense. Samuel continued to move in his slow steady clockwise motion. The two new lovers were enjoying each other very much. Kora and Samuel were both watching Samuel's insertion of his penis into Kora. They both watched Samuel's long hard black penis disappear under Kora's dark brown curly pubic hair. Then it reappeared and disappeared again. They watched this motion in sexual excitement. As they looked up at the same time, they kissed and their tongues moved around and around each other's mouths. Kora started to feel fulfilled in a way she had never felt before. She tightened up her grip on her man and continued kissing him fervently with her eyes closed. Kora's natural lubrication made the young lovers' first time together a very pleasant experience.

The more Samuel performed his slow-motion lovemaking stroke, the harder his penis became. Kora was feeling better and better to him. Samuel soon forgot he had a young virgin lover. He became selfish and slowly stopped his rotating movement and gradually started moving in a gyrating in and out motion. He started taking his penis out of Kora's vagina so the tip of it was on Kora's clitoris, then ramming his penis deeply into her again. He repeated this violent motion over and over. Kora did not like Samuel's vicious stroke. She tensed up in pain again. Samuel did not stop. Kora contained her echoes of pain and anger. With an outburst of strength, she pushed Samuel away from her and herself away from him. As soon as Kora pushed Samuel out of her she looked at Samuel and moved her open hand toward his face with force. SMACK! Went Kora's hand against Samuel's face.

She then said in an angry whisper, "Why are you trying to hurt me!?"

Samuel quietly replied, "I am sorry. I didn't mean to hurt you."

Kora started to get off the well wall. Samuel's penis was still erect and he wanted to finish what they had started. As Kora started to climb off the wall, Samuel moved closer to her, preventing her from climbing down.

He said, "Look Kora, I am sorry I got carried away. I promise you that will not happen again."

Kora repositioned herself back on the wall and looked Samuel in his eyes, giving him her silent approval to continue making love to her. Samuel moved closer with his hand on his penis.

As Samuel reentered Kora she gently said, "Baby, please go slow."

Samuel smiled and said, "I will baby, I will."

Kora was still extremely wet. Samuel's penis eased deeply into Kora again with no resistance. Samuel started his slow motion stroke again and the two kissed and enjoyed each other. Again, as Kora felt good to Samuel, he slowly increased his stroke, rancorously gyrating in and out of Kora. She wanted to beg for Samuel to stop, but just as she was about to, she started to enjoy Samuel's violent stroke. Samuel's throbbing hard penis was touching parts of her vaginal cavity that had never been touched before. This caused Kora to breathe heavily. With her mouth open, she tried her best to withhold her screams of passion as Samuel continued to use his sun-baked slave-built body to put every ounce of passion into every stroke. With each stroke Samuel seamed to go harder and harder, faster and faster, deeper and deeper. Kora could not contain herself. She started to scream and her lover anticipated her action by reading her body language. Samuel quickly moved his hand from Kora's thigh and covered her mouth. He tightened his grip just enough to muffle his lover without hurting her.

After Samuel had to silence his aficionada's cries of excitement, he changed their lovemaking position. Samuel put his hand behind Kora's head. Then he pulled her head into his chest and held it there tightly to continue to muffle her echoes of delight. He then put his other hand under her thigh and lifted it in the air. With one of Kora's calves against the well wall and her toes curled, the other was behind Samuel's arm and in the air. The pale bottom of this elevated foot was also arched and curled. Kora held Samuel firmly with both arms.

With Kora's leg elevated, Samuel was able to move even deeper into Kora's cavity to give her more pleasure then she was getting before, as if that was possible. Now Samuel's hand was not on Kora's mouth. She knew she could not scream, so she grabbed her lover tighter. Samuel's gyrating angle changed after Kora's leg went up. He was now moving against Kora's clitoris. With each stroke in her moist vagina, Samuel's erect penis was giving Kora the sensation of going deep inside her and stimulating her clitoris at the same time. Kora then began to feel like she was about to

9

explode. With Kora's pulse increasing, Samuel was feeling better and better with each gyration. He was starting to sweat against Kora's face. This turned her on even more.

Samuel was feeling the same. His penis was more erect then it was when he began. He was holding Kora tight and gyrating hard. His pulse was also high. Samuel felt himself about to release his juices inside Kora. He grabbed Kora's long brown curly hair and pulled it down so her head went back. As he released himself, he grunted and bit his lip to keep from screaming with pleasure. Kora released herself as Samuel pulled her hair. To maintain her sexual silence, Kora dug her nails into Samuel's back and pulled both hands in a downward motion until her high pulse orgasm was complete.

After their partnership in climatic experience, Samuel fell to the ground, taking Kora with him. He held her as he moved toward the grass beneath them placing Kora on top of him. The two of them lay there for a moment, then Kora slowly got up and started putting her clothes back together. Samuel watched her and he was still in awe from her beauty. Kora saw Samuel lying on the ground and gave him a look that made him get up and start putting his pants on. Kora started pumping her well water. Samuel wet his hands with Kora's water and wiped off his genitals. At this moment, Kora realized their current situation. Everyone in the Big House was asleep. Kora was always the last one asleep and first one awake. Their secret was safe with Kora, but Samuel was a different story. Samuel was married and his time away from his wife was unaccounted for. Also, Samuel now had to come up with a reason to explain the fresh deep scratches on his back. As Kora stood there wondering how her lover would explain all of this, Samuel pulled up his pants. He kissed her and disappeared into the night.

Chapter Three

Maggie

As Samuel walked back to his slave quarters, his mind was racing. What would he tell his wife Maggie? Samuel and Maggie had jumped the broom one year ago. Maggie was a field hand like Samuel. She was one year younger then Samuel and a good wife. Samuel always felt that their marriage had been arranged. Before they were married, the elders told Samuel, Maggie would make a good wife. No one knew for sure if the raping of Maggie as a child was the reason her and Samuel did not have any children yet. It had only been a year since they had intercourse for the first time. As Samuel thought about all this, there was one constant thought on his mind, Kora. Never before had he witnessed anyone so beautiful, tender and loving. Not only was Samuel thinking about what he would tell Maggie, he was also thinking about what he would do about his future with Maggie and Kora. Samuel felt like his mind was on fire. As all these contemplations went through his mind, he lost his place on the farm. Before he knew it, he was upon his front door.

Maggie was born on Tom's plantation. She was 5'3" tall, with thick jet-black kinky hair. Maggie also had full African lips and a nose with flaring nostrils. She was petite with small but firm breasts, a small waistline and large, firm hips and thighs. Her parents, Arthur and Yolanda, were field hands Tom had purchased as teenagers from a slave auction. Arthur and Yolanda had two children after they were married on Tom's farm. Their oldest son was named John. John was four years older than Maggie. Arthur constantly rebelled against Tom and the head slave master Charles. He was often whipped for giving Charles an "evil eye." Arthur was not a good worker. He did not like being a slave and his attitude showed his discontent.

Arthur shared his disgruntlement with his wife. Yolanda supported her husband. The two started talking to the other slaves about a revolt. The slaves on this small farm out numbered Tom and his family. Arthur and Yolanda saw no reason why he had to endure their inhumane life style. They made the mistake of trying to recruit any slave

11

that would listen to them. It was not long before one of the slaves informed Tom of Arthur and Yolanda's plot. Tom decided that he had had enough of Arthur and Yolanda and came to the conclusion they were more trouble than they were worth.

Tom sold Arthur and Yolanda to different plantations. He broke up Maggie's family. Maggie was only six. Her brother John was ten. Maggie and John were devastated by the removal of their parents from their life. Another slave family on the plantation took the two children in.

During the next two years John and Maggie worked hard on the farm. Arthur had included his son in his revolutionary ideas. Arthur planted a seed in his son that grew for two years before John decided he could not take being a slave and living without his father any longer. John was only fourteen when he ran away. He was gone only two days before Tom's hired slave catchers brought him home.

The day Maggie's brother was brought home in shackles would resonate in all of the field hands' minds for the rest of their lives. Tom had had enough with Arthur's family and decided to make an example out of young John. Charles and a few hired hands gathered all the African workers in front of an old oak tree. Kora was told to wait in the master's house. She did not witness the brutal beating that John was about to endure. Charles strung John up by his hands. His feet were two feet off the ground. Charles instructed all the slaves to look at John. He told them if they took their eyes off him they would be next.

Charles stood ten feet from John's strung-up body with his whip in his hand. John was determined not to cry. He had seen his father get whipped before and Arthur didn't cry. Charles perfected the slave master's art of implementing corporal punishment. He whipped Arthur and several other slaves several times. He had never whipped a child before, but he did not hesitate to follow Tom's orders. Charles straightened his right arm and positioned it behind his head and parallel to ground. With his right hand wrapped around the base of the whip, Charles stepped forward with his left leg. He shifted his weight from his right side to his left side as he stepped forward. He then moved his right arm forward with his left leg. As Charles bent his left knee, all his momentum moved forward and transferred into his whip. Charles's whip whistled as it cut through the air. When the end of the whip found John's back, the whistle ended and a loud cracking sound echoed through the crowd. The whip cut into John's back and tore away his flesh. John tried to hold in his pain but he could not contain himself. As his blood and flesh splattered from the whip's contact, John bellowed in agony. Charles dragged the whip back along the ground then behind his head until his arm was parallel with the ground again. He again stepped towards John's body.

Whhhhpt! went his whip. "Ahhhhhhw!" screamed the young boy!

Charles dragged his whip back and told everyone, "Keep yo' eyes on him! This is what happens to disobedient niggers!"

John turned his head to beg Charles for mercy.

He gasped for air and cried out, "Please masa Charles, I no run no mo. I be one good nigga! Please stop masa Charles! I be good!"

Charles did not listen to the boy's cries for mercy. With John begging, Charles dragged the cowhide behind himself and took another human tissue destroying step toward John. Charles's cowhide flogger screamed through the air and struck John on the side of his face. John's left eyeball was knocked out of its socket. John screamed in an even higher pitched voice. Charles smiled and repeated this horrific action. Charles beat little John until John was too weak to cry any more. As Charles exhausted himself, John moved less and less. Each blow from Charles's flay left a little less life in the young boy's body. After several more blows, John's body hung motionless from the oak tree. There was a pool of blood and flesh underneath John's corpse. Charles realized he had beaten John to death. He and the other hired hands prepared to leave the scene. Charles ordered John's body not be touched. John's torso was left hanging

13

from the tree for a week to remind everyone what happened to a slave that tried to escape.

After her brother's death, Maggie was left with the memories of her parents being unwillingly removed and the atrocious death of her only sibling. When she was ten years old, Charles decided Maggie would make a good virgin lover. Tom gave Charles permission to move Maggie into her own cabin so Charles could have his way with her whenever he wanted. For the next six years, Charles visited Maggie three or four times a week. Each night he called on Maggie he demanded that she cook for him and provide him with sexual pleasures.

After Samuel arrived on the plantation, the elder slaves convinced Tom Samuel and Maggie could bear strong healthy young children. Tom agreed and instructed Charles to leave Maggie alone and allow Samuel to marry her. Just as the elders anticipated, Samuel marrying Maggie saved her from being raped and abused for the rest of her life. Samuel knew Chares resented him for marrying Maggie. He was not afraid of Charles. He was smart enough to act like he was cerebrally deficient. Also, Samuel was not on the farm when John was killed. He had not been placed in a mental prison with the other slaves.

Samuel gathered his thoughts and opened the door. He walked in and saw his wife in the kitchen washing dishes. Samuel also noticed his plate of food on the dinner table.

His wife turned to him and said, "We need water."

Samuel didn't have to go back to the well to get the water. The co-slaves kept the local fount full through the day. Samuel grabbed a bucket and went to the local watering hole. Everyone was in for the night. Samuel was alone has he filled his bucket. He went back inside his shack and poured the water in their kitchen tube. He sat down to eat his cold dinner, waiting for his wife to question him. The questions never came. Samuel ate his dinner and put his plate in the basin for his wife to wash. Usually,

14

Samuel and Maggie would relax, talk and make love during this time before going to sleep.

Samuel got in the bed first. He was on his back with his shirt off when Maggie came to bed. He lay in the bed with his massive arm up and his hand under his head. Samuel never slept with a shirt on because he only had two shirts. He knew that if he put a shirt on it would look suspicious. Maggie climbed into the bed with nothing but a shirt on.

As she put her head on her man's chest she asked him, "Tired baby?"

He replied, "Yeah."

Maggie started to rub her man's torso. Samuel held her hand to make her stop. She just looked at him then rolled over and fell asleep.

The roosters always awakened the slaves in the morning. Maggie got up first. She bathed then started breakfast. Samuel stayed in bed until he smelled breakfast. Once Maggie's cooking reached his nose, Samuel put on his ragged trousers and torn shirt. He sat at the table with Maggie wondering if she had seen his scratches.

Maggie fixed Samuel's plate then sat down to eat with her husband.

Samuel ate and said with his mouth full, "These some good eggs woman. You sure make some good breakfast."

Maggie smiled and said, "Thank ya."

Then she changed the subject by saying, "You know I had to give Mandy some o' my pick'ns again yesterday. I don't know what wrong wit dat girl. She just pick so damn slow. She always come up low. We get'n tired of help'n her."

15

Samuel looked up and said, "Come on na, none of that talk. Y'all know Charles will beat her again if she low. Y'all just go have to work with her."

Maggie replied, "Yea, you right. I swear, every time Charles beats one a us we aw feels it." Maggie then smiled and said, "I just don't think dat girl was meant to be in no tobacco fields."

Samuel looked at his wife and said, "Non of us was meant to be in dem damn fields!"

Maggie looked surprised and said to her husband, "What you say? Don't let masa here you talk like that. What wrong with you? You know better."

Samuel just looked at his wife as she washed the dishes. He approached her from behind, put his arms around his wife, then hugged and kissed her. He walked out the door and headed toward his plow. The sun was up and in his face. It felt good on his black body. Samuel waved at other slaves while he continued toward his workstation.

In the summer months Samuel was a plow slave, the most physically challenging job on the farm. His job was to push the plow and turn over the dirt so the tobacco could be planted. Everyday, Samuel got behind this massive object. The plow had two sharp blades that were curved and in the ground. The blades were attached to several pieces of wood that formed a crate. The crate had two handles that Samuel stood between. Samuel had to push up on the handles with his legs. This caused a downward pressure on the crate, thus pushing the curved blades further in the ground. Samuel then had to push forward with his legs and back. The forward motion caused the blades to go into the ground and move forward. As the crate moved forward, it turned over the soil in its path. Samuel also used his arms to steer the plow. As Samuel started his daily duty, he pushed with his legs and the plow uncovered the earth in its trail. Samuel could not wait for his first water break.

Maggie finished the breakfast dishes and headed to the tobacco fields. She approached Charles, the overseer, to get her tobacco-picking bag. Maggie put the bag over her left shoulder and it hung off her right side. She then walked to the middle of the pasture and started picking tobacco.

The slaves were not allowed to converse with each other while they worked. However, soon after they started picking, one of the women would start singing soulful melodies that put the colored folk on a rhythmic pace.

> *Sum body call'n my name*
> *hum humm hum,*
> *Sumbody call'n my name*
> *Hum humm hum,*
> *Oh could it be?*
> *Hum humm hum*
> *"Maybe it's my Jesus call'n out for me.*

It was Negro spirituals like this that set the work pace for the tobacco pickers. It also made the day go by faster. Maggie had the best voice on the farm. As Maggie sang, Charles the overseer sat on his horse and watched the field hands work.

Charles was a short unattractive white man with a nasty disposition. He planted himself upon his horse every day and never came down. He carried a whip and a gun. All the slaves were either victims of or witnesses to his lashings.

Maggie was forced to work with her six-year molester and manipulator. Maggie was terrified of Charles. Maggie knew Samuel protected her. She felt safe with him and loved him dearly. She was concerned about her marriage. Lately she was feeling distant from her husband. About a month ago, Maggie and Samuel were lying in bed together. Samuel shocked Maggie by telling her he was thinking about running away.

17

Maggie thought about John and told him not to talk like that. Now, when she reflected, she could pinpoint that moment as the start of their mental separation.

Now Maggie had another problem. She saw the scratches on her man's back when Samuel rolled over in his sleep. Samuel's back had several whip lashing scars from Charles beating him. The scars looked like snakes on Samuel's back. They were long and twisted and turned from his shoulder down to his buttocks. Kora's scratches were not nearly as deep and did not inflict nearly as much pain. Samuel had four scratches from Kora on each shoulder. Kora's scratches were fresh and still bleeding when Maggie noticed them. They covered Samuel's older back lashings from the short white overseer with the Napoleon complex. Maggie also smelled the scent of another woman on her man. She didn't know what to do. She was only seventeen. She had never had this problem before. Maggie had no one to talk to about the problems in her marriage.

At first it seemed like Samuel and Maggie were a good couple. Samuel was a good protector and Maggie needed protecting. However, Samuel was physically and mentally strong. Maggie was not. Samuel would act like his cerebral capacity was lower then Charles and any other white man he came across. Samuel wanted to go home and have a companion he could confide in. He was disturbed about the fact that he could not share his true feelings and dreams with Maggie. Samuel knew if and when he decided to leave the plantation, Maggie would not leave with him. He wondered if Kora would leave with him. Samuel decided to share his dreams of freedom with the master's child.

Chapter Four
The Plot

The next day, as the sun approached its highest point in the sky, Samuel knew it was time for his first water break. He looked out to the middle of the field and saw a narrow but firm figure carrying two buckets of water over her shoulders. He had never envisioned Kora like this before. Kora had carried those buckets for years and mastered the art of serving water to ten slaves three times a day. For the first time, Samuel noticed her form. The plywood across Kora's neck never tilted to the left or to the right. Neither pail dipped up or down. Samuel saw a graceful T moving toward him. He became excited as his newfound love stood next to him and squatted. Kora had served Samuel water before but this time was different. This time Samuel wanted desperately to tell Kora he loved her. He struggled to get his water without saying anything to Kora. Samuel drank his water and gazed into Kora's eyes while he drank. Kora smiled back at him. Samuel's spoon hand was shaking when he took his second drink. He spilled half of the water in the spoon. When Samuel finished drinking Kora squatted, secured the buckets, stood up and walked away. Samuel looked straight ahead daydreaming about himself and Kora. Unfortunately, Charles noticed Samuel standing in the middle of the field. Charles came toward Samuel on his horse with his whip drawn.

He yelled at Samuel, "Hey boy, stop daydreaming and get back to work!"

Whispt went his whip. The whip tore Samuel's shirt and cut into his back. Samuel had received lashings from that whip several times before. No matter how many times Samuel was lashed with that long piece of cowhide, he never got used to the pain. What made Samuel even angrier was the fact that he knew he could kill Charles. Here was this little man inflicting pain on him. He knew he could overtake Charles any time he wanted to. He had to control his feelings and make Charles feel superior. When Samuel felt the whip rip into his back, he quickly became alert again.

19

In his state of cerebral inferiority, Samuel bellowed out, "Iza sorry masa Charles! I don't know what came over me!"

Samuel quickly got under the plow and started pushing. He felt the blood dripping down his back. He pushed his anger down to his legs while he pushed the plow. This was Samuel's outlet. This was how he dealt with the unjust microcosm that he lived in. The irony was that the pressures of his world made him a better worker.

As the sun set, Samuel headed home for the evening. He and Maggie arrived together at their cabin. They were tired and happy to see each other. They entered their home to relax, unwind and prepare dinner. Once inside, Samuel lay down while Maggie started dinner.

Samuel asked his wife about Mandy, the slow tobacco picking worker, "How did Mandy do today?"

Maggie replied, "OK, Rachel help ha today."

Samuel asked, "Why didn't you help ha?"

Maggie responded in a higher pitched voice, "I did not want to come up showt."

Samuel looked at his wife and said, "You never showt. You the best tobacco picker on the farm. Why didn't you help ha? You know what happens if she come up showt. Why didn't you help ha?"

Maggie began to get angry. The thoughts of her husband with another woman combined with her husband questioning her infuriated Maggie.

Maggie loudly said, "I said I didn't wont to come up showt!"

Samuel just looked at his wife. He knew she was frustrated and not to bother her. He lay back and waited for dinner to be prepared. The two didn't talk as they ate. After dinner, Samuel headed for the door.

Maggie asked Samuel, "Where you go'n?"

Samuel replied, "To talk to Harold."

Harold was Samuel's best friend. The two of them often sat under their favorite tree and talked about their lives on the farm. They dreamed of being free. They often discussed running away when the time was right. Samuel liked talking to Harold. This was the only time Samuel could express himself freely. He wished he could talk to his wife like he talked to Harold. As Samuel greeted his friend, he noticed that he seemed anxious.

He looked at Harold and said, "What you so happy 'bout, Harold?"

Harold smiled and said, "I got the word."

Samuel hoped it was the word he thought it was, but didn't want to guess, so he asked, "What word?"

"The word" Harold said again smiling.

Harold paused and looked at his friend. He noticed Samuel was not smiling and seemed to be getting a little upset. Harold wisely realized he should stop teasing his friend and confirm Samuel's thoughts.

With content in his voice Harold said, "She coming, Sam. She coming."

Samuel looked at his companion with a firm, serious stare and said, "Harold stop given me half a story and say what you mean!"

Harold composed himself, took a deep breath and said to his comrade, "Harriet Tubman is come'n Sam, she come'n!"

Samuel and Harold had heard rumors about a woman with a gun and a nasty disposition going from farm to farm and leading slaves to freedom. Up until now, Samuel thought these were just rumors. He wished they were true but he didn't get his hopes up. Harold had been on his master's brother's farm for the past week. He was helping out until Tom's brother Michael returned from a Virginia slave auction with another worker or two. When Michael returned, he was in a wagon with an older slave named Eli. Eli and Michael had two slaves shackled to the wagon with them. Michael's farm was about ten miles from Tom's. Michael didn't feel like taking Harold back to Tom that evening. He was tired from their long ride. Harold was happy to stay overnight on Michael's plantation because he liked Eli. Harold often went to Michael's farm to help out or to take Tom to see his brother. He got to know Eli and the other workers on Michael's land. Harold had not had a chance to spend any time with Eli on this visit because Eli was in Virginia. Since Harold spent one more evening on Michael's farm, he had a chance to talk to Eli. Now, the next evening on his own farm, Harold met with his friend, waiting to give him the news.

Samuel expressed his doubt and asked Harold, "How you know she come'n?"

"Old man Eli told me," replied Harold.

Unlike Harold, Samuel never left Tom's farm. Harold was smaller and less threatening then Samuel. Harold could shuck and jive better than Samuel. Both Charles and Tom thought Harold was a good slave. One that knew his place. They gave Harold the less physical jobs when available. A few years ago, before he learned how to act in a non-threatening manor, Samuel was caught giving Charles a hard look. A look that

22

displayed his true feelings. A look that got Samuel beat with the whip. Samuel quickly learned how to be large and not be intimidating. Samuel did get to know Eli when Eli brought Michael to see Tom. He liked and respected Eli. The old man had a kind gentle demeanor and was very wise. Samuel knew you didn't grow to be old as a slave unless you were smart enough to play dumb or just stupid. Samuel knew Eli was not stupid.

When Harold said Eli told him Harriet Tubman was coming, Samuel began to smile. He knew it was true if Eli said it.

He grabbed Harold and asked, "Did that old man say when she come'n?"

Harold said, "Nope, but it be soon. He said we would hear a drum. He said we should start beat'n a drum every night so when we hear Harriet's drum it will sound normal to white folks. We will know we ain't beat n the drum and we will meet at this tree."

Samuel said smiling, "I'll talk to Robert. I think he got a drum."

The two men set their schedule to take turns beating the drum at night. Samuel returned home to his troubled marriage. Maggie and Samuel didn't talk much. They just went about their everyday routine as if each other were invisible.

Samuel was not spending time with Maggie. When he was not beating the drum, Harold was providing love making music for his friend as he made love to Kora under the moonlight in the grass next to the water well. Samuel and Kora were getting very close. Their late night encounters allowed the two young lovers to not only satisfy each other sexually, for the first time they talked to each other. They had established a means of communicating with body language. They corresponded like this for years. It felt good to hear each others thought for the first time in six years.

23

Samuel and Harold thought they had a very good plot to be prepared for Harriet's arrival. Harold and Samuel agreed to alternate beating the drum every two days one week and every other day the next week. If a slave from the Underground Railroad came while one of the two men were playing the drum, they agreed to get the other one and leave the farm with their families immediately. Harold had no family. Harold always assumed Samuel would bring Maggie.

One evening Samuel said to Harold, "Harold, if Harriet comes you can find me at the well."

Harold asked Samuel, "Why are you at the well at night instead of wit' yo' wife?"

Samuel replied, "I just need some time to myself. I like to lay in the grass and look at the stars and dream of being free."

Harold didn't question his friend. After a few weeks, the two men met under the tree one evening. The same tree they always congregated under. The same tree they played the drum under. They agreed to meet once a week to discuss any rumors they may have heard. This night Samuel confided in his friend.

As the two men stood under the tree they greeted each other and Samuel asked, "Heard anything, Harold?"

Harold replied, "Nope, you?"

"No, but I need to tell you something," Samuel said as he stood about two feet from his comrade.

Harold anxiously asked, "What?"

Samuel looked his friend straight in the eyes and said without hesitation, "I ain't take'n Maggie with us. I'm take'n Kora."

Harold looked in shock. The two of them agreed not to tell anyone about the anticipated gathering with Harriet and the railroad. They did not know whom to trust. Harold certainly didn't trust a house slave.

In anger Harold asked, "Why in hell you take'n that high yellow house bitch? Nigga, is you crazy?"

Samuel was a little surprised by Harold's reaction. He expected Harold to be upset and was prepared for his response. What he was not prepared for was the way Harold spoke to him. Harold was always a mild mannered man with a good disposition. He was very easygoing and everyone liked Harold. Samuel had never heard Harold speak to anyone like this.

Calmly Samuel said, "Harold, don't call her a bitch again. I love Kora. She ain't no threat. If I thought she would sell us out I wouldn't even tink about bring'n her."

Harold was still amazed and he asked, "So you ain't told ha yet?"

"Not yet. I'm gona tell ha tonight," Samuel replied.

Harold still had several questions.

Curiously he asked, "Dat where you been when I'm play'n?"

Samuel replied, "Yep, I been meet'n ha at the well. I'm on my way over dare now."

Harold trusted his friend. He knew Samuel would not jeopardize their escape under any circumstances. Harold watched as Samuel faded off the hill into the night.

As Samuel approached the well, he saw Kora pumping her water. She noticed her man and stopped pumping and threw her hands around him.

"Hey baby!" Kora expressed in joy.

Samuel smiled and said, "Hey woman. How you be?"

"I'm fine." Kora replied as she kissed her man. Samuel broke off the kiss and looked at Kora. She was surprised. Kora and Samuel always made love at the well. They didn't waste a lot of time. As soon as Samuel showed up, they would be in the grass, or Kora would be on the well wall with Samuel between her legs.

Samuel said to Kora, "I need ta talk ta ya."

Kora knew this was serious.

"What is it Samuel?" she asked.

Samuel took Kora's hand and proceeded toward the well. He sat in the grass with his back against the well. He looked up at Kora and took both her hands to invite her to sit with him between his legs. Kora accepted his invitation.

As she sat with her back against his chest and his arms around her she again asked, "What is it baby?"

Without wavering Samuel said, "I'm leave'n."

He got quiet to see how Kora would react.

She turned to look at him and asked, "When we leaving Samuel?"

Samuel was quiet for a moment then replied, "Soon Kora. Real soon."

Kora then turned 180 degrees, wrapped her legs around her man and kissed him passionately. Soon after their encounter, Samuel was home with Maggie. Maggie was becoming more and more bitter. She knew Samuel was seeing another woman. She never confronted him about it. Samuel stopped making love to Maggie. As Samuel and Kora grew closer, Samuel and Maggie grew further and further apart.

When Samuel came home, Maggie asked, "Where you been?"

"With Harold," Samuel replied.

Maggie was very upset with her husband. He claimed he was with Harold every night.

"You been spending a lot of time with Harold. How come you ain't been home?" Maggie asked.

Samuel was surprised. Maggie never questioned him.

"I just didn't want to come home. I can talk to Harold. I don't think I can talk to you," Samuel said.

Maggie was confronting her husband like she never had before. She was tired of being alone at night while her man was out spending time with another woman.

"What you talk to Harold 'bout, be'n free? You gon' mess around and get you and Harold killed," Maggie said.

Samuel didn't feel like arguing with his wife. He was trying to just keep peace in his home.

"We don't talk 'bout be'n free. We just talk," Samuel said.

Maggie just looked at Samuel as he lay down on the bed and didn't say another word. Maggie was also tired of arguing. She decided to go to bed herself without talking.

In the morning, the two woke up and moved through their morning rituals without speaking to each other. Maggie still cooked for Samuel. The two didn't talk as they ate their breakfast.

As Samuel left for his plow Maggie asked, "You coming home tonight?"

"Yes," Samuel replied.

Samuel decided he would spend one night at home with Maggie to try to keep her happy. Over the next few weeks, things didn't change much. Samuel and Maggie still were not communicating. Every night Samuel was either with Kora, beating the drum, with Maggie or talking to Harold.

One evening, Samuel was having another encounter with Kora. It was a quarter moon with few stars in the sky. As Kora looked up at the black sky with the occasional starlit sparkle, she felt her back moving back and forth against the cool long green Delaware grass. Her man was pulsating on top of her in his nice steady motion that she loved. She loved his motion and she loved her man. While the two of them were enjoying each other's bodies, they heard the familiar sound of a beating drum. Samuel immediately stopped enjoying being inside his new lover. He withdrew from her and sat up on his knees.

He looked down at Kora and said, "It's time."

Kora was surprised when her man stopped sexually satisfying her and she was more surprised when he said, "It's time." *How did he know it was time* she thought? Kora didn't say a word. She just gathered herself together and quickly dressed herself again.

Samuel pulled his pants up and said, "Harold ain't beat'n that drum. It a different beat."

The two of them moved up the countryside towards the large old tree Harold and Samuel had gathered under so many times.

When they arrived, they saw Harold standing under the tree with another man.

When they got close Harold said, "This it man, you ready?"

Samuel replied, "I been ready for dis all my life."

Samuel studied the other man. He was short but muscular. His arms were almost as big as Samuel's. He was dark, very dark. He was dressed in field hand clothes like Harold and Samuel wore. Samuel looked the stranger straight in his eyes and extended his hand.

He simply said, "Samuel."

The stranger shook Samuel's hand and replied, "Leonard."

He looked at Kora and asked, "Why y'all bring the house nigga?"

Samuel kept his calm appearance and said, "She alright. She wit me. Dis Kora."

"Kora huh, she ain't gon' like this at all. Harold, you told ol' man Eli it was three ah you. You never said nut'n 'bout one of you being the house bitch!" Leonard expressed.

29

Before Harold could say anything, Samuel interrupted the two men and firmly stated, "Her name is Kora. It ain't Harold's fault, he didn't know 'til a lil' while ago I was bring'n Kora."

Leonard told Samuel, "You have to explain dis to Harriet. Let's go"

Leonard led the way as the four of them headed into the woods and disappeared in the trees. The farm the three lived on didn't have any fences they could not climb. There were no chains or shackles keeping them on the farm. None of the farms had anything enclosing their slaves. Any slave could walk off any time they wanted. The image of little John was still fresh in all the workers' minds. Inhumane acts like the killing of little John terrified all workers of African descent and placed them in a mental prison.

No one talked as the four field hands continued their escape deep into the woods. They moved quickly in a single file line. Samuel held Kora's hand to make sure he did not lose her. To his surprise, she had no problem keeping up. After moving swiftly for about fifteen minutes, Leonard stopped his fleeing train and made a low then high pitched whistle. He did this a few times. When he stopped, there was silence for a moment, then they could hear the sounds of other people moving in front of the foursome. Samuel saw two shadows come from behind the trees.

One figure said, "That you Leonard?"

"Yeah, it me," Leonard replied.

Chapter Five
Harriet

After Leonard responded, the tension was a little lighter. Samuel, Kora and Harold were now escaped fugitives. The three former properties of Tom Johnson anxiously awaited their introduction to the modern Moses, Harriet Tubman. Kora saw several shadows come from behind the trees and shrubbery in front of them. Kora counted five other bodies. The three of them and Leonard made a total party of nine. Kora stood there wondering how all these runaways would make it to freedom. Where would they go?

As these thoughts ran through her mind, a firm and aggressive female voice said,

"Who brought da mulatto house gal?"

Samuel replied, "She wit me. Dis Kora."

The voice they were hearing was the voice of the savior they were waiting for. It was Harriet in the flesh.

Harriet looked at Samuel and asked him, "Who told you you could violate da code and tell da house gal?"

Samuel studied Harriet for a moment, she was about 5'5", 130 pounds. She had black and gray hair in two French braids. She was wearing a long black skirt with a gray cotton shirt and she had black boots on. Harriet was also holding a black bag about one foot long and six inches wide with a rope hanging from it. For the first time in his life Samuel, felt intimidated. He dared not let it show.

He looked Harriet straight in the eye like he always did and said, "We can trust her. After all she wit us ain't she? I mean, she escape'n too, right?"

Harriet paused for a moment. Then she pulled the material on the left side of her garment back and revealed her pistol. Harriet looked at the three newbies.

She said, "From here 'til freedom, y'all's with me. Dare's no turn'n back. No quit'n. All y'all do as I say. I been done this befo' and I knows how to get us all to freedom. I got two rules, do as I say and no talk'n."

Samuel was relieved to know that Kora was accepted. He was also concerned and curious. It was late fall now and snow would be coming soon. They needed shelter, shoes, winter clothes and food. As these thoughts went around in Samuel's head, he was confident that Harriet would provide, protect and lead them to freedom.

Harriet Tubman did not invent the Underground Railroad, but she was its best ambassador. The Underground Railroad consisted of Quakers and abolitionists that provided safe houses from Georgia all the way to Canada. Harriet had the most dangerous job on the Railroad. Harriet went into the south once or twice a year and led slaves to Canada by hiding them in the safe houses. This took a lot of courage. Harriet had been a slave herself in Delaware. She had to be very brave to return to the inhumane environment a few times a year to lead people she didn't even know to freedom.

Harriet did not start out leading strangers. She escaped slavery herself and returned for her niece Kissy in 1850. Kissy and Kissy's husband accompanied Harriet on her first few trips for freedom. On Harriet's second voyage into the south, she helped Kissy's children escape. Other slaves heard about Harriet and wanted to come along. Harriet never refused anyone. She never let anyone turn back. It is estimated that between 1850 and 1860 Harriet helped nearly 300 slaves to freedom.

Harriet only moved her crowd at night. This is why she made most her tours of freedom in the fall. The nights were longer and it wasn't as cold as it would get in winter. It would usually take Harriet about one month to get her multitude of southern African Americans to Canada. That evening after her introduction, Harriet guided her group to the home of an abolitionist named Thomas Garrett. Thomas owned a safe house in Wilmington, Delaware.

Thomas Garrett was happy to see Harriet. He welcomed her and her nighttime traveling companions. He gave them supplies, sandwiches, water, boots and a change of clothes. They eight light because they had to move fast. They took just enough to get them to the next safe house.

As soon as Harriet passed out the supplies everyone was ready to leave Delaware. Harriet didn't like being south of the Mason Dixon line and the ex slaves didn't like it either. Harriet intentionally gave Samuel his supplies last.

After she gave Samuel his late night snack, she handed him another bag and said, "Hurry up and eat yo food. Drink all yo water, you gone need it. Then tie this bag 'round yo' waist. Put the bag over yo' butt and make sure you ties it tight."

Without any questions Samuel quickly consumed the sandwich and drank the water. Then he tied the bag around his waist as Harriet instructed. Harriet lined up her escaping class of Negroes single file with Samuel at the rear. Kora was in front of him. Harriet returned to the back and pulled out a dinner fork Tom Garrett had given her. When Samuel saw the fork he turned around to face Harriet.

She said to him, "Calm down big boy. I ain't gon' hurt you. I just needs to slow down da dogs." Samuel trusted Harriet. Harriet put her arm on his shoulder and guided Samuel forward in the direction of the other escapees. She then moved her hand off Samuel and put it on the bag resting on Samuel's butt. Harriet took her other hand with the fork in it and stabbed the bag three times, putting nine small holes in the bag. Pepper started seeping through the holes immediately. Harriet looked at Samuel and pushed him to his left until he was in the position she wanted him in.

She then said, "I needs you to move from side to side while we runs. Run to one side until you sees in front of me."

Then she pulled him back to his right until he was in the position she wanted him in again and said, "Then runs to yo' other side 'til you can sees in front of me. If you see or hear any dogs holla to me up front. Can you handles that?"

Samuel quickly replied, "Yes ma'am."

Harriet then walked to the front of the line and said, "We will follow the North Star to Canada."

After years of dreaming about being free, the eternal indentured servants were dreaming no more. They were finally on their freedom run. Harriet led the way and everyone traveled in a single file line. While they retreated further and further away from their plantations, the bag of pepper over Samuel's butt covered their tracks with his zigzag motion. Samuel now understood why Harriet put him in the rear and gave him the bag. He was the strongest. If they had an encounter with slave catchers it was most likely going to come from behind. Samuel also realized that the person in the back needed more energy to keep up with the group and move from side to side. Kora was in front of Samuel and had no problem staying in front of him. The years of physical labor made all the freedom seekers mentally and physically strong. Strong enough to push their bodies when fatigue set in.

The group now had shoes and food in their stomachs to give them the energy they needed to make it to the Pennsylvania state line by dawn. For the next six hours, the wood runners didn't stop moving toward the North Star. Just as the sun started to come up, Harriet's group came upon a river. The other side of the river was Pennsylvania. The current was swift and the group hesitated. Harriet demanded they cross the river because it was now day break and she knew slave catchers would be coming after them with dogs and horses soon. Harriet had crossed this river several times, but she did not want to leave the posse for fear that they would turn back.

She ordered them, "Y'alls get across, I'm right behind ya. I done it befo', it ain't that deep, now gets!"

No one moved. Just as Harriet considered going herself to show everyone the river could be crossed safely, Kora walked in front of the crowd and headed for the water. Samuel wanted to stop her but he trusted Harriet and he let the woman he loved so deeply go forward. As Kora waded into the water she realized how cold it was. It was late fall and the early winter breezes chilled the water Kora moved through. Kora did not stop. She moved further into the river until the water was at her waist. She held her sack of supplies above her head so that they didn't get wet. Kora could not swim, as could none of the other slaves. This is the reason they were so afraid to cross. As Kora reached the other side, Harriet instructed her not to go on shore but to wade downstream. After everyone watched Kora cross the river, the rest of the group didn't hesitate to follow her. Samuel and Harriet took up the rear.

As they crossed, Harriet told Samuel, "Dat's one strong, brave woman you got dare."

Samuel just glanced at Harriet and smiled. He was so proud of his baby that he could hardly contain himself. The former laborers were just a few feet away from free land for the first time in their lives. Harriet also instructed them not to step foot on the land they had desperately desired for their entire lives. She told them to follow Kora upstream. Harriet let Kora lead her group in the water for nearly five hundred yards. Once Harriet thought they were far enough away from their Delaware trail, she instructed Kora to go onshore and the others followed. Once on free land for the first time in their lives, the former slaves were in a state of euphoria. They stretched and all smiled and looked up towards the risen sun. Harriet let them gathered themselves together on the shore for a moment, then led them into the forest because they were in the open and the sun was now up. They went into the forest and changed out of their wet clothes. They threw their drenched attire into the trees to keep them out of the hounds' scent. Harriet continued north to the next safe house. Everyone including Harriet had just run twenty miles in six hours. All of them were tired. The field hands pushed through their physical state of exhaustion and continued to the next safe house.

The group's next stop was in Marcus Hook, Pennsylvania. Now on free land, Harriet moved with her excited freedom seekers during the day through the woods nonstop until they made it to Marcus Hook. Quincy Manley was a farm owner in Marcus Hook. He was also an abolitionist and safe house provider for the Underground Railroad.

Harriet guided her congregation to Quincy's farm. Once there the newly freed slaves were allowed to rest. Everyone settled in the barn and was given blankets, food and water. The continuous fast pace they were on had caught up with them. All the marathon runners, including Harriet, were experiencing cramps, aches and pain as fatigue set in. Some vomited and couldn't eat. Others lay on the ground in pain as their legs locked up with cramps. Harriet and Quincy knew what to do. Quincy had tea ready for the exhausted ex-slaves along with all his other prepared recuperating supplies. As the tea, water, food and rest set in, everyone started feeling better. They didn't talk much, but you could sense the overwhelming joyful mood that the group was in. As the moon rose again, they didn't have to get up and run this time. They all fell asleep under the moonlight for the first time as freed humans.

Chapter Six
The Day After

Back on Tom's plantation, Charles realized that Samuel and Harold were missing. He immediately went looking for Maggie, to question her on the whereabouts of her husband and his friend.

Charles found Maggie in the apple orchard and asked her, "Where is Samuel?"

Maggie replied, "Don't know. He didn't come home last night."

Without hesitation, Charles slapped Maggie and knocked her to her knees. He then pulled out his whip and proceeded to flog Maggie.

As he whipped her in front of all the other workers, he said, "You lying black bitch! I'm gon' beat the truth out of you! Now where are they?!"

Maggie was still on her knees with Charles towering over her on his horse. She tried to protect herself by placing her arms in between Charles's vicious lashings and herself. Charles's whip tore through Maggie's sleeves and ripped into the flesh on her arms and torso.

Maggie screamed in pain and said, "Please Masa Charles, I don't know where they went! Samuel didn't tell me nuth'n!"

After five or six lashings, Charles realized that Maggie was telling the truth. He also realized that, with Samuel gone, Maggie was all his again. He went to the big house to give Tom the bad news with a smirk on his face. When he walked into the house, he was surprised that Kora did not great him. No one greeted him.

Charles took a few steps inside the mansion and loudly said, "Hello, Tom, you here?"

Tom came downstairs quickly. He had a look of concern on his face.

He said to Charles, "Kora is missing."

Charles said, "I think Samuel and Harold took her."

Tom asked, "They're gone too?"

Charles replied, "Yes."

Tom then asked, "Did you talk to Samuel's wife, Maggie?"

Charles said, "I just finished trying to beat it out of ha. She don't know nuth'n."

Tom replied, "Charles, I must say I am disappointed in you. I hired you to control my Negroes and now three of them are missing."

Charles said, "You don't need to be disappointed in me. I'll get them niggers and Kora back. They will pay for run'n, and they better not hurt Kora!"

Tom quickly said, "Yes, yes man. Well, don't just stand there talking about it, start looking for them!"

Charles said, "I'm going to need to get together some slave catchers and hounds."

Tom replied, "There are only three of them. You only need to hire two slave catchers with hounds."

Charles agreed and left the house to find two of his friends to help him hunt down Samuel, Harold and Kora. Charles found his two friends in the local saloon. They gathered their hounds, mounted their horses and went back to Tom Johnson's plantation. It didn't take long for the dogs to pick up the runaways' scent. The hounds led the three men on horseback into the woods in the direction of Thomas Garrett's farm. As they approached the Garrett farm, they came across another posse of slave catchers. The other group outnumbered Charles and his friends three to one.

The groups met and Charles asked, "Y'all look'n for runaway niggers too?"

Someone from the larger posse replied, "Yes, and I think they went to that there farm."

The man pointed his rifle toward the Garrett farm. All the men and hounds rode off in a hurry toward the farm. With the dogs barking and horses hooves rumbling in the ground the men arrived on Tom Garrett's front porch. Tom was expecting them. He and Harriet had anticipated being pursued by slave catchers.

Tom walked out onto his porch unarmed and said to the posse, "Y'all to late, they gone."

One man dismounted from his horse and asked, "We looking for a bunch of running niggers. You seen them?"

Tom said, "I just told you, they gone."

With his rifle in his hand, the leader of the posse walked onto Tom's porch and confronted him.

He said, "Tell me everything that happened."

Tom said, "Ok. Ten niggers with guns came into my house last night. They took clothes, food and more guns. They went north toward the river."

The leader didn't say anything. He just mounted his horse again and headed north. The hounds picked up Samuel's pepper trail and started sneezing. The hounds sneezed out the pepper for a moment, then off they all went. They arrived at the riverbank and the hounds lost the scent. The posse crossed the river on horseback, but the hounds still could not pick up the scent. The posse searched up and down the river for hours trying to pick up Harriet's trail. They never did.

The men then returned to Tom Garrett's farm to get more details about the slaves escape. Once again, the group's echoes announced their arrival. Tom greeted the posse on his porch one more time.

He said to the group, "Y'all didn't find them?"

The leader Douglass dismounted again and said, "We lost the scent at the river. Your story sounds a little farfetched. You said the niggers had guns?"

Tom replied, "That's right. There were nine or ten of them and they all had rifles."

Douglass looked at Tom and said, "Now where the hell you suppose niggers learned how to use guns and then got the gumption to run a way and rob white folks? Just don't sound like niggers to me."

Tom said, "I agree with you, Sir. But trust me, my wife and I were more surprised than you when they woke us up with a barrow to our heads. Besides, it's been done before. Twenty years ago in Virginia, a nigger named Nat Turner led a slave revolt and killed over sixty white folks."

The group shook their heads, indicating that they had heard of the famous Nat Turner.

Douglass said, "We are sorry you and your family had to go through this."
Charles bellowed out, "Did they have a half-breed woman with them?"

Tom replied, "Yes, she was tied up. They were upset with her because she was slowing them down. I heard them say if she could not keep up they would kill her."

Douglass left Tom's porch and said, "Let us know if you hear anything."

Tom said, "I will, and you do the same."

With that being said, the group rode off Tom Garrett's land. Tom was convinced his safe house secret was still safe. Everyone else returned to their own farms empty-handed. Charles and his friends went back to Tom Johnson's farm to give him the bad news. Charles went inside while his friends waited outside. Tom Johnson came downstairs and eagerly waited for Charles to give him an update on his escaped workers.

Charles said, "Bad news, Mr. Johnson. They met up with some other niggers in the middle of the night. They robbed Tom Garrett at gunpoint and went northeast. We lost them at the river. Tom Garrett said they had Kora at gunpoint and may have killed her."

Tom Johnson was very disappointed with Charles.

He asked Charles, "Negroes robbing white folks with guns? Charles, you work with them all day. You didn't see this coming?"

Charles responded by saying, "No one could see this coming. Niggers just don't act like this. This was well planned. They met up with other niggers from other farms around here and went to Pennsylvania."

Tom Johnson said, "Yes, I see your point Charles. Even I would never anticipate a good slave like Harold taking Kora."

Charles said, "I think Samuel may have put Harold up to it. I always had my eye on Samuel. That big nigger was just too stubborn."

Tom Johnson asked, "When you noticed his defiance, what did you do to control him?"

Charles said, "I beat him! He seemed to be getting better. Not to rush you Mr. Johnson, but two of the slave catchers are outside waiting to be paid."

Tom Johnson said, "Yes, yes of course."

He went to the kitchen and returned with two small bags filled with silver.

Tom Johnson said to Charles, "They do realize that since they didn't catch them and were only gone a few hours, they have not eared a full day's pay?

Charles said, "They will be disappointed, but I'll tell them."

Charles gave his friends their compensation. They were disappointed, but went to town to buy some liquor. Charles agreed to join them after he checked on the other slaves. Charles went to the apple orchard. It was fall now, and tobacco-picking season was over, but the apples grew until early winter. Charles found the other workers picking up apples and asked where Maggie and Mandy were. Charles was informed that the two women had gone back to Maggie's shack to tend to her wounds. Charles went to Maggie's shack, smiling all the way. Samuel was gone now and Charles had his African lover again. Charles opened Maggie's door and found Maggie sitting at a table in the middle of the room. There was a bucket on the table and Mandy was cleaning Maggie's wounds on her chest and arms. Maggie did not have a shirt on.

Charles walked in and said, "Mandy, Maggie don't need yo' help no mo'. Get back to work!"

Maggie saw the look in Charles's eye. She knew what Charles wanted. She begged Charles not to hurt her anymore.

She pleaded to Charles and said, "Please Masa Charles, not now. I'm still hurt'n from the beat'n you put on me dis morn'n."

Charles had one thing on his mind.

He replied to Maggie's cries, "Shut the fuck up you black bitch. You ain't hurt'n no mo'. It been a long time since I had me some a yo' black ass! I been wait'n for this a long time!"

Maggie quickly realized how she could appeal to Charles.

She said to him, "Masa Charles, with my arms and chest all cut up I cain't love you like I should. Not now. Give me until tonight and I will make you happy, I promise."

Charles was walking toward his half-dressed ex-victim when she said this. He stopped in his tracks, thought for a moment and decided he would rather be drinking with his buddies now anyway. Charles knew that, with Samuel gone, he had plenty of time to have his way with Maggie.

Charles turned around and said, "I'll be back tonight. Mandy, get back to work!"

Maggie said, "Masa Charles, I need her to help me heal my wounds so I can give you plenty of good love'n tonight."

Charles said, "I want me some dinner too. You remember what I like. I'll be back, don't disappoint me!"

Charles slammed the door and rode off.

The women heard him ride off and breathed a sigh of relief. Mandy continued bathing Maggie.

Mandy said to her, "You know Maggie, you always been there for me. I don't think I ever thanked you."

Maggie said, "No need to thank me girl, you just keep bathing me up. It feels good. I never knew being touched by a women like this could feel this good."

Mandy replied, "I never knew you liked being bathed by a woman. I never bathed a woman before. I do kinda like it."

Maggie then said, "Ya know Mandy, I use to lie to Samuel about help'n you. I use to tell him I didn't help you and he would get so mad talk'n about (Maggie imitates Samuel) *Why you didn't help ha, you know what happens if she come up short.*"

The two women laughed.

Mandy said, "Girl, you sound just like him. Why you lie to him 'bout help'n me?"

Maggie replied, "Cause I didn't want him to know I had feel'ns fo' you."

The two women kissed and embraced each other. Mandy helped Maggie remove the rest of her clothes and Maggie got in the tub. Mandy bathed Maggie and the two women climbed into Maggie's bed. They then kissed and caressed each other until a few minutes turned into a few hours.

Maggie said to her new female lover, "You need to go now baby. I feel much better. Thank you."

Mandy said, "I'm worried about you. When Charles was beat'n you this morn'n I wanted to kill him."

Maggie replied, "Don't worry about Charles, I learned how to keep him happy. Befo' Samuel came into my life, I learned how ta feed Charles and fake love'n him. Girl, I act like his little wee-wee feels so good. I be scream'n like I cain't take no mo'. He loves that. He be say'n stuff like (she imitates Charles), *Yeah, you like this white dick don't you girl?* I tell him, *Yes, Masa. Yes.* He be eat'n that shit up."

The two women laughed again for a few minutes.

Then Mandy said, "You sound just like Masa Charles, too."

Maggie replied, "You know I was with him a few years. I know what that little man likes."

Mandy asked, "Are your arms OK to cook for him and hold him?"

Maggie said, "No. They still hurt'n. I need you to help me with dinner."

Mandy then asked, "Sure girl, anything fo' you. What you gon' do about yo' fake love'n him?

Maggie replied, "I'll have him bring me some liquor. Girl, I'll get so drunk I won't feel any pain or his little wee-wee!"

Again Mandy laughed and helped Maggie get dressed. Mandy then wrapped Maggie's arms and the cuts on her torso in bandages. Mandy also cooked dinner while Maggie rested. Maggie continued to recuperate and wondered how she could be so happy when she suffered through so many atrocious events in her young life. Now Charles was back in Maggie's life in a way she accepted, but opposed to his presence in her home. Maggie's concern about Charles's raping her was minimal. She knew how to handle Charles. The years she was with Charles, Maggie learned how to control Charles with sex and alcohol. Now, for the first time in her life, Maggie had someone she truly loved, Mandy. Maggie thought she loved Samuel, but he didn't understand her and eventually he left. Mandy understood Maggie. It was Mandy's family that took Maggie and her brother in after their parents were sold. Maggie cried in Mandy's arms as a child when Charles beat her brother to death. Mandy and Maggie were the same age and they were best friends. Maggie glanced at Mandy cooking in the kitchen and fell asleep knowing why she could be so happy after so many bad things happened to her.

Maggie's rest was interrupted by Charles bursting through the door, intoxicated.

He saw Maggie on the bed and slurred, "Bitch, what you do'n on da bed? Get ya ass in da kitchen!"

Maggie said to her drunken rapist, "Dinner is ready Charles. I'm in the bed wait'n for you."

Mandy walked past Charles and out the door.

Charles staggered to the table in the middle of the room. Maggie got out of the bed and helped Charles to the table. She held him and endured the pain from the wounds he had inflicted on her. Maggie held Charles up and pulled the chair out as Charles plopped down into it. She fixed him a plate and joined Charles at the dinner table. Maggie didn't put a lot of food on Charles plate because she knew he was too drunk to eat. Charles ate his dinner and swayed to the bed.

Maggie said, "Baby, I want sometin' to drink. Did you forget I love you better when we both been drink'n?"

47

Charles sat on the bed and smiled. He removed a fifth of rum from his jacket pocket.

Charles leaned back on the bed, straightened his arm with the rum in his hand and said, "I ain't forgot nuth'n!"

Maggie took the rum out of Charles hand and sat on the bed. She drank the rum and Charles rubbed her chest. Maggie pulled back in pain and lay down.

She said to Charles, "Baby I'm still hurt'n from this morn'n. Rub me down there while I drink my rum. It's been a long time since I had my rum with you. I missed you two."

As Maggie told Charles to rub her down there, she pulled her skirt up and revealed her vaginal pubic hair. Charles was infatuated with Maggie's black body. He loved her petite physic, full-figured hips and robust, firm thighs.

When Maggie showed Charles her jet black pubic hair, Charles remembered how much he loved being inside this beautiful black African. Charles took his pants off and Maggie continued to drink her rum. Maggie and Charles often drank before having sex. The years Maggie was with Charles, the bottle comforted her and allowed her to deal with Charles having his way with her every night. When Samuel married Maggie, she stopped drinking abruptly. This caused her to go through withdrawal. Maggie desperately wanted a drink. She confided in Samuel what Charles did to her and why she started drinking. Samuel understood but refused to help her continue drinking. Instead, he tied her to the bed while he went to work. He checked on her throughout the day. Charles knew why Maggie was not at work. He had been instructed by his boss Tom to let Samuel and Maggie mate to try to conceive children to provide more farm hands. Tom referred to Samuel as a "big black buck." After going through alcohol withdrawal for nearly a week, Maggie recovered, alcohol free. She did not have another drink until now.

The rum removed Maggie's pain. Charles completed the removal of his pants. He lay in between Maggie's thighs and proceeded to place his erect penis inside Maggie. Maggie stopped him.

She said to him, "Baby, you forget how much better it is when you get me wet first?"

Charles smiled and kissed Maggie. He loved her soft, full lips. He then kissed her neck and pushed her shirt up. Once Maggie's shirt was up, Charles saw what he had done to her. He could not bear to look at the damage he had done to Maggie. He pulled her blouse back down and proceeded to rub his hand in between Maggie's thighs. Maggie sighed and arched her back. Charles inserted his middle finger into Maggie's vagina. He moved his finger in and out of her vagina and rubbed Maggie's clitoris while he kissed her again and again. Maggie moaned from his touch. She kissed Charles back, rubbing her lips against his white face like he liked. She licked his lips with her tongue. Maggie held her blouse closed with her shredded arm. Mandy had done a good job of cleaning her wounds and putting bandages on Maggie's arms. In bed, Maggie learned how to get Charles to satisfy her before they had intercourse, because intercourse with Charles was not satisfying to Maggie. Charles removed his finger and placed it on his erect penis again.

Maggie grabbed his hand and said, "Huh-hun. I'm not ready yet, baby."

Maggie pulled his hand to her mouth and licked the index finger that Charles had been fondling her with. Charles also licked his finger while Maggie licked it. Maggie stopped licking his finger and kissed Charles. As she kissed him, she pushed his shoulders down toward her hips. In her early years with Charles, Maggie learned how to turn Charles's vicious attacks into a sexually pleasing experience. She started manipulating Charles into pleasing her when she was supposed to be pleasing him.

Maggie held her blouse with her other bandaged up arm as Charles moved his head past her arm and to her beautiful vagina. Maggie had jet black long kinky pubic hair on her vagina and a brown labia. Charles kissed Maggie's labia and licked the outer area of her vagina. He then used his thumbs to spread her labia and licked the inside area of Maggie's vagina. He started from the back of her vagina and licked her to the top, resting his tongue on Maggie's clitoris. He licked her clitoris from the bottom to the top. He then placed his tongue back on the bottom of Maggie's vagina and repeated this act several times. Charles could taste Maggie's juices starting to moisten her vagina. Charles started to lick Maggie's clitoris only, and inserted his index finger inside Maggie's vaginal cavity again. Maggie arched her back again and moaned. She put her hand on the back of Charles's head and pulled him toward her. Charles continued to perform intercourse with his finger as he tasted Maggie's vaginal juices. He stopped licking her clitoris and started gently sucking it. Maggie held her shirt closed with one hand and held Charles's head with the other. Maggie felt herself about to reach her peak. Her vagina was extremely moist now. She was moaning and holding Charles's head tighter. She locked her legs with her feet elevated and released herself as Charles continued sucking her clitoris and using his finger to have intercourse with her.

Maggie and Samuel had not had sex in a while. When Samuel and Maggie did have sex, Samuel did not lick Maggie's vagina. Maggie did not miss Charles's tongue while she was with Samuel because Samuel had a large penis and always made her have an orgasm from intercourse. This was the first orgasm Maggie had that was not self-induced in a long, long time. She loved it. Right then and there, Maggie made up her mind that she was going to use sex to get whatever she wanted from Charles. Maggie knew how to make Charles feel like a man. She screamed out Charles's name with passion and unlocked her legs, placing her feet on the bed and elevating her hips. She stopped holding his head and now pushed him away from her. Charles stopped performing intercourse with his finger and placed both hands under Maggie's robust black hips, locking his head in between her legs against her will, or so he thought. Maggie passionately pleaded with Charles to stop.

She said, "OK OK OK baby, please stop."

Charles said with his tongue on her clitoris, "Shut up, I ain't stop'n 'til I'm good and ready!"

Maggie smiled and placed her elevated hips back on the bed on top of Charles's arms. She still pushed his head away, but not as hard. Maggie felt herself about to release her juices again. She moaned and reached her second climax. Now, Maggie was tired of Charles licking her. She was ready to fake enjoying having intercourse with him so he could reach his peak and go to sleep.

She said to Charles, "Baby, I want you inside me. Please baby, please come up top now."

Charles had been waiting for over a year to hear Maggie say this to him again. He stopped licking her vagina, moved his head past her blouse and her arm that hid her wounds. He then started kissing Maggie. He placed his hand on his erect penis and inserted it into Maggie. First, Maggie wondered if that was still his finger. As Charles kissed Maggie, he started gyrating and held Maggie's hips. Maggie then realized this was Charles's little penis in her. She proceeded to try to satisfy herself. Maggie tried to position her hips so that Charles's penis was rubbing against her clitoris. She lifted her legs with her knees bent and pushed her thighs at an angle to place her clitoris directly against Charles's penis. Maggie did get some pleasure, but she could not help thinking about being in the same position with Samuel, and how he penetrated her so deep while his penis rubbed against her clitoris. She always had good orgasms with Samuel. This was not Samuel. Charles was just the opposite. This little white man started gyrating harder and harder, going faster and faster, trying to go has deep as his little penis would let him. Charles was moaning as he enjoyed being in between Maggie's beautiful black hips again. Charles's body was elevated in the missionary position and he was pumping as hard and fast as he could. The bed was squeaking, and Maggie continued to hold her blouse closed with one hand.

51

Maggie placed her other hand on Charles's chest and as the bed squeaked louder and louder she moaned to him, "You feel so good, baby. Don't stop, baby. Don't stop!"

Charles continued to gyrate and he relaxed his arms and kissed Maggie. Maggie moved her hand from Charles's chest to the back of his head and placed her tongue in his mouth. Their tongues explored each other's mouths and Charles continued to gyrate. Maggie kissed Charles and closed her eyes. She moaned to Charles how good he felt while she pretended Samuel was on top of her, ramming his long black penis deep in her vaginal cavity.

Maggie moaned again and said, "Charles, Charles, sssss oh Charles!"

Charles continued to kiss Maggie as he completely relaxed his arms. This placed his body directly on top of Maggie's. Maggie was still holding her blouse closed and Charles's body weight on top of Maggie's arm aggravated her wounds.

Maggie said to Charles, "Ouch baby, you're hurting my cuts! Get up. Baby. Get up!"

Charles did as Maggie asked. He got up on his knees and looked down at Maggie. His penis was still erect, and Maggie lay in front of him with her legs spread and black vagina exposing itself from the bottom of her shirt. Charles stuck out his index finger and rotated it in a clockwise motion, motioning for Maggie to get on her knees. Maggie knew what Charles wanted. She often wondered why Charles liked this position so much. She hated doing it on her knees with Charles because she could not feel any penetration. On her back, she may have reached another orgasm if Charles kept sliding his little penis against her clitoris. She moved on her knees as Charles silently requested. Once Maggie was on her knees, Charles inserted his penis into Maggie from behind. Maggie remembered the first time Samuel inserted his long black penis in her from the back. Maggie jumped away from him and told him he would have to go slow. She eventually got used to Samuel's size. Now she had to readjust from Samuel's long hard black penis to Charles's little white one.

Charles started gyrating behind Maggie. He looked down and loved the way his penis disappeared inside Maggie's round dark hips. He pushed his penis as far into Maggie as it would go and removed it and slammed it in her again. This caused a loud clapping noise. Charles gyrated as hard as he could, causing the bed to rock. The clapping got louder. Charles felt himself about to explode. He tightened up his grip on Maggie's hips and wished he could go deeper into her. Charles held his head up and exploded inside Maggie. As he released himself, he grunted and squeezed her hips as hard as he could. He fell to Maggie's side and caught his breath.

Maggie lay down with her back to him. She was so happy that her unsatisfying sexual experience was finally over. She knew sex with Charles would be better when her wounds healed. She knew she could manipulate her overseer in bed so she could have some sexual satisfaction. Yet she still missed Samuel. No other man made her feel like he did. Maggie knew Samuel was good for her.

For the first time she wondered if she had made the right decision by not supporting Samuel when he expressed his eagerness to escape. After all, Samuel was gone and Maggie was still a slave.

Chapter 7
After the Marathon

In the morning, on Quincy's farm, Harriet's runners were still recuperating from the marathon they had run the other day. Harriet's plan was to stay in a small suburb outside of Marcus Hook for a few days to rest, then continue moving northeast through Pennsylvania into New Jersey, New York and then Canada.

As the group rested, Samuel noticed that Kora was not feeling well. She was still vomiting and lying on the ground. Kora started vomiting as soon as they stopped running. Others had been vomiting, and Samuel assumed it was just fatigue. By the late morning, the other ex-slaves began to move around and show signs of life but Kora was still ailing. Samuel was becoming concerned. He lay on the ground and held Kora.

He asked her, "You OK baby?"

Kora replied in a low voice, "I don't feel good Samuel. I think I caught something."

Samuel looked up and saw Harriet walking toward them. Samuel and Kora were the only people in the barn. As Harriet entered the barn, Samuel noticed a look of concern on her face. Samuel was very nervous. He didn't know what Harriet would do if she found out that Kora was sick.

What Samuel didn't know was that Harriet had experience with most common illnesses. When Harriet was a slave, she attended to all the other slave's ailments.

As Harriet approached the two young lovers she asked, "How ya feel'n, gal?"

Kora replied, "Not so good. I think I be OK if I can rest a bit."

Harriet walked over to Kora and put her hand on her forehead.

With her hand on Kora's head she asked, "Tell me how you feel'n inside gal."

Kora replied, "I feels funny inside. I cain't keep nut'n in me."

Harriet moved her hand and replied, "Auhun, you ain't got no fever. Cain't keep nut'n down, huh? We gon' be here a few days. I keeps my eye on you. Keeps try'n to eat. You need food to help ya get ready to move when we leave."

As Harriet walked away she said to Samuel, "Come get some a these grits for you two. Make sure she tries to eat 'em."

Samuel and Harriet walked to a large kettle in the middle of the field where the grits were cooking. He returned with two large bowls of hot grits.

"Here baby, you need to eat sumtin'."

Kora replied, "Uut hun. I don't feel like eating, Samuel."

Samuel asked his lover again, "Just try baby. You needs to eat sumtin'."

Kora replied, "OK Samuel, I'll try to keep something down."

Kora blew on her hot grits and took a spoonful.

After a few spoonfuls, Kora began to feel better. She finished her bowl. She didn't vomit. Samuel consumed his grits also. Kora looked at her man and kissed him. Samuel held her tight and kissed her back.

Kora responded to Samuel by saying, "I should have never got you started."

Samuel looked at Kora and softly said, "How long it been?"

Kora knew what he meant. She always knew what her man meant.

She responded by saying, "A few days. You haven't been in me since we heard Leonard beating the drum."

Samuel looked at Kora with a facial expression indicating that he remembered.

He responded by saying, "Oh yeah, I remember now. That seems like such a long time ago. Come on baby, let's go off into dem woods where wes can be alone for a while."

Kora smiled at the thought of being with her man.

She looked at him and said, "I am feeling better, baby, but I am tired. I want to take a nap right here. Just hold me, Samuel. Take a nap with me."

Kora loved it when her and Samuel made love and he held her in his muscular arms, against his brawny chest. Every time Samuel was holding her after they made love, the moment was short because they were still on the plantation and they didn't want to take a chance on getting caught.

Samuel was not a cuddlier. He held Kora like she requested. He was aroused. After all, it had been a couple of days since he made love to Kora. As Kora lay on her back, Samuel was on his side. His left hand was on Kora's waist. He slowly moved his hand up her torso. As he fondled her breast, Kora moaned slightly. Samuel kissed her passionately. Kora put her hand on her lover's back and pulled him closer to her. Samuel stopped kissing Kora and swiftly picked her up and carried her behind a stack of hay where they could not be seen. Samuel gently laid Kora on her back. He laid his body on top of hers. Samuel looked into Kora's eyes and she silently accepted her lover as she always did when he aroused her. Kora was extremely attracted to Samuel.

It didn't take much for Samuel to arouse Kora. Samuel lay in between Kora's legs and kissed her while he massaged her breast. He lifted his hips, and slowly inserted his erect penis inside of her. She moaned and Samuel pushed himself further inside Kora. He started gyrating in a slow, smooth motion while he kissed her ardently. Samuel and Kora's sexual experience evolved from hot obsessive sex to passionate lovemaking. Samuel was now making love to his newfound lover. Kora could sense the difference. She enjoyed being with her man even more now.

After their lovemaking session, Samuel and Kora took a nap. After a few hours of rest, they woke up together. Samuel got Kora some hot tea and returned to their semi-private barnyard behind the hay stack. Samuel gave Kora the tea and rejoined his wife under their blanket. He stared at his beautiful aficionada as she sipped her tea.

Kora asked him, "Something on your mind baby?"

Samuel asked Kora, "How comes you talk like a slave to everyone but me?"

Kora sat back a moment, then asked her man, "Do you love me Samuel?"

Samuel was surprised and a little caught off guard by Kora's question.

Samuel responded by saying, "Why you ask me dat, women? You here, ain't you? You free just like me, ain't you?"

Kora replied by quickly saying, "All that is true, but you never told me you loved me. You just lead and I follow. It would be nice to hear you say you love me."

Samuel was impatient. He wanted an answer to his question.

He raised his voice slightly and asked Kora, "How the hell we get from you talk'n white, to me say'n I love you?"

Kora remained calm and said, "Do you?"

Samuel sighed and said, "Yes."

Kora replied, "Then say it."

Samuel took a deep breath and said, "Fine, I love you."

Now Kora responded with a little frustration in her voice. She said, "Is that how you tell me you love me? Say it like you mean it, Samuel!"

Samuel was even more surprised by Kora's tone. Kora had never raised her voice to him before. Samuel also wasn't good with words. He was a man of action. He knew he had to do whatever it took to keep Kora happy.

Samuel paused and complied with his girlfriend's wishes, "Kora, I cannot imagine being free witout you. I love going da bed wit' you, I love wake'n up wit' you, I love being inside you, I love talk'n ta you. What I am try'n to say is, I love you."

With a tear in her eye, Kora kissed Samuel.

Samuel looked at her and said, "Now will you answer my question?"

Kora calmly replied by saying, "That's easy, I love you too."

Samuel had another confused look on his face. He was getting frustrated.

He asked Kora, "That's nice to hear, but what the hell do that have to do with you talk'n white?"

Kora smiled at her man and kissed him on his forehead.

She said to him, "When I talk to you, I am being myself. I am very comfortable with you."

Samuel was glad he was getting some answers to his questions and getting to know his girlfriend better.

Seeking more information, he asked, "Where you learn to talk like that?"

Kora responded, "Anna taught me."

Samuel asked, "Why don't you talk white all the time?"

Kora told Samuel, "Negroes already look at me funny. Just because I wasn't in the fields or shacks with you all doesn't mean I wasn't a slave. They look at me and treat me different because I don't look like you all. Imagine what they would say about me if I talked like a white slave owner. They might kill me!"

Samuel understood why Kora spoke in proper English with him now. He still had a few more questions for Kora.

He asked, "What else did Anna teach you?"

Without hesitation Kora responded, "She taught me how to read, write and do arithmetic."

Samuel was shocked.

He said to Kora, "Damn, Kora. She taught you all that?"

Kora replied, "Yes."

The two continued talking for the rest of the evening. As the others came into the barn, Kora and Samuel fell asleep together on their own secluded space behind their haystack.

The next morning the sunrise woke Samuel up. He washed up at the farm's well and headed out to get some firewood. When he returned with enough firewood to keep everyone warm on the chilly fall day, Kora was up. Samuel returned to the barn, anxious to check on Kora. As he entered the barn, he looked in the direction of the hay stack Kora and he used for a wall. He heard Kora moaning in discomfort. He quickly walked around the haystack. Samuel witnessed Harriet bent down tending to Kora as she was on her knees vomiting into a bucket. Harriet had her hand on Kora's back and looked up at Samuel.

She said to him, "Glad you got some firewood, now yo' wife here need some tea."

Samuel abruptly went to the firewood he had just gathered. He noticed that Leonard had started a fire already. Samuel was glad he was with this group. Samuel thought some slaves would become lazy after they were free. He thought if their master wasn't there to make them work, the work would not get done. This was not true with the runaways Samuel was with. The slaves still didn't talk much, but if something needed to get done, someone just did it. Samuel filled the teapot with water and put several tea bags supplied by the Manleys in the water. The fire was hot. It only took a few minutes to boil the water. Samuel returned with the teapot and a teacup. Kora was not regurgitating anymore. She was lying on her side and holding her stomach. Samuel gave the teapot and teacup to Harriet. She fixed Kora a cup of tea.

She told Kora, "Here gal, drink this. It will calm yo' insides down."

Harriet then walked toward Samuel and led him out of the barn by his arm.

60

Harriet looked at Samuel and said, "Yo' wife is with child."

Samuel didn't know what to say. He just stood in front of Harriet with a strange look on his face.

After a few moments Harriet smiled and asked Samuel, "You OK boy? You look like you seen a ghost."

Samuel quickly snapped out of his trance.

He responded by asking, "Do Kora know?"

Harriet said, "I doubt it. This her first child, she don't know what go'n on. She scared. I told you so you can tell ha."

As Samuel gathered his senses, his freedom movement attitude returned.

He asked Harriet, "So, where this leave us? I mean we cain't be run'n to Canada with no baby."

This is what Harriet liked about Samuel. No matter what happened, he was always concerned about the status of the group.

Harriet replied, "Go be wit' ha. We can talk later."

Samuel was afraid of Harriet. He didn't show it but she was the first person he met that ever intimidated him. Samuel had heard stories about Harriet and her no slave left behind rule. He didn't know what Harriet would do if he and Kora couldn't complete the journey. Samuel felt a little better after he saw Harriet comforting Kora, and the sight of a rare smile on Harriet also relaxed him slightly. He walked back to the barn to return to

Kora. She finished her tea and was asleep. Samuel lay next to Kora without waking her. He was on his back with his hand behind his head. This was his thinking position. He had a lot to think about.

Chapter 8
Settling Down

Samuel looked up at the blackness that covered the barn roof. He enjoyed the cracks in the roof that allowed the sun's rays to warm his face. This reminded Samuel of his days on the plantation, when he walked to the field and the sun hit his face. That was one of the few pleasant memories Samuel had of the place he was running away from. As Samuel lay on his back, Kora's voice interrupted his thoughts.

She placed her hand on his chest and said, "You up, baby?"

Kora sounded better, and Samuel was glad to hear her pleasant voice.

He responded by saying, "Yeah."

Kora asked him, "Something on your mind, Samuel?"

Samuel, still deep in thought, said, "Yeah."

Kora felt that her man had something on his mind. She decided to let him think. She attempted to get up and felt faint. Samuel quickly came out of his inert state of contemplation. He grabbed Kora to make sure she didn't fall. Kora put her hand on her head and lay back down. Kora was very concerned about her health. She did not feel well and did not know why.

She looked at Samuel and, with tears in her eyes, said, "What's wrong with me Samuel? i can't even stand up. It's almost time to leave. How are we going to keep up with the group if I can't even stand up?"

Samuel never was a man of many words. He just looked at Kora and said, "You with child now, baby."

With an astonished expression on her face, Kora asked him, "Is that why I haven't been feeling well?"

Samuel simply replied, "Yeah."

Kora lay in the hay and tried to relax. In her calm state, she realized that their future was unclear. The one thing that was clear was, whatever she was about to go through, Samuel would go through it with her. That thought brought her comfort.

She looked at Samuel and asked him, "What are we going to do when everyone else leaves?"

Samuel said, "I need ta talk ta Harriet 'bout dat. You OK for now?"

Kora said, "Yes."

Samuel went to find Harriet. It didn't take him long. Harriet was on her way into the house to talk to Quincy.

Samuel stopped her and said, "Good morn'n Harriet."

Harriet replied, "Hello Samuel. How is Kora dis morn'n?"

Samuel told Harriet, "She not feel'n well. Still cain't keep nut'n down. I don't think we can leave with y'all."

Harriet already knew that those two couldn't continue on their journey to freedom. She had a plan. Harriet always had a plan.

She told Samuel, "I'm gona talk to Quincy about you two stay'n on as field hands. Dat mean you gon' have to work to earn yo' stay."

Without hesitation Samuel replied, "Shoot woman, I been work'n all my life. If it's one thing I know how to do, it's work."

As they walked toward the house, they saw Quincy walking toward them.

They met on the walkway and Harriet introduced Samuel and Quincy to each other, "Quincy, dis Samuel. Samuel dis Mr. Manley."

Quincy extended his hand and said, "Nice to meet you, Samuel."

Samuel had never shook a white man's hand before.

He hesitated, then shook Quincy's hand and replied, "Nice ta meet you too Mr. Manley. Yo' barn need a new roof."

Quincy was a little surprised at Samuel's bold statement. He thought about it for a moment.

Then replied, "Do you know anything about building roofs, Samuel?"

Samuel replied, "I puts up a few in my day."

Quincy asked Samuel, "It only takes about a week to put on a good roof. Harriet tells me you and your wife are with child. I could use a good field hand if you're up to it."

Samuel smiled and said, "Yes, I'm up to it. I can get started on your roof right away."

Quincy agreed by saying, "Come with me, I'll show you where the tools are."

Samuel and Quincy walked to a barn on the other side of the farm. This was the first time Samuel had a chance to explore the farm he had been residing on for the past three days. It was a beautiful farm. Quincy raised award-winning riding horses. Quincy's farm was larger then the one Samuel had been living on for the past six years.

On Tom's farm, Samuel did everything for his master. He was a very good field hand. He was hard working and a fast learner. As he walked Quincy's land, he looked around and made note of things he could improve or repair. Samuel didn't see any crops, just animals.

He asked Quincy, "You grow any crops on your farm?"

Quincy replied, "A few. Crops take a lot of manpower. I don't have a lot of field hands. Just my two sons and our hired hand Kevin. I can't pay you, but I can give you, your wife and your expected little one food and shelter."

As they went into the supply barn, Samuel looked around and smiled. He gathered wood, a hammer and nails. He put them in a wheel barrow and proceeded to the barn that Kora and Samuel would call home for the next year or so. Samuel had the wheel barrow loaded with a lot of wood. The barrel looked very heavy. Quincy was impressed by Samuel's strength and willingness to work.

After Samuel made his first trip to his new home with the supplies, he checked on Kora and sought out Harriet again. He had one more thing to ask her. He found Harriet talking to the others about the rest of their trip up north.

He pulled her to the side and said, "I want ta thank ya for all ya done fo' us. I need one mo' fava from ya."

Harriet asked, "What's that Samuel?"

Samuel told Harriet, "Kora and I ain't married. I was hope'n you would marry us before you leave."

Harriet replied, "I'd be happy to marry you two. Y'all's a fine couple."

Samuel smiled and said, "I'll tell Kora. When you want to do this?"

Harriet replied, "Tonight. Dat way we can get everyone together for da wed'n."

Samuel was very happy. He smiled all the way back to his barn. He could not wait to tell Kora the good news. When Samuel returned to the barn, Kora was with Harold and Leonard. They were eating chicken with boiled onions. Kora had a plate for Samuel also. Samuel was hungry and happy to see his friend. He sat on a crate and Kora brought him his plate.

Harold said to Samuel, "Man can you believe we ran dat far, dat fast?"

Samuel, with his mouth full, replied, "Naw, I never imagined we could run like that."

Leonard joined in by saying, "Shit, we run'n fo' freedom. We gon' run some mo' too."

Harold said, "Yeah, but not like that. We on free land now."

Leonard quickly replied by saying, "Harriet say we ain't totally free 'tils we gets to Canada."

Kora didn't say anything. She never did. When everyone finished eating, she took their plates to the well to wash them. As Kora took the plates to the well, Leonard watched her.

He told Samuel, "Dat one fine high yellow house bitch you got, man. How you pull dat off?"

Samuel had never liked Leonard. Samuel and Leonard had similar personalities. They were both headstrong and very determined.

Samuel was silent for a moment, and then he said, "I ax you befo' not to disrespect her."

Leonard didn't care much for Samuel either. He thought that Samuel was selfish and had put everyone at risk by bringing Kora.

Leonard looked Samuel right in the eyes and replied, "I'm just payin' you a compliment. Nigga, is you too dumb to know a compliment when you hear it?"

Before Leonard finished his sentence, Samuel was off his crate and ready to fight. Harold was sitting in between Leonard and Samuel. He jumped up as Leonard responded to Samuel. Harold wasn't about to let his best friend get into a fight at a time when everyone had to pull together. Samuel was larger than both Harold and Leonard. He reached across Harold and grabbed Leonard's shirt collar. Harold held Samuel back with one hand and Leonard back with the other. Samuel let Leonard loose and pushed Harold almost ten feet away. Samuel was very angry and his adrenalin level was very high. He was stronger then usual. Now, no one was between Samuel and Leonard. Samuel had to turn his body to his left to move Harold. Leonard saw this as an opportunity to strike the first blow. As Samuel brought his body back to a frontal position, his peripheral vision picked up Leonard's left arm moving in a hooked motion toward his head. Samuel saw the punch coming and bent his knees to get under it. In one movement, Samuel ducked under Leonard's left hook and took hold of Leonard's groin. With Samuel's left hand on Leonard's genitals, Leonard became less aggressive instantly. He moved both hands toward his crotch and bent down. Samuel used his cat-like quickness to punch Leonard in the chest as Leonard bent down. This knocked the wind out of Leonard. His legs became weak and, in less then two seconds, Leonard was defenseless. Samuel secured Leonard's shirt in his right hand after punching Leonard in the chest. With Samuel's left hand controlling Leonard's lower half, and his right hand controlling Leonard's upper half, Samuel shifted his weight to his legs. The same legs he used to push his plow for the last six years. As he shifted his weight, Leonard's body moved with him. Leonard was almost knocked unconscious by Samuel's chest blow. Samuel pulled Leonard's upper body with his right hand. He then used his massive arms and muscular torso to pull Leonard's stunned body over his head. Samuel then used his legs to stand up and lift Leonard's body in the air. He took one step forward and threw Leonard's body toward the ground. Samuel looked at Leonard's body with a killer's expression on his face.

Harold watched in amazement. He knew that Samuel was strong, but he had never witnessed his friend in this kind of rage. No one ever saw Samuel like this. On their plantation, Samuel's anger was controlled. He also had an outlet. His daily farm duties allowed Samuel to release his anger and stress. It had only been a few days since Samuel had been working on Tom's farm, but here in Pennsylvania, Samuel had no outlet. Samuel moved toward Leonard. Harold quickly positioned him self between his friend and Leonard.

Harold stood face to chest with his friend and said, "Come on, man. He had enough. Come on. Let's go fo' a walk. Show me dis big, beautiful farm. "

Samuel silently agreed by letting Harold guide him out of the barn. As the two men walked, Samuel started to calm down. He started feeling better. Harold was trying to make small talk to help Samuel relax.

He started by saying, "Damn man, dis is one big-ass farm! How many slaves you think they needs here?"

Samuel responded by saying, "It big, but the ground ain't soft. Ol' man Tom's farm was close to the river. The ground was soft. Good fo' grow'n tobacco."

The two walked and talked for about thirty minutes. When they returned to the barn, Kora was returning at the same time. The barn was empty. Leonard was gone.

Samuel said to Harold, "Thanks for calming me down. I needs to talk to Kora now. Do you mind give'n us a few minutes Harold?"

Harold replied, "No problem, man. I'll see you later."

Samuel walked into the barn and approached Kora. She was sitting on a crate, mending some garments for the other runaways. As Samuel approached her, she looked up and smiled.

Samuel stood about two feet away from her then said, "I need ta talk to ya."

Kora stopped sewing and said, "Sure Samuel, what is it?"

Samuel said to Kora, "Stand up a moment."

Without saying a word, Kora put her sewing needles down and stood up in front of her man. Samuel sat on the crate and guided Kora to his lap. Kora sat on her man's lap and put her arm around him. Samuel was nervous.

He looked at Kora and said, "Kora, I have sumtin' ta ask ya."

Kora didn't say a word. She didn't want to interrupt her man. She kept quiet and continued to look him in his eyes.

Samuel hesitated a moment, then said. "Well I been think'n. We together now and I ain't go'n nowhere without you. I told you I love you. Now I think we should gets married."

Kora looked at Samuel and asked him, "Samuel, did you just ask me to marry you?"

Samuel said, "Yes."

Kora started crying. Sobbing, she bellowed, "Yes! Yes! Yes, I'll marry you!"

The two hugged again. Kora pulled herself together and asked, "When we getting married?"

Samuel replied, "Tonight. Harriet is marrying us befo' she leaves."

Kora said, "So we are not leaving? You plan on staying here and raising our child?"

Samuel said, "I already talk'd to Quincy. He said he can hire us to work as field hands. Dat means we do da same things we did on our old home."

Kora raised her voice slightly and firmly said, "I am not carrying water to the field hands."

Samuel responded by saying, "You can work in the house cooking an cleaning. That is, if you up to it, and the workers can get they own water."

Kora smiled and kissed her man. She moved her leg over Samuel's waist so she was straddling him. They kissed passionately.

As they kissed, Harriet walked into the barn and said, "Y'alls stop dat. Y'all have plenty of time for dat later."

The two stopped kissing. Kora moved her leg back to the front side of her man's lap.

As Kora looked at Harriet, Harriet asked, "Did Samuel give you the good news?"

Kora replied by smiling and saying, "Yes."

Harriet smiled back and said, "I talked to da others. Dey all thinks we should do da wed'n at sunset. We will do the wed'n right here in da barn. I'll leaves you two alone 'til its time"

Kora and Samuel just looked at each other and embraced the moment.

Samuel said to Kora, "How you feel'n baby?"

Kora responded by saying, "Fine. I am very happy, Samuel."

Samuel kissed her on the forehead and said, "I means, how yo' stomach feel'n?"

Kora responded by saying, "I'm fine Samuel. I feel OK."

Samuel asked Kora, "You want to go fo' a walk, baby?"

Kora happily said, "OK. Lets go."

Kora and Samuel walked slowly around the farm. Kora started feeling queasy. She told Samuel she needed to take a break. She walked to a nearby bush and vomited. After Kora regurgitated the contents of her stomach, she was weak and dizzy. Samuel supported Kora while they walked back to the barn. The sun was setting behind the trees on the western horizon. Kora was looking forward to lying down behind their haystack. While they were walking, Harriet gathered everyone for the wedding. All the escaping slaves were there, even Leonard. Quincy and his family were also in the barn, waiting for the soon-to-be newlyweds to arrive.

Samuel and Kora walked into a barn filled with all of their new friends. As they entered, several people lit lanterns to provide light for the upcoming ceremony. Samuel looked around at everyone. He noticed a broom in the middle of the barn floor. Samuel had jumped the broom before. He was well aware of what was about to occur in his new home. Kora didn't feel well and it showed. Samuel was still holding her up. She was slightly slumped forward with her head down. Samuel knew Kora needed rest. Before he could say anything, Harriet walked up to Kora and pulled her hair off her face.

As she pulled Kora's hair back, Harriet asked her, "You OK, gal?"

Kora weakly responded by saying, "Yes. I can do dis. I wants to marry Samuel."

Harriet said, "Come on. I'll marry y'all befo' dis child pass out."

Samuel nodded his head in agreement with Harriet.

Harriet started the ceremony by saying, "Do you Kora…"

Harriet hesitated for a moment. She then asked, "I'm sorry, what y'all last name?"

Samuel said, "Don't know, we never tought about one."

Harriet asked, "Y'all want to go with yo' master last name?"

Kora perked up and responded by loudly saying, "No!"

Harriet said, "Well, we better thinks of sometin' while this child is alert."

There was silence as everyone tried to think of a last name.

Chapter Nine
Mister and Misses?

Everyone was quiet for a moment. They were trying to think of a good last name.

Harold said, "How about Barns?"

Samuel asked, "Where you get that name from?"

Harold responded, "Cause we in a barn."

Everyone laughed.

Samuel said, "Barns is OK, but I wants a name that means sometin'."

Harriet came up with a good last name. She said, "How about Freeman?"

Kora smiled and Samuel looked at his bride and said, "Freeman is a fine last name."

Harriet said, "Good, now we got that out the way, let's get on wit' it."

Harriet started the marriage vows again, "Do you Kora Freeman take Samuel Freeman to be your husband – to live together after God's ordinance – in the holy estate of matrimony? Will you love him, comfort him, honor and keep him, in sickness and in health, for richer, for poorer, for better, for worse, in sadness and in joy, to cherish and continually bestow upon him your heart's deepest devotion, forsaking all others, keep yourself only unto him as long as you both shall live?"

Kora, weeping, responded and said, "I do."

Harriet looked at Samuel and said, "Do you Samuel Freeman take Kora Freeman to be your wife – to live together after God's ordinance – in the holy estate of matrimony? Will you love her, comfort her, honor and keep her, in sickness and in health, for richer, for poorer, for better, for worse, in sadness and in joy, to cherish and continually bestow upon her your heart's deepest devotion, forsaking all others, keep yourself only unto her as long as you both shall live?"

Samuel looked at his crying bride and said, "I do."

Harriet then said, "I now pronounce you husband and wife. Jump the broom and kiss each other!"

Harriet stepped back while Samuel and Kora jumped the broom. They then kissed. The others in the barn started playing music. Quincy had an old banjo that he started playing. Harold was beating on an old hollow log. Felix, a younger runaway, was playing a harmonica. Everyone started dancing and clapping. This was the last night that they would be together. This gathering was a wedding celebration and a farewell party. Kora, the guest of honor, was not feeling well. She went to a crate against the wall and sat down. Samuel was with her.

He asked her, "You OK, Mrs. Freeman?"

Kora said, "I like the way that sounds, Mr. Freeman. I'm OK. Just a little tired."

Samuel found a crate and joined his wife. He put his arm around her and she put her head on his shoulder.

Harriet walked over, she looked at the newlyweds and said, "Y'all looks real happy."

Kora smiled and said, "We is. Thanks for everytin' Harriet."

Harriet smiled and said, "Please forgive me, Kora, but I needs to talk to yo' new husband."

Kora smiled and removed her head from Samuel's shoulder. Samuel got up and walked outside the barn with Harriet.

As they walked, Harriet said, "We gon' be leave'n soon. Y'all got everything here y'all needs to survive 'til I gets back."

Samuel asked, "When will that be?"

Harriet responded, "One fall. I cain't not say when, but one fall. When I do come back, we will see if you and yo' family can come with us. Now I don't usually leave folks behind, but y'all's special. Y'all be fine, but you gots to be careful. Remember we ain't that far from yo' old plantation. Watch out fo' slave catchers. Don't be out after dark. Quincy will keep an eye on y'all."

Samuel was silent. He didn't say anything. He just walked with Harriet and listened.

Harriet continued, "Quincy said he will teach you da trade of be'n a blacksmith. Now that you free, you need a trade."

Before Samuel realized it, the two were back in front of the barn again. Everyone had calmed down. They were relaxing, waiting for their leader to give the word to run again. When they saw Harriet, they stood up. Samuel looked at Harriet and silently said goodbye as he walked into the barn to be with Kora.

Harriet said, "One mo' ting Samuel, if anything should happen and y'all have to leave, go to Philadelphia. They got lots of abolitionists, Quakers and freed Negros there. They will help you."

Samuel smiled and went toward the barn. Before he entered Harold approached him from behind.

He said, "Hey man, I ain't leave'n without say'n bye."

Samuel turned around. He was happy to hear his friend's voice. He didn't know if this was the last time he would see his friend. Samuel and Harold were friends for years. Until Samuel fell in love with Kora, Harold was the only person he trusted. Samuel knew it was Harold that had connected the two of them with the Underground Railroad. Samuel knew he would still be on Tom Johnson's farm if it wasn't for Harold. Now he had to say goodbye to his friend.

Samuel calmly said, "Goodbye Harold, good luck to y'all."

Harold laughed briefly, then replied, "We don't need luck. We got Harriet. She makes her own luck."

Samuel said, "Yeah, I guess you right. Harriet will take care of y'all."

Samuel hugged Harold and walked into the barn. As he entered, he turned around one more time to take one last look at everyone. They were all walking off the farm with Harriet. Samuel wondered if he would see any of them again. Kora was already lying on the haystack that the two used for a bed. Samuel joined her. He held his new bride as they fell asleep.

Samuel was awakened by the sunrise. He got up and gathered firewood. He dug a hole in the middle of the barn. The hole had a circumference of approximately five feet. It was about three feet deep. Samuel stacked firewood about three feet high from the pit of his ditch. He then swept away all the hay within ten feet of the cavity. Now, the barn ground had a fifteen foot dirt circle with a three foot hole in the middle of it. Kora's morning sickness temperately interrupted Samuel's morning chore. He tried to comfort

Kora. He could not do much but hold her as she regurgitated into a bucket beside their bed. Samuel realized Kora needed her tea. He lit his barn fire and left the barn to fill the teapot with water. He returned and made his wife some tea. She began to feel better immediately.

Kora slowly walked to the well to wash up. While she was bathing, Samuel walked to Quincy's house. After her bath, Kora joined her husband at Quincy's home. Quincy gave the two a large supply of grits, oats and tea bags for breakfast. Samuel carried the month's supply of breakfast back to the barn. He doused the fire with water, realizing he shouldn't have lit it. He returned to the house to get some breakfast. When he returned, he looked through the kitchen window and saw Kora hard at work preparing breakfast for Quincy and his family. Samuel sat on the porch step waiting for Quincy. Kora came out on the porch and gave her husband a large bowl of grits. Samuel looked at his wife. She looked tired and was moving slowly. Samuel watched her as she went back into the house to serve her other family. As Samuel ate his grits, his mind was on fire. He was mad his wife was working when she should be resting. He started to compare his new live to his life as a slave. He saw too many similarities. He realized that he had just arrived here and decided to give their new farm a chance. Kora came back on the porch to get her husband's empty bowl. Quincy came out to the porch and put his hand on Samuel's shoulder.

He asked Samuel, "Are you ready to do some work?"

Samuel replied, "Yes sa."

As Samuel and Quincy walked to the other side of the farm, Quincy explained what was expected of him and how Samuel would be compensated.

He told Samuel, "Like I said yesterday, I can't pay you, but you and your family can have all the food you need and stay as long as you need. As far as what I need you to do around here, it's just farm work, which you seem to be good at. I will also teach you

78

the trade of blacksmithing. With a trade, you can provide for your family as a free man. I will also need you to go to town to get supplies. You ever been on a wagon before?"

Samuel replied, "No sa."

Quincy said, "Well that is just one more thing I can teach you. For now, I need some repairs on the farm."

Samuel was prepared to make Quincy's repairs. He had already observed several informalities in his new home. Quincy and Samuel walked to the supply barn. Quincy explained what he needed Samuel to work on.

Quincy told Samuel, "Now every morning I expect you to feed the chickens, pigs, horses and cows. While you are feeding the animals, Kora will be in the house cooking breakfast. After you finish feeding them, come on the porch to get your breakfast. After breakfast, I will tell you what we will work on. For now, I need you to put up a new fence around the whole farm. I know it is a project that will take some time. Let's see how your daily chores go and then we will talk about blacksmithing."

Samuel gave his usual nod indicating that he understood. The chore of putting a new fence was not an easy one. It consisted of a lot of manual labor. First, Samuel had to gather the wood from the supply barn. He put the wood in a wheelbarrow and pushed it to the area he was working on. Once he arrived with the wheelbarrow, he had to remove the section of the old fence that he was replacing. Then he had to put in the new post with fresh mud in the hole. After the posts were in place, Samuel had to put up two five-foot two by fours from post to post. This was Samuel's routine for the next several days.

Kora would bring Samuel his lunch every day around noon. Samuel was not happy with their current living condition. To him it didn't seem like they were free. Samuel didn't complain or express his discontent to anyone. He shut down to everyone, even Kora.

Samuel and Kora used to talk at night. Now Samuel just went to sleep. Kora knew something was wrong with her man, she just didn't know what.

One evening, after the two went to bed, Kora put her head on Samuel's chest and asked him what was on his mind. Samuel realized that he had shut his wife out and it was not her fault. He decided to open up to Kora.

He said, "I don't feel free, do you?"

Kora replied, "Yes baby, I feel free. Why don't you?"

Samuel explained to Kora, "We do'n the same shit we did on da plantation. We ain't get'n paid. You are working yo' ass off in this white man's kitchen when you should be rest'n. If you was pregnant on masa Tom's farm he would work you just like Quincy is. So tell me woman, how you feel so free?"

Kora replied, "The difference is, baby, if we don't do the work now, we have to leave. If we didn't do the work on Master Tom's place, we would get beat, or worse. See baby, now we have a choice. That's what being free means. "

Samuel responded by saying, "I guess you right, but I thinks we can do better. If we has a choice, I choose to leave."

Kora let Samuel know they were not leaving by saying, "Samuel, I'm in no condition to leave. After the baby comes we can talk about leaving. Hopefully over the next few months Quincy will teach you how to be a blacksmith like he promised."

Samuel agreed with his wife. Kora consistently surprised him with her strength and knowledge. Samuel told Kora she was right, then he kissed her on her forehead. Kora moved her head up and kissed her husband on the lips. Feeling aroused, Samuel moved from under Kora and laid his body on top of hers. She spread her legs to accept him. The two made love, then fell asleep.

Chapter Ten
The Lord Gave, The Lord Took Away

Harriet and her group had arrived on Quincy's farm in late September. It was now early November. The days were getting shorter and the nights were growing longer. In the past month, Samuel and Kora had done what was expected of them. Every morning when the sun came up, they awakened and proceeded with Quincy's instructions. Constructing a new fence was a two-month job. Samuel completed it in one month. He also put a new roof on the house and on both barns. Samuel's slave days were not far behind him. He felt as if he had never left. Just as Samuel's anger made him the best field hand on the plantation, his anger also made him the best field hand Quincy had ever seen. Samuel worked very efficiently. He did everything correct the first time. He made no wasted movements while working. Samuel took a lunch and Kora started bringing him hot tea twice a day. Quincy was impressed with Samuel's efficient work methods. He decided that Samuel had earned the right to learn to be a blacksmith. One morning after Samuel finished eating his oatmeal, Kora came onto the porch and gave him a cup of tea. As she took his empty bowl, Quincy came onto the porch.

He said to Samuel, "I like the way you work Samuel. I think it's time you started learning how to be a blacksmith."

Kora heard Quincy say this and smiled as she returned to the kitchen. Samuel nodded and finished his tea. The two men went to another area of the farm where the horses were housed. Quincy instructed Samuel to wait outside. He then went into the stable and returned with a fine stallion.

Quincy asked Samuel, "Samuel, have you ever rode a horse before?"

Samuel replied, "No sa."

Quincy said, "Well, I will teach you how to mount, shoe and ride a horse. The rest of the month you can work in the fields in the early part of the day and I'll teach you about horses in the later part of the day."

Samuel nodded. He and Quincy discussed what Samuel needed to work on during the day, and Samuel was off to work. Every day, six days a week, Samuel would work on the farm in the morning and come to the stable by noon for his lessons. By December, Samuel could mount, fit and ride a horse. Samuel was feeling much better about his living conditions. He was riding a horse now. Slaves didn't ride horses. For the first time in his life, Samuel began to feel like a man and not a slave.

It was now the middle of December. Christmas was approaching. Winter had settled in. Quincy gave Samuel a coat and boots so he could continue to work outside. Kora was now in her second trimester. Kora was also working closely with Quincy's wife Amanda. Amanda was very fond of Kora. She often let Kora work sitting down so she could get off her feet. Christmas was the most celebrated holiday of the year in Quincy's home. Samuel and Kora knew how to prepare Christmas dinner. They had participated in the preparation of Christmas dinner since they were children.

On Christmas morning, Samuel killed and skinned a pig and a turkey. Kora baked both animals with all the trimmings. Quincy invited several friends and relatives over for dinner. Everyone admired the food. Several people claimed this was the best Christmas dinner they had ever tasted.

Kora was extremely tired on Christmas evening. Preparing Christmas dinner for ten people was not an easy task. A few hours before dinner was served, Kora asked Amanda if she could lie down for a moment. Amanda was surprised. Kora had never requested a break before. Amanda granted Kora her wish. Kora took her break and returned to serve dinner. After dinner was served, Amanda noticed for the first time that Kora was moving slower than usual. After dinner, Amanda assisted Kora in the kitchen. There wasn't much to clean up because Kora was also an efficient worker. On her plantation, Kora also learned to be well organized. Years ago, Kora realized that if she cleaned up the kitchen while she cooked, she would have less of a mess to clean up after everyone finished eating. Kora was gaining weight rapidly in her second trimester. Kora's feet were starting to swell and hurt. She was not working at her usual efficient pace. Kora's request for a break was what made Amanda began to realize that Kora needed a maternity leave.

Amanda thought about Kora's condition. Amanda realized that if Kora did not take care of the house, she would have to. Amanda and Kora had connected while Kora was working in the house. Amanda liked Kora. Not only was Kora naturally beautiful, she was very mild mannered, gracious, pleasant and a good worker. Just as Kora won over her runaway slave companions, she won the admiration of Amanda. Amanda could no longer watch Kora suffer.

After Christmas dinner Amanda went to Quincy to discuss giving Kora some time off. Quincy was not receptive to the idea of letting Kora stay on the farm without working. Amanda pleaded her case to Quincy. Amanda reminded Quincy that with the money he was saving by not paying Samuel, Kora and Samuel's room and board were more than covered. She also told him that she could take care of the house. She had taken care of it before and she could take care of it again. Reluctantly, Quincy agreed.

The next morning, Samuel and Kora started their daily duties. Amanda met Kora in the kitchen to inform her she could return to the barn to rest. Kora was confused. No white person ever expressed any type of kindness to her before. Kora thought she was being punished for asking for a break.

She said to Amanda, "Please Mrs. Manley, I sorry I asked fo' a break. I was a little tired with the baby and all but I'z fine now."

Amanda responded, "Kora, you don't understand. You are not being punished. You need a break. Take some time off until your baby is born."

Kora stood in the middle of the kitchen in shock. Amanda walked up to Kora and put her hand on Kora's shoulder. Kora returned from her brief state of shock. She went back to the barn. She lit the barn fire and started reading the Bible that she had taken from Master Tom's plantation. Around noon, Samuel went to the house for lunch. Amanda informed Samuel his wife was in the barn resting. Amanda gave Samuel two plates of chicken and beans. Samuel took the plates to Kora and ate lunch with his wife.

During their lunch, Kora expressed how happy she was. Kora could not believe that a white person could be this nice to her. Now Samuel knew they were free. His wife was resting while she carried his child and Quincy was teaching Samuel a trade that he needed to earn a living as a free man.

Samuel was working in the stable with Quincy during the winter. In the first half of the day, Samuel was still taking care of the farm animals. In the second half of the day, Samuel was in the stable shoeing, saddling and grooming Quincy's premium riding horses. Quincy noticed that Samuel was a natural with the animals. Samuel loved being around the horses and they loved him. Quincy allowed Samuel to show his prize-winning riding horse to prospective buyers.

Samuel's brief life as a freed man had left him very satisfied. His wife was resting and having a healthy pregnancy. Samuel's job duties were expanding each month. Quincy took Samuel into town and introduced him to several other Quakers that Quincy received supplies from. He then allowed Samuel to run errands regularly.

As the rainy days of spring returned, Samuel was looking forward to becoming a father. It was now May, and Kora was due any day. One day, Samuel went into Marcus Hook to pick up supplies for the farm. As he returned to the farm, Quincy's son Alex met him at the farm entrance. Alex was on his horse and on his way into town to find Samuel. He was excited to see him.

Alex told Samuel, "Samuel, it's Kora. She is having your baby."

Samuel's face lit up with enthusiasm. He immediately asked Alex, "Where is she?"

Alex turned his horse around and said, "In the barn."

The two men rode off toward the barn as fast as they could. Alex on his horse and Samuel in his wagon. They approached the barn, dismounted and walked into the doorway. They saw Quincy walking toward them. As Quincy walked out of the barn, he put his hands on Alex and Samuel. He motioned for them to come back outside with him.

Quincy said, "Come on boys, we need to wait out here. Amanda can take care of Kora."

Samuel was very nervous. He didn't say much. He just kept pacing back and forth. Then Kora screamed in pain. Everyone heard her. Samuel started to go inside the barn.

Quincy stood in front of him and said, "Calm down, Samuel. Amanda can take care of Kora. If Amanda needs us, she will call us."

Samuel did not say a word, he just started pacing again. After about an hour, the three men were tired of standing. They decided to sit under a nearby crabapple tree. Inside the barn, Amanda was helping Kora bring a new life into a free world. Kora was on her back, lying on top of a bed of hay. Her legs were spread and her hands were on her stomach. Amanda was by her side, trying to comfort her. Amanda was wiping the sweat from Kora's head with a damp cloth. Amanda also had towels waiting to wrap Kora's newborn in. As Kora felt her contraction move from her uterus to her vaginal cavity, she moaned in pain. Kora's contractions were only a few minutes apart. Her birth canal was widening has her body shifted her unborn baby's body to the birthing position. After nine months, Kora was ready to deliver her and Samuel's child. She screamed in pain as the baby started moving down her birth canal. Amanda held her hand and encouraged her to push. Kora screamed and pushed, screamed and pushed, then screamed and pushed some more. Kora managed to push their child out of her uterus and into her birth canal. Amanda was in between Kora's legs, waiting with blankets to catch the child. As Kora pushed, she took small intermediate breaks to catch her breath, then she pushed and screamed again. As she pushed, Amanda saw the baby's head.

Amanda told Kora, "I can see the head Kora. Push, Kora, push!"

Kora pushed with all her strength. The baby moved through her birth canal on to Amanda and her waiting blanket. Amanda gently grabbed the baby by its shoulders, supported its head and helped it through the canal. Amanda removed the child as Kora breathed a sigh of relief. Then Amanda cut the umbilical cord and wrapped the child in her waiting blanket. She crawled up Kora's side until she was able to place the child on Kora's chest and into her immediate, anticipating, outreached arms.

Amanda looked at Kora with the child in her arms and said to her, "You did it, Kora. You did it."

Kora smiled and said, "Thank you Amanda. Fo' everythin'. Where's Samuel?"

Amanda said, "He's outside. I'll get him."

Amanda walked outside to get Samuel. She stayed outside with her son Alex and her husband Quincy. Samuel walked inside anxiously to see his wife and their newborn child. Kora was on her bed of hay with a blanket over her and their separately wrapped child in her arms. Samuel smiled from ear to ear. He had never felt more satisfied in his life. Here was this beautiful woman that loved him and gave him the greatest gift a woman can give a man, a beautiful healthy newborn child.

Samuel walked up to his wife and new member of their family. He kneeled down beside them and put his hand on Kora's head. He kissed her on her forehead.

He said, "You did real good, baby. Real good."

Kora said, "Thanks, Samuel. We never talked about a name."

Samuel smiled and asked, "Is it a boy or girl?"

Kora paused and joyfully told her husband, "It's a boy. You want him to be a junior, don't you?"

Samuel asked, "Why you tink dat? You tink you know me, don't you?"

Kora replied, "Oh I know you alright Samuel Freeman. I know you. I think Samuel Freeman Junior is a fine name."

Samuel said, "Then Samuel Freeman Junior it is."

As Samuel said this, he looked down and noticed Samuel Jr. sucking on Kora's breast. Kora was feeding their child for the first time. They gave Junior a few minutes to finish his first meal. Then they placed him in a crib that Samuel had made. Junior fell asleep pretty fast and so did Kora. Samuel knew she needed her rest. He just lay on his back for a moment looking at the roof. Then he got up and invited Quincy and Alex in to see his son. The three men stood over Samuel's son and admired him in his manger.

Spring turned into summer and the next few summer months were very enjoyable for everyone on the farm. As Samuel Jr. grew, Kora returned to work in Amanda's kitchen and took her son with her. Kora was feeling much better when she returned to work. Her efficient, hard-working manner returned. Samuel Jr. was a happy baby. He sat on the kitchen table and watched Kora and Amanda work. The two women consistently acknowledged his presence with phrases of love and affection.

Samuel Freeman Junior strongly resembled both of his parents. His skin was golden brown, he had sandy brown hair and his mother's light green eyes. Junior was a long, lean baby with a hearty appetite. Kora and her son developed an early method of communication. If he was hungry, he held out his hands and smiled. Kora picked him up, sat down and allowed him to nurse as she covered him with a blanket.

Samuel's daily routine didn't change. He worked on the farm early in the day and he was either in the stables or in Marcus Hook getting supplies in the afternoon. Samuel worked hard all day and came home to a loving wife and his infant son every night. In the evening, Samuel and Kora ate dinner and played with Samuel Jr. until they went to bed. Every day Samuel became more and more content with his life. He had almost everything he wanted.

Samuel lived near the Delaware border and slave catchers were in abundance. Samuel lived by the unwritten curfew that Harriet had advised him of. Whenever he was in town, he was sure to return to the farm by dusk. This was his only discomfort. Samuel's biggest fear was getting caught by a slave catcher and removed from his newfound freedom and family. He began to contemplate leaving Quincy's farm. Samuel preformed his daily duties and considered his options every day.

He thought, if he did leave, where would he and his family go?

On a hot day in August, Samuel was in Marcus Hook when he witnessed something he never thought he would. He walked into a store for some saddles and horseshoes. Samuel was now a regular with this merchant. He consistently purchased supplies for Quincy on credit with the owner who was a friend of Quincy's. As he walked into the store, he noticed another Negro making a purchase with cash. This stood out in Samuel's mind for two reasons:

1. Samuel never noticed any other Negroes in Marcus Hook.
2. This Negro was paying for his merchandise with cash and he could count.

When the man turned around, him and Samuel observed each other. Samuel walked up to the man and extended his hand. The two men greeted each other and went outside to the storefront to chat for a minute. There were not a lot of Negroes in Marcus Hook, Pennsylvania. Marcus Hook's proximity to the Delaware border and reputation for housing slave catchers made it appear uninhabitable for most ex-slaves. This runaway's name was Donald. Donald was from Virginia. He told Samuel that he had been a free man for almost two years now, and he was in town to get some supplies and to see if he could find a contact for Harriet Tubman. Donald had heard that Harriet came through Marcus Hook on her way back to the south. He was also informed that there were several abolitionists and Quakers that assisted her. This made Marcus Hook a very dangerous but tempting place for runaway slaves that were determined to get the rest of their families out of bondage. Samuel didn't tell Donald about his knowledge of Harriet's plans. Samuel was looking forward to seeing his friend Harriet whenever she returned. Samuel did not know or trust Donald. He told Donald he had no knowledge of Harriet Tubman. He wished Donald well and went back into the store to complete his purchase. Samuel returned home to his family. That evening Samuel told Kora about his encounter with Donald. Kora agreed with her husband's decision not to confide with a total stranger.

The rest of the summer went by very fast. Samuel and Kora went about their daily duties as normal working class people. Samuel's fear of getting abducted by slave catchers grew more and more until the day came when he decided it was time he discussed moving with his wife. That same day, Samuel was in Marcus Hook getting equipment again. Samuel had a large order. It took him an hour to load his wagon. As he was leaving town, he noticed it was getting close to dusk. Samuel began to get concerned because his wagon was heavier than usual this afternoon. He calculated it would take him twice as long to get home. Samuel was halfway home when he noticed another wagon on the side of the road. Samuel recognized the occupant of the wagon and he stopped. The wagon on the side of the road had a broken wheel. It was occupied by one of Quincy's business associates. The man's name was George Thompson. He owned the feed store Samuel purchased the farm animal's food from. Samuel stopped his wagon and got out.

He said to George, "Mista Thompson, I gots a spear wheel in my wagon. I'll puts it on for ya."

George replied, "Why thank you Samuel, that's very kind of you."

That was not the answer Samuel wanted to hear. Samuel usually didn't carry an extra wagon wheel, but today it was one of his supplies. The spare wagon wheel was on the wagon's floor. Samuel would have to remove half of his load to get to the wheel. As soon as Samuel saw George broke down on the side of the road, he knew that he was getting home well after dark. He was hoping George would tell him he was fine and would not need his help. This was not the case. George needed Samuel's help. As Samuel unloaded his wagon, George unloaded his. The two men had changed wagon wheels before. They knew the process. Changing a wagon wheel is an intense two-man-minimum labor job. The wagon with the broken wheel had to be empty. The wagon with the broken wheel needed to be as light as possible because one of the men had to hold up the wagon while the other one changed the wheel. By the time Samuel got to his extra wheel, the sun was resting on the horizon. George emptied his wagon and Samuel rolled the wheel to the side of his wagon. Samuel then walked to the rear of the wagon on the broken wheel side. With George next to him and kneeling down in front of the damaged wheel, Samuel looked at George and George nodded, indicating that he was ready. Samuel bent his back, secured the wagon's axle, then straightened his legs. The wagon was heavy. Samuel had to put all of his strength into this squat. Once his legs were straightened, the wagon was elevated enough for George to remove the old wheel and replace it with the new one.

Fortunately for Samuel, George had changed a wagon wheel before. Because of George's experience, Samuel only had to hold the wagon up for a few minutes. After the wheel was changed, the two men reloaded their wagons. George thanked Samuel and rode off, leaving Samuel alone on the dark dirt road. Samuel was very uncomfortable. He was never out this late. Samuel was also angry with George. All the citizens of Marcus Hook knew slave catchers were prevalent in their city. The sheriff was also a Quaker and an abolitionist. He provided some protection for the few Negroes in Marcus Hook. Everyone knew the sheriff could not protect the runaways all the time. All Negroes were advised not to be out after dark. Samuel knew George knew about the unwritten Negro curfew. Samuel felt George left him alone without any regard for his safety after Samuel helped him. This thought did not sit well with Samuel. As he rode his wagon home his worst nightmare came true.

Samuel heard a voice behind him say, "Let me see yo' papers boy."

Samuel froze. He was paralyzed with fear. He could not move. He brought his wagon to a halt and heard the man ride along his left side.

The man said again, "Boy, did you hear me? Let me see your papers."

Samuel knew what this man wanted. Slaves that were legally freed were required to keep their freedom declaration papers on them. This prevented them from being confused with escaped slaves. Samuel knew that if this man was asking for his papers he must be a slave catcher. The fact that Samuel did not have any papers declaring him a free man didn't matter. Slave catchers were known for destroying legally freed slave's freedom papers and returning them to slavery for a bounty.

Samuel heard this man approaching on his left side and he thought about Kora and his son, Samuel Jr. Samuel's mind was racing. His focus on his family allowed him to overcome his fear. He had to quickly come up with a plan. Samuel decided to act like an individual of lesser intelligence. He looked to his left and saw the man on his horse five feet away staring at him. Samuel quickly sized him up. This man was short and thin. A weak frail man Samuel thought. Samuel knew he could and would kill him.

Samuel said, "I'z got my papas right hear sir."

Samuel reached into his shirt as if he was getting the papers. Samuel pulled his hand out of his shirt and climbed out of his wagon. He walked up to the man on his horse and held his hand up like he had something in it. It was dark and the man could not clearly see that Samuel's hand was empty. The slave catcher reached down toward Samuel's hand to get the paper work. Samuel seized his opportunity to save his own life. He grabbed the slave catcher by his arm. This individual had very thin arms. Samuel's massive hand covered the skinny slave catcher's entire arm by his elbow. Samuel then pulled him off his horse. The man yelled and hit the ground with a loud thud. The slave catcher looked up from the ground at his worst fear. This five foot five, one hundred and thirty pound white slave catcher was looking up at a six foot four inch two hundred and twenty pound ex-slave determined not to go back. As the man hit the ground, Samuel realized that he was no longer the victim. Now he was the executioner and this slave catcher was about to become Samuel's first victim. Samuel looked down on his target and saw Charles. In this brief moment, Samuel thought about all of the times that Charles had physically abused him. Now there was no plow for Samuel to take his rage out on, no Harold to calm him down. Samuel released his fury by driving his knee into his assailant's chest. As Samuel's knee crushed his sufferer's ribs, the would-be slave catcher let out a loud, high-pitched screech. Samuel seized his victim's collar and every piece of white flesh immediately above it with both his hands. The man tried to scream but, as Samuel applied pressure to the victim's neck, the slave catcher felt his esophagus being crushed. Now Samuel's wounded assailant's air circulation was cut off from his brain. As Samuel looked down on the injured party, he saw his victim's eyes open wide as the slave catcher realized he was looking death in the face. The slave catcher made one last attempt to save his life. Samuel's assailant grabbed Samuel's massive arms and tried to remove his death grip. When Samuel's sufferer could not remove Samuel's grip, he dug his nails into both of Samuel's arms and scratched Samuel in a downward motion as hard as he could. Samuel did not even feel the little man's last desperate effort to free himself. Samuel lifted his hands with the slave catcher's throat in them and plummeted him back to the ground several times, banging his victim's head on the ground with each stroke. This ferocious pounding caused his prey's skull to crack open. The slave catcher was gasping for air with his mouth open and tongue out. The severe concussion caused Samuel's assailant to have a seizure. Samuel's perpetrator started having convulsions and his jaw locked shut and severed its own tongue. Samuel raised his prey's head one last time and the bloody tongue hit Samuel in his face. Samuel moved his arms in a downward motion one more time and opened his hands. His former assailant's body hit the ground one last time and lay there, motionless.

Samuel was in shock for a moment. He stood there, staring at the Caucasian and his bloody hands. As his adrenalin level lowered, he felt pain in his arms from his prey's scratches. This brought Samuel to his senses. Samuel came to and realized what he had done. He quickly picked up the body and threw it into the shrubbery on the side of the road. He then tied the man's horse to his wagon and proceeded home. Samuel's wagon was still full. He thought about unloading it and then decided it would take him too long to unload his wagon again. His wagon stayed full and Samuel's ride home seemed like an eternity to him. His mind was spinning. He knew he had a big problem. He had killed a white man. If he were caught, he would surely be hung. Getting caught was not an option. As he entered the farm, he knew what he had to do.

Chapter Eleven
Escaping their Escape

Samuel entered the farm and hoped that no one noticed him. It was late and everyone was in the house. As Samuel approached his home/barn, his adrenalin level increased again. Samuel was concerned about Kora and Samuel Jr. He knew they had to leave immediately. On his way home, he decided to take Harriet's advice and take his family to Philadelphia. Before Samuel went into the barn, he walked to the well to wash the blood off his arms and hands. Then he walked into the barn and saw Kora sitting on a crate, feeding Samuel Jr.

Kora looked at her husband and asked him, "Hey Samuel, where have you been?"

Samuel proceeded toward them and Kora saw the scratches on his arms.

She gasped and asked him, "What happened Samuel?!"

Samuel looked at his family and as calmly as possible he said, "We have to leave this place, NOW!"

Kora was stunned. Samuel never told her how dangerous going into Marcus Hook was because he didn't want his wife to worry. Now he had to quickly ask Kora to leave the place they called home. Samuel demanded that Kora start packing.

He said, "Come on woman, start packing, I'll explain everytin' whiles we get our stuff together."

Kora saw how serious and upset her husband was. She knew that something terrible had happened. She decided it would be best to do as her husband requested and allow him to give her the details at his own discretion. She placed their son in his crib and started getting together everything she thought they needed.

Samuel looked at his wife and barked at her, "What the hell you do'n woman?! We ain't go'n on no vacation! Just takes what we needs fo' now. We has to travel light."

Kora looked at Samuel as he ran outside to the wagon. Her husband was acting very erratic. She began to get even more worried. She walked to the doorway of their barn and looked at Samuel. He was untying his victim's horse.

Kora asked him, "Samuel, where did you get that horse?"

Samuel responded, "Don't worry about that now. Just grab a few clothes, some food an' a cook'n pot. We gots to go!"

Kora returned to the barn and did as her husband requested. She gathered a few clothes for her, Junior and her husband, some fruit, grits and a cooking pot. Samuel came back into the barn.

He looked at Kora's collection and said, "That's my girl."

Then he laid out two blankets, one on top of the other, on the middle of the ground. He put everything in the middle of the blankets and tied up the corners with a rope. He slung their self-made traveling bag over his shoulder and started walking toward his attacker's horse.

He looked at Kora and said, "Come on baby, get Junior and let's go!"

Kora was confused and upset about the fact that her husband was in this rage and would not explain to her why he was uprooting the family all of a sudden. Kora trusted Samuel. She had followed him off the plantation and he had been a good provider for them so far. She knew he would always protect her and Junior. She did as he asked without question. Once outside the barn, Samuel told Kora to get on the horse with

Junior. He then led the horse with his family on it off the farm and toward a new life in Philadelphia.

Samuel was a planner. He was always plotting his next move. When he met Donald a month ago in Marcus Hook, Donald told him he lived in Philadelphia. Samuel engaged Donald in small talk to get directions to Philadelphia. Before Donald left, Samuel knew the direction and riding distance of his new home. Donald told Samuel all he did was follow the river for a day on his horse. Samuel was with his family and walking while they rode the slave catcher's horse. Samuel estimated it would take them two or three days to get to Philadelphia. However long it took it was too long for Samuel. He wanted to get far from Marcus Hook as soon as possible.

Samuel approached the nearby river and led his family upstream by walking in front of the horse while guiding them. He walked in the shallow edge of the water just as Harriet had instructed Kora to do a year ago. Samuel knew that this would keep the sheriff and his posse from tracking him. Samuel was extremely paranoid. In his mind, he saw the citizens of Marcus Hook discovering the slave catcher's corpse, realizing he must have killed this man, and coming to Quincy's farm with a lynch mob, looking for him. He continued to move through the night. Kora didn't say one word. Junior was asleep in her arms.

The three slowly and silently moved up the river for hours until the sun began rising behind the traveling fugitive and his family. Once Samuel noticed the sun's reflection in the water awaiting his footsteps, he turned around to see the dawn. Samuel's plan was to travel upstream at night, like Harriet, and rest in the forest during the day. As the sun came up, Samuel led his family into the trees on the banks of the river. He assisted Kora off of the horse with Junior. He then untied the blankets and laid them out for his family to lie down on. Kora was exhausted. She had stayed awake riding all night while Samuel walked upstream. Her buttocks and thighs were very sore. Kora did not complain. She did not say a word. She just lay on the blanket with their son in her arms. Junior was awake now. It was time for his morning feeding. Kora started feeding him while Samuel gathered firewood. Samuel started a fire and placed a pot with water in it on the fire. While he waited for the water to come to a boil he walked the horse to the river to allow it to graze and drink. When Samuel returned, Kora was stirring the grits with a stick. Samuel did not notice the stick in their pot of grits. Samuel Jr. was sitting up, watching his mother stir as she watched him and the grits. Junior looked at his father and smiled. The child started laughing and held his hands out for his father to pick him up and play with him. Samuel fulfilled his son's request. He picked his son up, spun him around, and lifted him in the air several times. Junior expressed his happiness by smiling and giggling as he looked up at the treetops. Junior's joy made Samuel forget about all his concerns for a moment. Samuel was so happy to make his son laugh that he was smiling and laughing himself. Kora observed the two and also smiled as her son expressed his joy.

She then said, "Breakfast is ready."

Samuel stopped spinning and secured his son against his chest. He walked over to Kora and sat on the blanket with his family.

Kora told him, "In our rush, I forgot the bowls."

She then looked at Samuel to see how he would respond. Samuel was looking at their son in his arms. He looked up, gently kissed Kora on the cheek and said, "You did real good, baby. Real good."

Kora placed the pot of grits with the sick in it on the ground in between herself and Samuel. The two adults looked at each other for a moment. Then Kora started laughing vigorously. She tried to keep her laughter muffled by covering her mouth. She leaned back and lay on her back with her hand over her mouth and continued laughing.

Samuel looked at his wife, waiting for her to tell him what was so funny.

She finally composed herself enough to tell her husband, "We ain't got no spoons either!"

Samuel started laughing also. Not as hard as his wife, but he did find it funny. Here they were, running for their lives, hungry, with a pot of hot grits and no bowls or spoons. Regardless, they were together and they were happy. The two paused for a brief moment. They decided to let the grits cool off for a while, then eat with their hands. Samuel knew this was the perfect time to tell his patient wife why they were here. Whenever Samuel had to engage in a difficult conversation, he approached the situation the same way he approached all difficult situations he faced, head on.

Samuel looked Kora in the eye and told her, "Thank you."

Kora giggled and said, "For what? Making you eat with your hands?"

Samuel replied, "No, fo' trusting me. Fo' following me without question."

Kora realized that her husband was serious and the mood quickly changed from a jovial moment to a somber one.

Kora responded by saying, "I love you, baby. I'll always follow you."

Samuel said, "I know. We here cause I killed a man. A slave catcher caught me on my way home. He was going to take me back to the south. I couldn't let him take me away from you two."

Kora was silent. Now she knew why Samuel made them leave. She understood and supported her husband's difficult decision to leave. She placed her finger in the grits to see how hot they were.

She looked at Samuel and asked him, "Are you hungry baby?"

99

Samuel smiled, continued to hold Samuel Jr., put his hand in the pot, removed a handful of grits and proceeded to eat the grits out of his hand. Kora did the same. The two ate their breakfast together in a joyful bliss, just happy to be together. After breakfast, Kora lay down to get some rest. Samuel stayed up to keep watch and entertain his son.

Before Kora went to sleep, she looked at Samuel and asked him, "Where are we going, Samuel?"

Samuel replied, "Philadelphia."

Kora just looked at her man, smiled, and went to sleep.

Samuel stayed awake. He was too tense to sleep. He enjoyed spending time with his son. He also kept an eye out for the Marcus Hook sheriff and his gang. Samuel was sure the sheriff knew what he had done by now. He did not think that the sheriff could track him in the river, but he was still too paranoid to sleep. For the next several hours, Samuel lay on his back with his son on his chest. He tried to unwind, but he couldn't, so he just relaxed and bounced Junior on his chest. Junior soon fell asleep on top of his father. He woke up a few hours later, agitated. Junior had his hands out and he was starting to cry. Samuel knew that his son was hungry. Kora was still asleep. Samuel placed Junior on the blanket and watched him. Samuel was curious. He wanted to see where his five-month-old son's instincts would take him. Junior crawled to his mother as she lay on her side with her back to them. He didn't have far to go. Kora was right next to them. Junior tried to pull himself up Kora's back. He was trying to reach his mother's breast and drink his lunch. Kora felt Junior pulling on her side. She awakened, looked over her shoulder, and slowly moved away from her son so she could turn on her back to feed their child.

While Kora fed Junior, she looked at Samuel and said, "Don't look at me like that, Samuel."

Samuel asked, "Like what?"

Kora smiled and responded, "Like you wish you were on top of me instead of Junior."

Samuel did not have a lustful look in his eye. He did have a look of appreciation on his face.

He responded to Kora by saying, "Woman, please. I ain't think'n about love'n right now."

Kora quickly and firmly asked her husband, "So what you trying to say, Samuel?"

Samuel said, "I didn't mean it that way. I means I got a lot on my mine and love'n ain't one of them. I was just look'n at you feed Junior and realizing how lucking I am."

Kora finished feeding Samuel Jr. and placed him on the blanket.

She then looked at her husband and said, "Please, I'm the lucky one. Any woman would be lucky to have you. You said you have a lot on your mind. Care to talk about it?"

Samuel hesitated, then he said, "I know I did da right thing. I know if I didn't do what I did I be backs down south by now. I just don't know why do'n the right thing feels so wrong. I keep see'n him in my head, over and over and over. I sees my hands squeeze'n his throat, squeeze'n the life out of him. I cain't get him out my head."

Kora got on her knees and crawled behind her husband.

She then hugged him from behind and told him, "You are right, baby. You did what you had to do. Time will heal all your wounds. You are not a killer. That is why you are struggling with what happened last night. You will be OK. Just give it some time."

Kora kissed Samuel on his cheek. Samuel smiled and leaned back. Kora laid down on her back with Samuel's back in her lap. The two lay on their blanket looking at the treetops. After talking with Kora, Samuel was able to fall asleep. Samuel fell into a fast, deep sleep. Kora eased out from underneath Samuel and played with Samuel Jr. while her husband rested.

Samuel slept until the early evening. He woke up hungry and well rested. Kora was by his side, watching Samuel Jr. fall asleep for the evening. Samuel stood up, stretched and gathered some firewood again. Then Samuel started a fire while Kora prepared the pot, water and grits. The two cooked and ate the stick-stirred grits with their hands again.

As they ate, Samuel asked Kora, "You ready to move again, baby?"

Kora responded, "I guess. It is so peaceful here."

Samuel said to his wife, "Remember, we are on the run, not a vacation. We needs to get to Philadelphia."

Kora asked, "Why Philadelphia?"

Samuel replied, "Cause other ex-slaves like us lives in South Philadelphia. We going to South Philadelphia, find jobs and settle down."

Kora gave her usual smile of approval. Then the two packed and continued Northeast with the night's darkness blanketing them. They followed the river upstream. This time, Samuel walked on the shore to make better time. He was sure no one could have followed them from Marcus Hook. Kora stayed awake, held Samuel Jr. and rode horseback the rest of the night. Samuel led his family throughout the entire night. Samuel's legs were in perfect condition to make the walk from years of pushing his plough though Master Tom's fields. When dawn came, Samuel knew that he was close to their destination. Through the sun's early light, Samuel noticed a cattle-herding fence not far off the river's bed.

Samuel knew where there was a fence, there would be a farm. He decided to take a chance and ask if he could do a day's work for a meal and a place to stay overnight. Samuel brought his family within yelling distance of the fence. He left them with the horse and told Kora if anything happened, she was to take Junior and continue Northeast without him. When Kora kissed her husband, she knew it was not goodbye. She knew after overcoming all the obstacles they encountered since they left the plantation, this short, unknown adventure would not take her husband away from her. Samuel climbed the fence and proceeded cautiously toward a house he saw in the middle of the farm.

While he walked, he heard a voice call to him.

The voice bellowed, "Hey you."

Samuel stopped walking and turned toward the voice.

Samuel focused on and then made eye contact with the individual calling to him. This person proceeded toward Samuel and Samuel walked toward the person to meet the individual halfway. As the two people approached one another, the blurry shapes of the two bodies came into focus for each other. Samuel could see this was another Negro male approaching him. Once Samuel was about three feet away from him, he stopped walking and so did the other person. Samuel could clearly see that this man was a field hand. He was dressed in field hand clothes and had a physique like a field hand. The two men sized each other up for a moment. The man Samuel was looking at was an older gentleman, about five foot ten inches tall, dark skinned and he had a thick grey beard. Samuel was still on guard. The other individual looked like Samuel, but Samuel still did not know or trust this person.

The other man said, "What you dewn here, boy?"

Samuel replied, "Look'n fo' work."

Then Samuel extended his hand and said, "I'm Samuel."

The other person shook Samuel's hand and replied, "Jesse. If you look'n fo' work, I could use a hand around here. Come on, I'll takes you up to the house and ask my masa if it's OK. "

The two men walked up to the house together. They entered the kitchen and took their hats off.

Then Jessie walked to the stairs and said in a loud voice, "Excuse me, Masa. Can yous come down fo' a minute?"

Samuel heard someone moving around upstairs. Then he heard footsteps coming toward the steps. Each step echoed from the top going down. Samuel waited anxiously and nervously to see the person Jessie called Masa. After Samuel heard a few steps from the top of the stairs, he saw the boots that caused the wooden steps to announce Jessie's masa's arrival. Then he saw the blue overalls, and then the white man dressed in overalls and wearing a straw hat and boots.

The white man came halfway down stairs and asked, "What you want Jessie?"

When Samuel laid his eyes on Jessie's white masa, his first thought was to run. He was thinking that he had made a wrong turn somewhere and somehow ended up back in the south. Samuel did not run. He was very tense. Samuel stood in the kitchen of this northern slave owner, studying the relationship between Jessie and the white man, wondering how Jessie could be in the north and still be a slave.

While Samuel studied Jessie, the old slave replied, "This Samuel, he a field hand look'n fo' work. I could use a little help, Masa."

The white farmer came completely down the stairs and walked toward Samuel.

With a deep southern drawl he asked Samuel, "You ever worked on a farm befo', boy?

Samuel hesitated a moment. He was very uneasy. This farmer looked and spoke like a southern slave owner. The farmer stood there waiting for an answer with his thumbs stretching his suspenders.

Samuel replied, "Yes sa."

The farmer was chewing tobacco. He walked to the kitchen door, opened it and spit his tobacco from his doorway, over the porch and onto the adjacent grass. He then walked back into the kitchen and looked at Samuel. He looked Samuel up and down, studying him.

He asked Samuel, "What's yo' name, boy?"

Samuel replied, "Samuel sa."

Then the farmer asked Samuel, "Where you from, boy?"

Samuel said, "Marcus Hook, sa."

The farmer said in a harsh voice, "Bullshit! Ain't no niggers in Marcus Hook. Where you from boy?"

Samuel's adrenalin level was rising again. Samuel's mind was racing and his pulse increasing. For a moment he thought about running again. He decided not to run but see if the farmer would allow him to do some work.

He cautiously answered the farmer's question and said, "Delaware, sa."

The farmer replied, "Just what I thought. Another nigger on the run. Damn, with all you niggers running up north, how the hell they get'n any work done down south?"

Samuel and Jessie were quiet. The farmer then asked, "You got yo' family with you, boy?"

Samuel replied, "No sa. Just me, sa."

The farmer replied, "I thinks you bullshit'n me again boy. I don't trust niggers, Jesse get'n up in age and needs some help. You looks like you worked on a farm befo'. Follow Jessie, he will tell you what to do. I cain't pay you but I will give you some of the crops you picks."

Jesse and Samuel turned and walked out the door. The farmer followed them.

He spit in the grass again and harshly stated, "Jesse, no mo nigger workers. Too many niggers don't work well together. Y'all just wants to talk and bullshit all day. You hear me Jesse? No mo' nigger workers."

Jessie replied, "I hear ya, Masa. I hear ya."

Once the two men were away from the house and in the field, Samuel asked Jesse, "Jesse, how long you been with yo' Masa?"

Jessie replied, "Don't know. Long time, long time."

Samuel also asked Jesse, "You know you in the north and free, don't you?"

Jesse replied, "Of course I knows that, I ain't no fool. I stays with Masa cause he good to me. He take care of me."

Samuel could not believe there were slaves that were in the north and still did not want to leave their masters.

He then asked Jesse, "How y'alls get here anyway?"

Jesse said, "We from Virginia. Masa wife died from scarlet feva. Then Masa moved here and married his dead wife sister. He sold all his other slaves. I'z the only one came with him. But he good to me. Real good."

Samuel opened his mouth to ask another question.

Before his words came out, Jessie bellowed at Samuel, "You gon' ask me a bunch of questions or do some work!?"

Samuel calmly replied, "I just got one mo question, which way to Philadelphia?"

Samuel knew the way but he wanted to ask to see if Jesse would truthfully answer him. Jesse did by pointing northeast.

Jesse said, "Just keep follow'n the river upstream for a few miles. You will see a dirt road through the forest. Follow the road into Philadelphia."

Samuel replied, "Thank you."

Then he turned and walked off a slave owner's farm again, leaving one indentured servant to tend to the farm duties. Not two.

Samuel found his family just where he had left them. As he approached his family in the middle of the woods, he noticed his wife and son asleep on their blankets. Seeing them sleep looked very inviting to Samuel. He walked over to his slumbering wife and pulled her hair off her forehead. Kora awakened and quickly and sat up.

Samuel smiled and said, "It just me women. Go back to sleep."

Kora said, "You scared me, Samuel."

Samuel said, "I know. I sorry about that."

Kora asked her husband, "Did you find any work on that farm?"

Samuel said, "No. I want to rest a while. Then go to Philadelphia tonight."

As Samuel said this, he pulled back the blankets that covered his wife and child. He climbed under the blanket and held Kora as she lay back down. Samuel slept for several hours. He woke up in the late evening. Kora was up with Samuel Jr. when Samuel awakened. Samuel arose from his long, deep sleep well-rested and hungry. Kora greeted her husband.

She said to him, "Hey baby, did you sleep well?"

Samuel stretched and replied, "Yes, and I'm hungry. We got any grits left?"

Kora replied, "Yes. I'll make you a pot."

Kora made Samuel some grits. Samuel stood and picked up their son. He walked around their camping area with Samuel Jr. in his arms. Kora prepared Samuel's dinner. Samuel let his grits cool off then he put Samuel Jr. down and consumed his supper.

As Samuel ate he said, "I'm tired of grits. We needs to get to Philadelphia and get some real food."

Kora asked her husband, "How much further do we have to go?"

Samuel said, "Not far. We almost there."

Samuel finished his dinner and started loading up his family's belongings. It was dark now and late in the evening. Samuel was sure no one was tracking them, but he wanted to keep moving in the night's darkness. The three continued their journey up the river's shore. After walking for a few hours, they stopped to rest again. The family was living in the woods for the last night of their journey. Samuel decided to stop in the middle of the night to let his family rest in the woods one last time. Kora and Samuel Jr. fell asleep. Samuel stayed up and kept watch. After Kora and Junior awakened in the morning, Kora fed Samuel Jr. There was nothing for Samuel and Kora to eat because they were out of grits and fruit. If Samuel needed to, he could have found his family something to eat. Berries were prevalent in the forest they were traveling in. Samuel wanted to get to their destination. With their bellies slightly empty, Samuel made the decision to find the Philadelphia border and somehow get settled in. Samuel was uncomfortable with uprooting his family because he was not sure how he would find food and shelter for his family in Philadelphia. The only reason he choose Philadelphia for his family's new home was because Harriet recommended the city for a good place to escape to if he were in trouble. Samuel could not imagine himself in any more trouble than he was in now.

The three continued northeast in the woods as Jesse instructed them. It did not take long for Samuel to come to a clearing in the woods. As they walked out of the camouflage of the trees, they came upon a beautiful field of grassland. Samuel let their horse graze and gave Kora a break out of the saddle. Samuel looked into the northern horizon and noticed a road leading away from the river that guided them northeast. The family saddled up one more time, with Samuel continuing to lead his family on ground. They walked to and up the dirt road until they noticed a farm ahead. Samuel did not stop on this farm looking for food. He knew they were close to the end of this journey. The dirt road led past the farm and continued north. Soon after the three left the farm behind them, they came upon a large sign on the side of the road.

They stopped and Samuel asked Kora, "What's it say, baby?"

Kora smiled and said, "It says Philadelphia."

Samuel smiled and continued leading his family into their new home. He still had several concerns on his mind. He had to feed his wife and son and he still had to find shelter. Samuel moved forward knowing that somehow, everything would be OK.

Chapter Twelve
Philadelphia

The threesome headed north past the Welcome to Philadelphia sign on the side of the road. They noticed a small wooden shack less than a mile from the sign. Then they noticed another small home made of wood. The deeper they walked into the city limits, the more homes they noticed. After walking on the Philadelphia dirt road for an about an hour, they observed several buildings ahead of them on both sides of the road. Samuel eagerly picked up the pace.

He looked back at his family and said, "This is it. Philadelphia."

Kora smiled and observed their new surroundings. The road they were on opened up into a South Philadelphia neighborhood. At the entrance, Kora noticed a street sign that had the street name Bartram on it. There were two-story wooden buildings on both sides of the mouth of Bartram Street that went deeper than their eyes could see.

They arrived in Philadelphia in midday, mid week. There were a lot of people moving in and out of the buildings, caring packages, groceries and boxes. They were riding in wagons and on horses. Samuel and Kora were very surprised to see most of the people were Negros. The people of this South Philadelphia neighborhood were mostly first or second generation ex-slaves. Everyone in the black ghetto was in a state of euphoria. Samuel and Kora observed the enthusiastic Philadelphia hustle that bordered them. Kora noticed a storefront sign that said, Bartram Hotel.

Kora called from the horse to her husband and said, "Samuel there is a hotel."

Kora pointed to the hotel. Samuel led his family to the wooden fount and tied the horse up. He helped his wife and son dismount. Then they waited outside while Samuel went inside. Once inside, Samuel immediately smelled food coming from the kitchen. He ignored his grumbling stomach and walked to the front desk. There was a woman behind the desk. She noticed Samuel as he approached her. While Samuel walked toward the desk, he passed a few ladies.

Samuel courteously said, "Afternoon, ma'am."

He spoke to both women and continued toward the desk. The ladies looked at Samuel in his ragged clothes, smiled politely and watched him as he continued to move toward the desk. Samuel drew closer to the desk and examined the woman behind it for a moment. She was a Negro woman wearing a white blouse and a leaf green skirt. She had a brown bow holding her black hair in a ponytail.

Samuel said to her, "Hi ma'am, is the owner in?"

The woman said, "Yes. You looking for work?"

Samuel replied, "Yes. Is it that obvious?"

She said, "Oh, it's very obvious. What's you name?"

Samuel replied, "Samuel. Yours?"

The young lady replied, "Maxine. I'll get the owner for you, Samuel."

Maxine returned with a white woman with blond hair. She had a green bow holding her hair back. She also had a white blouse on with a brown skirt.

Maxine said, "Samuel this is Helen, Helen this is Samuel."

Samuel said, "Nice to meet you, ma'am."

Helen looked at Samuel and said, "You are right, Maxine. He does look like he could use the work. Samuel, you're in luck. Our janitor quit yesterday. You good with your hands, Samuel? "

Samuel smiled and replied, "Yes ma'am."

Helen looked at Maxine and said, "You hear that Maxine? He is good with his hands."

Maxine smiled and blushed.

Helen then looked at Samuel and asked him, "When is the last time you ate something, Samuel?"

Samuel replied, "Last night."

Helen said, "If you're hungry, Maxine can fix you something. She is a very good cook."

Maxine was silent and continued to blush.

Samuel said, "I am hungry, but I am not alone. My wife and son are outside."

Maxine stopped blushing.

Helen looked at Samuel and said, "Oh, I didn't realize you were a family man. Do you and your family have a place to stay?"

Samuel replied, "No ma'am."

Helen said, "Well, don't let them stay outside. Bring them in. Let's meet them."

Samuel walked outside and found Kora sitting on the storefront bench holding Junior.

He looked at his wife and son and said, "Come on inside. The owner wants to meet us."

Kora smiled and tried to wipe her face off as she stood up. Samuel opened the door for them and they entered the hotel. Kora walked in first, holding Samuel Jr. in a blanket. As soon as she entered, Helen and Maxine were behind the counter staring at her. Samuel reentered the hotel behind his wife and child. Kora was wearing a brown shirt and grey skirt that she had made herself. She did not have a bow. Kora did not possess the beautiful fall-colored garments Helen and Maxine were wearing. Kora had no bow to put her hair in the stylish ponytail that the other women were wearing. Kora's hair was down and very long. Samuel and Kora's clothes showed their recent travels. As Kora approached these two well-dressed, beautiful woman, she made sure that she held her head high. She walked up to the desk with her worker garments on, son in arms and husband by her side. The three arrived at the desk at the same time.

Samuel said, "Helen, Maxine, this is my wife Kora and our son, Samuel Jr."

Helen said, "Hello Kora. Nice to meet you."

Kora smiled and said, "Nice to meet you also."

Helen then said, "Your husband tells me you all are looking for work and need a place to stay."

Kora responded, "Yes ma'am, that's correct."

Helen said, "I told Samuel we can use a janitor. I guess we can always use another maid. Can you do house work?"

Kora responded, "Yes ma'am."

Helen then said, "Kora, can you go into the kitchen and cook us all something to eat? If your food is decent, you can start tomorrow."

Kora responded ,"Yes ma'am, just show me the way to your kitchen."

Helen said, "Sure. Maxine, will you show Samuel the servant quarters?"

Kora followed Helen into the kitchen with Samuel Jr. in her arms. Samuel went outside to the horse and retrieved his family's belongings. Samuel returned to the hotel lobby and saw Maxine waiting for him. The two went upstairs to Samuel and Kora's room. Maxine let Samuel in, and then proceeded back downstairs.

On her way to the stairs she said, "I hope your wife can cook."

Samuel smiled and said, "She can."

Samuel looked around the room. It was small, and had one dresser and a mirror. There was a bed on the opposite wall from the dresser. There was also a door that led to the bathroom on that same wall. Samuel sat on the bed and heard it squeak as the mattress lowered from his body weight. Samuel had not been in a bed since he was on the plantation over a year ago. That bed was not as comfortable as this one. Samuel rested his head on the down pillow for the first time and fell asleep immediately.

Helen led Kora into the kitchen. There were two other women in the kitchen when Helen and Kora walked in with Junior in Kora's arms. Helen introduced Kora to the other Negro employees. She said, "Kora, this is Wanda and Debbie."

Debbie was a very attractive woman in her mid twenties, petite and with a chocolate complexion. She also had a thick, kinky afro. Wanda was Debbie's older cousin. She was in her upper twenties and was also dark skinned. She wore her hair in two French braids. Wanda was also a lot larger then Debbie and Kora. Wanda was tall, about five foot seven inches. Wanda was a very busty and hippy woman. She carried her full figure well. Wanda was larger than the other Negro woman workers and she knew it. Wanda was bitter because she did not have anyone in her life. When she saw Kora's high yellow skin, long hair and petite hourglass figure she immediately disliked her.

After observing both women for a moment, Kora smiled and said, "Nice to meet y'all."

The two ladies smiled and Debbie said, "Your son is adorable. What's his name?

Kora replied, "Samuel Junior."

Debbie walked to Kora and started tickling Junior. The child laughed.

Kora said, "Here, you want to hold him whiles I fix us dinner?"

Debbie said, "Sure, I'd be happy to."

She then took Samuel Jr. Helen walked out of the kitchen and left Kora to complete her test. Kora looked around the kitchen. She saw everything she needed to fix a mouth-watering dinner that would surely give her family a place to stay. The hotel had a few farm animals in the back to keep a fresh supply of meat on hand. Kora went into the back and grabbed a chicken. On her way into the kitchen, she put her hand around the chicken and snapped its neck. Once in the kitchen, she cut the chicken's head off and hung it upside down on a pot rack hanging from the ceiling. The chicken was hanging and draining over a bucket. While Kora waited for the chicken to drain, she started to boil some broccoli on the wood-burning stove in the middle of the kitchen. The other women just watched. They too had been tested before. Kora found some potatoes in a cabinet. She washed them and put several into the warm oven. Kora found some lettuce and other green vegetables in small garden that the hotel maintained to keep fresh vegetables on hand. She gathered some cucumbers, tomatoes, onions and green peppers. She placed all her vegetables on the counter and washed her hands and the vegetables. She then went to Debbie to get her son. Kora knew it was time to feed Junior. She sat in a chair with Junior on her chest and proceeded to feed him. While the chicken drained, the potatoes baked and the broccoli boiled, Kora relaxed for a moment and rested while she fed their son. She was sleepy and very hungry.

Debbie asked Kora, "Where you from, Kora?"

Kora replied, "Marcus Hook."

Debbie replied, "Well you look like you know what you dew'n. We got work to do ourselves. Come Wanda, lets go."

The two women walked upstairs to continue working, leaving Kora and Junior alone in the kitchen. The chicken finished draining and Kora took it down. She then plucked all the feathers out while she held Junior in her arm. Junior was used to clinging onto his mother. Kora had often moved around Amanda's kitchen with Junior in her arms. After she plucked the chicken, Kora placed Junior on the floor in between her feet to make sure he could not crawl away. Junior was also familiar with this position. His mother often placed him on the floor if she needed both hands free. He played with her ankles and skirt while he waited for his mother to pick him up again. Kora placed Junior on the ground so she could cut the chicken into several pieces. She cut it into legs, breasts, wings, backs and included the neck. After she carved up the poultry, Kora picked up Junior. She then found some eggs outside with the chickens. Kora returned to the kitchen sink and, with Junior in her arms again, she washed the chicken in the basin, cleaned the kitchen sink, and then placed Junior in the kitchen basin. The potatoes and broccoli had been cooking for around an hour now. They were done and Kora was almost finished with dinner. Kora removed them from the oven and added wood to the oven to increase her fire. She found a deep frying pan and some bacon fat from breakfast. She placed a large amount of bacon fat in the deep frying pan and placed the pan on the open fire. While the bacon fat melted and filled the kitchen with an appetizing aroma, Kora cracked the eggs in a bowl. She then seasoned the eggs with

salt and pepper and beat them. Kora dipped the individual chicken pieces in the eggs.
She then covered the chicken pieces in flour and placed them into the waiting hot bacon
fat. The poultry made a sizzling, popping noise as each piece went into the hot grease.
While the chicken fried, Kora cut up her vegetables and made a salad for an appetizer.
She also melted some butter and mixed in honey and a bit of lemon. Kora placed her
honey lemon dressing over her salad. She continued to look at Junior who was safe in
the clean kitchen sink while she worked over the hot stove. Junior just looked at his
mother working. Kora was sure that when Junior grew up, he would know how to cook.
He spent most of his time watching her cook. After Kora cut and tossed her salad, the
chicken was floating in the bacon fat. Kora removed Junior from the basin, cleaned out
the kitchen tub again, and placed Junior on the ground for a moment. She kept an eye
on him and removed her chicken from the grease. She placed the chicken in the
kitchen basin to drain and cool off. She then picked Junior up and went out of the
kitchen with Junior in her arms. Helen and Maxine were waiting in the dining area.

Helen said, "Smells good. What we having?"

Kora said, "Salad, fried chicken, broccoli and baked potatoes."

Helen said, "Fried chicken, that's my favorite. How did you know?"

Kora responded, "Oh, that's everyone's favorite."

Kora asked Maxine to hold Junior for a moment, then went upstairs to get her husband.
She knew that Samuel was hungry. Neither one of them had eaten all day. Samuel
was asleep.

Kora awakened him and said, "Get up and wash up baby. It's time to eat."

Samuel got up, and went downstairs and out the back. There was a fresh water supply
in the back by the animals. Samuel did as his wife asked. He then joined Maxine and

Helen in the dining room. They were not alone. It was approaching suppertime. The Bartram Hotel served dinner regularly. Wanda and Debbie were in the kitchen preparing for the evening rush as soon as Kora completed her test. Kora entered the dining room with a large salad bowl. She placed it on the table and allowed their son to rejoin her in her seat with their other three eagerly waiting dinner companions.

After everyone finished eating their salad, Maxine said, "The dressing on this salad is sooo good. What is it, Kora?"

Kora replied, "Oh, just some honey and lemon."

Kora got up to get the main course. She placed Junior in Maxine's arms again. Kora looked at Samuel and asked him to help her, and the two of them went onto the kitchen. When they returned, Samuel was holding a bowl of fried chicken and Kora was carrying the broccoli and baked potatoes. Kora went back into the kitchen and returned with some butter, salt and pepper. Kora placed Junior in her lap again and everyone started to fix their plates.

After one bite of Kora's fried chicken, Maxine said, "Kora, this chicken is very good."

Kora said, "Thank you."

There wasn't much conversation at the dinner table. Everyone was enjoying Kora's meal very much. After they finished eating, Kora went into the kitchen to finish cleaning up. Wanda and Debbie were moving in and out the kitchen serving the other customers. Helen stayed at the table with Samuel.

She said to him, "Samuel, in the morning we can come up with a list of repairs for you to make. I hope you are as good a handyman as your wife is a cook."

Samuel replied, "I am."

Helen then said, "OK, I'll pay you and your wife fifty cents apiece per day, and I'll give you three room and board."

Samuel stood up, smiled and said, "Thank you and goodnight, Helen."

Then he went into the kitchen with his wife and son. Kora was working hard to get the kitchen clean. She wanted to be alone with her husband. Kora noticed Samuel in the doorway. She walked toward him and said, "Samuel, please take Junior upstairs. I'll be up in a moment."

Samuel did as his wife asked. Once Samuel was back in their room, he opened the bottom drawer of the dresser. He placed a blanket in the empty drawer. He then placed Junior on the blanket. He kept his eye on Junior to make sure he was comfortable and secure. Once Samuel was sure his son could not get out the drawer, he sat on the bed and waited for his wife to come upstairs. He did not have to wait long. Kora finished cleaning up the kitchen and went outside to the well to wash up. She returned to her husband refreshed, tired and sexually excited. Kora had not made love to her husband since they left Marcus Hook. Samuel anxiously awaited her also.

Kora walked in, Samuel smiled and said, "That was a great dinner, baby."

Kora returned Samuel's smile with one of her own and said, "Thank you, Samuel. I'm glad you liked it."

Samuel said, "Junior is asleep. Come on over here on da bed with yo' husband, baby."

Kora replied, "I plan on getting in the bed with my husband, that is my clean husband. Samuel, go take a bath!"

In a surprised tone Samuel replied, "A bath! Woman, you crazy! I ain't take'n no bath!"

Kora anticipated her Samuel's reluctant attitude. She quickly replied, "You stink, Samuel! If you want to get in that bed with me you will have to wash. Now get!"

Frustrated and defeated, Samuel replied, "OK, OK, woman, you win! I'll take a bath!"

Samuel stood up and headed into the kitchen to get some hot water for his bath. Samuel made several trips to fill the tub with a mixture of hot and cold water to make a very warm, relaxing tub of water. Samuel got undressed and slowly sat in the tub. He started to wash himself and Kora came into the bathroom. She kneeled down next to him and started washing her husband's chest.

Samuel looked at her and said, "I'm wash'n, I'm wash'n."

Kora jovially replied, "I know you are. I figured you ain't washed in so long, you might need help."

Samuel responded, "I don't know why I got ta take a bath to get some lov'n."

Kora laughed at her husband and said, "I told you why. You stink, Samuel!"

Samuel looked at Kora and asked her, "Baby, is fifty cent a day apiece a lot of money?"

Kora said, "Not really, why?"

Samuel replied, "That's what Helen said she will pay us, plus free room and board."

Kora responded, "That's not too bad with the free room and board, but we can do better. This is not a bad start. You need to find a job blacksmithing."

Samuel was tired. He had walked several miles that day, and it was starting to catch up with him. He decided to keep quiet and sit back and let his wife bathe him. After Kora bathed and dried Samuel off, the two went to bed. Their bed had a handmade down quilt and down pillows on it, luxuries that Samuel had never experienced before. Kora was used to a nice bed and linen. On the plantation, Kora stayed in the big house and lived a plusher lifestyle than the field slaves. Yet this did not stop Kora from falling in love with a field slave.

The two got comfortable in bed and Kora looked at Junior across the room. He was sleeping peacefully. Kora then looked at Samuel and asked him, "So, what do you think of Philadelphia?"

Samuel replied, "It's OK so far."

Kora said, "I have never seen so many Negroes dressed so well and looking so happy. Maxine, Wanda and Debbie, they act like they like working for white folk."

Samuel replied, "Maybe they do like working fo' white folk. After all, they ain't slaves, ya know."

Kora said, "Yeah, maybe you're right. I hope we are as happy working for white folk as they are."

Samuel said, "I'm sure everything will be fine."

He then kissed Kora and tried to move on top of her. Kora positioned herself in between her husband's body and the bed. The two kissed, but Kora interrupted their built-up passion to tell Samuel something that had been on her mind for a while.

She said, "Samuel, I want you to do something for me."

Samuel said, "I'm trying to do something for you, but you keep stopping me."

Kora said, "I'm serious Samuel."

Impatiently, Samuel replied, "Alright, alright Kora. What is it you want me to do for you?"

Kora said, "I want us to start going to church together."

Samuel thought for a moment and said, "OK."

Then he kissed Kora again.

Kora interrupted their passion again and said, "I'm not finished yet."

Samuel looked at Kora and sighed. Then he said, "What else, Kora?"

Kora responded by saying, "If this is our new home, we need a solid foundation with God in our new community."

Samuel asked Kora, "Where you get'n all this from?"

Kora asked Samuel, "All what?"

Samuel replied, "All this talk about God and community."

Kora said, "From the Bible, baby. You will read it too."

Samuel said, "You mess'n wit' me, right? You know I cain't read."

Kora said, "Of course I know you can't read. I'll teach you. I want to teach you and anyone else that can't read. You need to learn how to count also. If you plan on being a blacksmith, you will need to count your money."

Samuel just looked at Kora for a moment. Then he asked her, "Is that it? Anything else?"

Kora kissed Samuel and said, "No baby, that's it."

Kora wrapped her arms around her husband and kissed him passionately. The two made love and fell asleep in each other's arms.

Chapter Thirteen
The Bartram Hotel

Samuel and Kora awakened before dawn. Samuel retrieved warm water from the kitchen to wash up with while Kora fed Samuel Jr. Kora and Samuel then proceeded downstairs with Samuel Jr. in Kora's arm to begin their new daily chores. Kora entered the kitchen with Debbie and Wanda. The three women greeted each other and started to prepare breakfast for the hotel guests.

Kora was beating eggs while Junior sat up on the counter in front of her. Wanda was warming up the wood burning stove. Wanda looked at Kora and said, "Kora, did you sleep well last night?"

Kora responded, "Why yes, yes I did. It has been a long time since I slept in a bed that comfortable."

Wanda chuckled and said, "Funny, it didn't sound to me like you two slept much."

Kora was a little caught off guard.

She responded to Wanda by saying, "Excuse me? What are you talking about?"

Without thinking about it, Kora was talking in her proper English tone. She did not even notice it, but Debbie and Wanda did.

Wanda replied, "We heard you and your man doing your thing last night. Girl, you sure yo little proper ass can handle all that man?"
Kora was beside herself. She did not know what to say. She never had anyone challenge her for Samuel before. Kora tried to compose herself, but the more she thought about it, the more angry she became.

Finally, she responded to Wanda's disrespectful comments by saying, "Oh, I can handle him alright, and just because yo' old fat ass ain't got a man, don't think you can take mine, cuz trust me girl, he ain't going nowhere!"

Wanda immediately responded to Kora by saying, "Bitch! Who you call'n old and fat?! You little high yellow heifer! Don't make me come over there and kick yo' ass!"

Kora turned to face Wanda with a fork in her hand and said, "Come over here if you want to, see what happens!"

Debbie interrupted the two irate women and said, "Ladies please, we got to finish breakfast."

Kora and Wanda knew Debbie was right. They needed to finish breakfast. The women did not say anything to each other while they worked diligently to finish the morning meal.

Samuel met Helen in the lobby while the ladies prepared breakfast. Helen was excited to see Samuel. She was anxious to go over Samuel's new daily duties.

She greeted Samuel by saying, "Good morning Samuel."

Samuel replied, "Hello Helen. How are you this morning?"

Helen responded, "I am fine. Are you ready to get some work done?"

Samuel said, "Yes. Yes I am."

Helen started to discuss Samuel's new job duties with him.

She said, "There are several things I need you to do. You can start by bringing our guests hot water for their baths. This will keep you busy every morning. After our guests are taken care of, you can get some breakfast. After breakfast, you can make any necessary repairs on the hotel."

She paused to see if Samuel had any questions. He did not.

Samuel looked at Helen and said, "I better get started on the hot bathwater."

Samuel went through the kitchen on his way to the back to check the firewood bin. Once in the kitchen, Wanda and Debbie looked at him and spoke.

The two ladies said, "Good morning Samuel."

Samuel smiled politely and said, "Hello Ladies."

Then he went out the back door to check the bin. Samuel noticed that the bin was low. He returned to Helen in the lobby.

As he went through the kitchen again, Wanda asked him, "Are you going to get us some more firewood, Samuel?"

Samuel replied, "I'm going to talk to Helen about that now."

He then found Helen in the lobby. He said to her, "We need more firewood."

Helen responded to Samuel by saying, "We are expecting a delivery later this morning."

Samuel informed Helen how he could help her by saying, "I can save you some money. Just buy an ax and I will keep the bin full myself."

Helen smiled and said, "OK Samuel. Let's go to the hardware store and buy an ax."

Samuel and Helen went across the street to purchase the ax. Helen agreed to allow Samuel to use the hotel wagon to get the firewood. Samuel put the ax in the back of the hotel wagon. Samuel's victim's horse was still tied up where Samuel had left it. After Helen went back into the hotel, Samuel tied the slave catcher's horse to the back of the wagon and led the hotel horse and wagon toward the city limits with Samuel's victim's horse forced to follow. Samuel had been in the forest twenty-four hours ago. He knew where to find plenty of free firewood. He moved down Bartram Street until the busy storefront environment was replaced with open countryside. Samuel was traveling by wagon now. He was no longer on foot. He now had a chance to relax with the sun in his face and observe the beautiful countryside that reminded him of the only thing he found pleasant about living in Delaware.

Samuel rode the wagon through the countryside and past the northern plantation that he had stopped at yesterday. Samuel tied the hotel horse and wagon to a tree and rode his victim's horse to the stream that he had followed from Marcus Hook. He set the horse free and walked back to his company wagon. He filled the back of the wagon with firewood and completed his journey back to the hotel. Samuel had enough wood to fill the bin and make another large pile next to it.

After he unloaded the firewood, Samuel went into the kitchen to get some breakfast.

Wanda asked him, "Can I get you some breakfast, Samuel?"

Samuel replied, "No thanks. Where's Kora?"

Wanda said, "I don't know, but if you're hungry, I can fix you a plate."

Debbie interrupted and said, "Samuel, your wife is in the lobby, talking to Helen."

Samuel said, "Thank you."

He then went into the lobby to talk to his wife and Helen. Samuel entered the lobby and found the two women talking at a table in the middle of the lobby.

Helen noticed Samuel first and said, "Hi Samuel. You back already?"

Samuel said, "Yeah. I'm back."

Samuel started to sit down at the table. Kora asked him, "Do you want some breakfast, Samuel?"

Samuel replied, "Yes please."

Kora went into the kitchen to fix him a plate.

Helen said, "Remember, you two need to eat in the servant room."

The servant room was not a room. It was a space in the kitchen with a table to provide an eating area for the workers. Samuel went back into the kitchen with Wanda and Debbie. He washed his hands and waited for Kora to feed him. Helen walked with Samuel into the kitchen to look at the firewood. When she returned, Samuel had just started eating his breakfast. Helen was exultant after viewing Samuel's hard work.

She walked over to the servant area and said, "Samuel, you got us enough firewood to last the rest of the week."

Samuel didn't say anything. He just smiled and continued eating his breakfast. After breakfast, Samuel returned to his hotel duties. He started making repairs and waiting on hotel guests. The Bartram Hotel housed mostly white people that could not afford a four star hotel in downtown Philadelphia. Samuel was asked to do some of the same tasks he did as a slave. He was asked to do things like shine their shoes, serve meals to guests in their rooms and empty their commodes. Samuel did not like waiting on the hotel guests. He did his job in his mentally inferior mode, saying things like, "Yes sa boss" or, "Yes'm ma'am" all the time with a smile on his face. As much as he disliked it, this is how he spent the second half of his day.

It seemed like it took an eternity for Samuel and Kora's first day to end. When dinnertime finally arrived, Samuel, Kora and Junior ate alone in the servant area. The three enjoyed each other's company like the happy family they were. Toward the end of their meal, Helen walked in and sat at the servants' table. Helen was satisfied with her new employees.

She asked them, "How did you two enjoy your first day?"

Kora and Samuel both had concerns about their new jobs but chose not to express them to Helen at that time. They both simultaneously said, "It went fine."

Helen responded by saying, "Good, I'm glad you two are happy. I have a few changes I need you to make. Samuel, you are working a lot with our guests. I am going to get you a hotel uniform. Kora, everyone raved about your cooking today. I do not need three women in the kitchen, so I am moving Wanda upstairs to be the full-time maid. Unless either one of you two have anything to add, I'm ready to call it a night."

Kora said, "So am I. Goodnight, Helen."

Samuel didn't say anything. He just looked at Helen, smiled and nodded.
Helen left and Kora, Samuel and their son went upstairs to their room. Once inside, Kora put Junior in the bottom dresser drawer and waited for him to fall asleep. Samuel lay on the bed and waited for his wife.

Kora walked over to the bed, looked at Samuel and said, "Bath."

Samuel got up and went back into the kitchen to warm up some water for his bath. Once his water was ready, Samuel took his clothes off and climbed into the bathtub. To Samuel's pleasant surprise, Kora walked into the bathroom, kneeled down next to him and started bathing her husband. Kora asked Samuel, "How was your day Samuel?"

Samuel replied, "Not too good. Most of the day I waited on white folk. You know I had to carry their shit outside! How about you, baby. How was your day?"

Kora responded, "Not so good either. I got into it with Wanda in the kitchen."

Samuel asked, "What was y'all fight'n about?"

Kora lied and said, "Kitchen duties."

Samuel then said, "Well, didn't Helen say she was moving Wanda upstairs?"

Kora smiled and said, "Yes."

Kora didn't like lying to Samuel, but she was not ready to tell him the truth. After Kora finished bathing her husband, she took her clothes off and joined Samuel in the tub. The cast iron tub was large enough for both of them. Kora sat in front of her husband and pressed her head against his chest. Samuel wrapped his arms around Kora and she fell asleep in her husband's arms.

Chapter Fourteen
Oh God

When the sun came up, the Freeman family awakened, ready to subject themselves to more degrading chores with undignified people. For Samuel, blacksmithing was the only job he had ever liked. As a blacksmith, he worked with horses. Samuel loved animals. He was a natural with them. Samuel didn't see himself working as a blacksmith any time in the near future. Kora was forced to work with Wanda's jealous attitude every day. Wanda was not in the kitchen with Kora, but the two women were in constant contact with each other. With all the unwanted circumstances surrounding Samuel and Kora, their marriage began to be tested. They had each other and a beautiful, healthy baby that was growing at a very fast, healthy rate. Despite his love for his son and wife, Samuel was becoming very easily agitated.

It was now winter, and Christmas was approaching again. Christmas was a holiday Kora usually looked forward to. This year, Kora was tired. The married couple worked long hard hours. She did not see Samuel nearly as much as she used to and when they were alone at night, she was too tired to make love to him. This made Samuel's temper worse.

One day when Kora came into the room after work, Samuel was leaving the bathroom and headed downstairs to empty the commode.

Kora asked her husband, "On your way back up, can you please stop by Debbie's room and get Junior?"

Samuel angrily replied, "Get him yourself, woman. I'm tired."

Kora responded to Samuel's tone with her own and said, "You tired? Like you the only one working around here! Hell, I'm tired too!"

Samuel said, "Kora, just leave me be!"

Kora told Samuel, "Huh hun, Negro. You cain't just choose not to be bothered when we have things to do as a family! Now your son need his bath! Go get him and clean him up!"

Samuel was standing in the doorway. He put the commode down and said to his wife, "Woman, who the hell you think you talk'n to? Don't you ever talk to me like that again!"

Kora yelled at Samuel, "What you gon' do if I do tell you to take care of your son?"

Samuel and Kora were allowing their tempers to take over. They were not thinking, just acting on angry emotion. As they yelled at each other with their door open, everyone heard them. Samuel stepped toward Kora and Kora grabbed the only thing she could find, a lantern. The glass was hot, but in her angry, adrenalin-filled state, Kora did not feel the hot glass burning her hand. She stood in the middle of the floor with her weapon by her side, ready to strike down the man she loved if he took one more step toward her. When Kora grabbed the lantern off the dresser, Samuel stopped in his tracks. He turned around and ran down the stairs and outside. Kora realized that her hand was burning and dropped the only light-providing lantern their family had. The lantern hit the wooden floor and its inflamed oil spread in a small circumference in front of Kora. Kora stood behind the small fire in shock. Debbie ran into the room and pulled Kora out into the hall. Wanda threw a blanket on the small fire and put it out. Debbie was now in the hall holding Kora. Kora was holding her hand and crying.

She was saying, "Oh my God. What have I done?"

Debbie took Kora into the kitchen to run some cold water on her hand and apply aloe vera sap to it. Once in the kitchen, Debbie got Kora some cold water and soaked her hand in it. Debbie left Kora's hand soaking in the water while she went to the aloe vera plant that they kept in the kitchen in case of burns. She broke off a branch and squeezed the sap into her hand. Kora then removed her hand from the bowl of water and Debbie rubbed the sap into her hand. Then she wrapped a bandage around Kora's hand.

Samuel went outside and was pacing up and down in front of the hotel in an angry rage.

While he was pacing, a familiar voice said, "Samuel, is that you?"

Samuel looked to see that it was Donald, the Negro he had met in Marcus Hook. The sight of Donald relieved Samuel's rage temporarily. He was happy to see Donald again.

Samuel said, "Don, that you?"

Donald said, "Yea man, it's me."

The two men embraced each other and Samuel said, "Man, it sure is good to see you. How you been?"

Donald replied, "I've been fine. Man what you do'n here?"

Samuel said, "My wife and I moved here about a few months ago."

Donald then said, "You OK? You look upset."

Samuel replied, "I'm OK. I just had a fight with my wife."

Donald then said, "Hell man, you need a drink. I'm on my way to the Last Stop Tavern on the other block. Come on."

Samuel didn't say anything. He just followed Donald. Samuel felt like he had to get away from that hell hotel he lived and worked in.

They walked into the tavern and the waitress greeted Donald. She said, "Hey Donnie boy, how you do'n tonight?"

Donald replied, "Hi, Deloris, I'm fine."

The tavern was filled with people smoking cigars and cigarettes. It had a thick fog of smoke that filled the room. The Last Stop Tavern also was not your regular tavern, it housed a brothel above the tavern. Donald led Samuel to a table and the two men sat down.

Samuel looked around and said, "I ain't never seen all these Negro women before."

He was referring to the waitresses. They were all Negro and all working girls posing as waitresses.

Donald said to Samuel, "They ain't never seen you before, either."

Donald noticed all the waitresses looking at Samuel and whispering and giggling amongst themselves. The waitress uniform was a red strapless top that covered their breasts and had white fringe around the curves of their breasts. They wore matching skirts that ended and flared out several inches above their knees. They also all wore black fishnet pantyhose and black shoes with medium-sized heels.

Deloris came to the table with two glasses of whisky and placed them on the table.

She then said, "Donnie, who's your friend?"

Donald said, "This is Samuel."

As she walked away, Donald heard Deloris say to her co-worker, "That's one fine man!"

135

Donald looked at Samuel and said, "The ladies here like you, man."

Samuel didn't say anything, he just stared at his drink and started reminiscing about Charles and his first wife Maggie. Charles was always drunk and smelled of alcohol. Charles was extremely harsh on Samuel when he reeked of liquor. Samuel also remembered how he had to tie Maggie to the bed while he was plowing the fields to get her over her alcohol addiction. The more Samuel thought about the only two people he knew that drank, the more knew he would never take a drink.

Debbie finished wrapping her friend's hand and Kora went back upstairs to their dark room. When Samuel didn't come home, Kora took Samuel Jr., wrapped him in a blanket and went looking for her man. Once outside her hotel, she saw no one. It was late and the streets were empty. She then walked to the other block that The Last Stop Tavern was on. Kora didn't know where Samuel was, but she followed her intuition and went where the action was.

Donald noticed Samuel not drinking and said, "Drink up, man. This one is on me."

Samuel didn't say anything. He just sat there quietly and thought about Kora and what he did to make her think about hitting him. He could not even remember what they were fighting about. Deloris came back and sat in Donald's lap. Samuel saw her whisper something in Donald's ear and the two of them laughed.

Then another waitress approached Samuel and said, "You want some company, big man?"
Samuel didn't say anything. He felt like he was about to choke from all the smoke. Samuel then stood up so fast he almost knocked the other waitress over. He moved quickly toward the front door.

Donald yelled, "Man, where you go'n? if you don't like Kim, they got plenty of other women to choose from. Come back."

Samuel could not reach the door fast enough. He burst through the front doors, closed his eyes and took a deep breath of the fresh night air. When he opened his eyes he saw Kora walking down the street carrying their son. He thought he was dreaming. He wiped his eyes to make sure that they didn't have smoke in them. When he opened them again, Kora was walking toward him and she did not look happy. Suddenly Samuel had the urge to go back inside. He thought it might be better to be in the choking cigar smoke than face his angry wife that had just caught him coming out of a bar.

Kora walked a few feet in front of the tavern porch and stopped in the middle of the street. Samuel didn't move. He didn't know what Kora was going to do or say. The two stood there looking at each other for a long minute.

Kora then said, "You ready to come home?"

Samuel replied, "Yes."

Samuel walked off the porch and Kora walked toward him. She stood directly in front of him with Junior in her arms. Samuel was glad Junior was in his wife's arms because that meant she could not hit him. Kora moved closer to Samuel and put her head on his chest.

She said, "I hate it when we fight, Samuel."

Samuel put his arms around his family and said, "So do I, baby. So do I."

The two walked back to their hotel together but apart. Kora knew they had not resolved their issues and they still had a problem. She decided that they needed help, and she knew just where to get it.

The next day after dinner, Kora told Samuel that she was going to a church Debbie told her about. It was cold outside, so she left Samuel Jr. with Samuel. The church was only a few blocks away. To Kora, it seemed like a long walk because she did not know where she was going and it was cold outside. Debbie gave her good directions and, within fifteen minutes, Kora was on the front steps of The African Methodist Episcopal Church of Our Lord. Kora stood at the bottom of the steps for a moment to observe the house of God. The church was a converted mid-size wooden two-story building. Kora walked up the steps and opened the doors. She could see that all the walls had been removed and that pillars had been put in place to support the second floor. As soon as she opened the doors, she saw a large open area filled with pews. There was a small stage in the back of the sanctuary.

The church seemed empty. Kora proceeded inside. She walked into the sanctuary where she saw several candles burning. Through the dim light the candles provided, Kora could see that the church needed repairs. The wood that the pews were made of needed a new finishing coat. Kora noticed several puddle stains on the floor from the roof's leaking. Also, the church was cold. In the back of the sanctuary was a large fireplace. The fire in it was dying out. Kora wondered if the church had a coal-burning furnace. Then, from the back room, a man entered the sanctuary. He noticed Kora and approached her. The man was a Negro and he was well dressed. He was wearing black wool pants, a grey cotton sweater, a wool coat, cowboy boots and he had his wool cap in his hand. To Kora, he looked to be about thirty years old.

He walked up to Kora and said to her, "Hello, I am the Reverend Marcus Lovejoy. Did you need some help, miss?"

Kora looked at the well-dressed reverend and hesitated. Kora had wanted to go to this church every since they had arrived in Philadelphia. She knew that her and her family needed God in their lives if they were ever going to have the life they truly desired.

After a brief pause, Kora said to the reverend, "Hello Reverend Lovejoy. My name is Kora Freeman. I came here today because I have never been in a church before and something inside me just kept telling me to come here. Well, I finally did."

The Reverend smiled and said, "You say you have never been in a church before. Sister, are you married?"

Kora said, "Yes Reverend. I am happily married and we have a beautiful healthy son."

The Reverend then said, "Yes, children are a true blessing. Where were you married?" Kora said, "In Marcus Hook."

Then the Reverend asked, "Who married you?"

Kora proudly said, "Harriet Tubman."

The reverend then said, "Let me guess. You and your husband were married in a barn."

Kora shockingly said, "Why yes, Reverend. How did you know that?"

The reverend said, "I have heard stories about an escaped slave that was returning to the south to free other slaves. As the stories go, you were not the first couple she married. You know sister, church can be anywhere that people worship the Lord. Did Mrs. Tubman read from a Bible when she married you?"

Kora responded, "Yes"

The reverend then said, "When she read from her Bible, she transformed the barn into a house of the Lord. So you see sister, you have been in a church before."

Kora said, "Well Reverend, I never thought of it that way before."

The reverend then asked, "Did she give you your last name also?"

Kora said, "Yes. Yes she did."

The reverend then said, "Freeman is a fine name for escaping slaves."

Kora smiled and said, "I couldn't agree with you more, Reverend. One reason why I think I was called to this church is because I have a lot to offer. Reverend, I can read, write and do arithmetic. I am willing to teach others to do the same."

The reverend smiled and said, "Oh, now this is truly a blessing, sister Kora. We have been looking for someone to school our local Negroes."

Kora smiled and said, "That's good, when can I start?"

The reverend laughed and said, "You're a little anxious, ain't ya?"

Kora said, "I just can't wait to do the Lord's work. I should have been here months ago." The reverend replied, "I'm glad you are so enthusiastic. Tell me sister, when and where do you work?"

Kora replied, "I work in the kitchen of the Bartram Hotel every day from six a.m. until nine p.m."

The reverend looked at Kora and said, "I heard the food at the Bartram is very good lately."

Kora quickly responded, "You heard correctly. I think I had a little something to do with that."

The reverend smiled and said to Kora, "You work long hours. When will you have time to teach?"

Kora said, "Between nine thirty and ten thrity every evening."

The reverend replied, "You seem to have it all figured out. How do you plan on getting people in here that late?"

Kora turned her head, looked at the reverend out of the corner of her eye and responded, "Why Reverend, I'll use my charm, of course."

The reverend said, "But of course. I can expect you tomorrow evening?"

Kora said, "I'll be here, Reverend. Before I go, I just have one more question."

The reverend said, "Sure, sister Kora. What is it?"

Kora asked the reverend, "Reverend, are you married?"

The reverend paused, slightly hung his head and said, "My wife passed away giving birth a few months ago."

Kora sympathetically said, "I'm so sorry Reverend."

Reverend Lovejoy replied, "Its OK, you did not know."

Kora then smiled and said, "Well I need to get back to my husband before he gets nervous. I've never been away from him this long before."

Both the reverend and Kora let out a slight laugh and walked out the door.

Once outside, the reverend said to Kora, "It's pretty late, I'll walk you home."

The two walked to Kora's hotel/job/home and talked about the format Kora would use to teach her prospective students. The reverend informed Kora that the church did not have many resources. The church did not have a blackboard or chalk. Kora offered to use some of her savings to buy paper and pencils. Kora then told the reverend that she would go from desk to desk, teaching each student. By the time they came up with their plan, the two of them found themselves on the front porch of the Bartram Hotel. The two wished each other goodnight and Kora went upstairs.

She walked into the room to find Samuel Jr. asleep in his drawer/crib. Samuel had fallen asleep on the bed with his clothes on. Kora knew that he had been waiting up for her and didn't make it. She leaned over her husband and kissed him on his forehead. Samuel woke up and smiled when he saw Kora.

He said, "Hey baby, you're back."

Kora said, "Yes, I'm back. I went to the church and met the Reverend Marcus Lovejoy. He seems like a very nice man. He is going to let me teach Negroes in the church every evening after work."

Samuel looked at Kora and with concern in his voice said, "Are you sure you can work all day and teach at night?"

Kora said, "Yes, I'm only teaching an hour every evening. I can squeeze another hour out of my day for the Lord."

Samuel then said, "But baby, that's an hour a day away from your family."

Kora quickly said, "No its not, because my family will be with me."

Samuel looked at his wife and said, "We will? When did you plan on telling me?"

Kora said, "I just found out myself."

Samuel replied, "Baby, you don't need me to go with you. I don't need to go to school. Most Negroes can't read and we get by just fine."

Kora angrily responded, "Samuel Freeman, I'm surprised at you. You have always been the type of man that wouldn't settle for getting by. That's why I followed you from Delaware to this rat-infested, rundown hotel. We are not going to be servants to the white man for the rest of our lives! You are going to learn to read, write and do math. You are going to be a blacksmith. We are not going to be here much longer, Samuel!"

Once again, Kora surprised Samuel with her strong will. Samuel knew that Kora was a very strong woman but he did not know how passionate she was about teaching. He knew he had to support his wife any way that he could. After all, she had always been there for him.

Samuel said, "OK OK OK Kora, I'll go with you."

Kora smiled and said, "I knew you would, baby. Now come on, let's get some sleep."

Samuel asked Kora, "Did you say 'rat-infested?'"

Kora replied, "Yes, I saw a rat in the kitchen this morning."

Samuel walked over to Junior and moved him from the bottom drawer to the middle drawer. Kora watched her husband care for their son as she got undressed and climbed into bed.

In the morning, Samuel and Kora once again started on their daily duties. After breakfast, Kora went upstairs to talk to Wanda. She found Wanda cleaning out one of the guest rooms.

Kora walked into the room and said, "I need to talk to you."

Wanda snarled and said, "We have nothing to talk about."

Kora told Wanda, "Yes we do. I want you to come to church with us tonight."

Wanda chuckled and said, "Go to church with you? You got me kicked out the kitchen and now I'm doing dirt work! Now you say you want me to go to church with you? Bitch please!"

Kora walked closer to Wanda and said in a low, peaceful tone, "I didn't get you kicked out the kitchen. That was Helen's idea. Ya know, you and I have more in common than you think."

Wanda asked her, "Exactly what do you think we have in common?"

Kora asked Wanda, "You were a slave before, weren't you?"

Wanda said, "Yes, Debbie and I ran away years ago. We heard Negroes could live a free life without fear of slave catchers in Philadelphia, so we came here."

Kora asked Wanda, "Did you have any children while you were on your plantation?"

Wanda took a deep breath and said, "Yes. A daughter. My master raped me then took my child and sold her away from me!"

Kora told Wanda, "I know how you feel. My mother was also raped by our master. I am the child of continuous unwanted sexual advances. My mother died hating my father, master. I too hated that white man. I lived in the Big House after my mother's death and I promise you, not a day went by that I didn't spit in their food."

Wanda let out a slight chuckle and said, "I guess we have more in common than I thought."

Kora replied, "Yes we do."

Wanda smiled and said to Kora, "I ain't eat'n yo' food no mo'!"

Kora also laughed and replied, "Don't worry, I don't do that no more."

Wanda and Kora were smiling at each other. Wanda asked Kora, "What time tonight?"

Kora smiled and said, "9:30. The African Methodist Episcopal Church of Our Lord. We can all leave here together."

Wanda replied, "That old rundown church."

Kora said, "It ain't the big house, but it is all we got. If you think it is so rundown, help us fix it up."

Wanda replied, "I'll see you tonight."

Kora returned to the kitchen feeling good about the fact that she turned a foe into a potential friend. Now there was just one more step to her completely winning Wanda over. Kora went into the kitchen to start lunch with Debbie.

During the lunch preparation Kora said, "Debbie, I am going to church tonight after work. I convinced Wanda to come with us."

Debbie replied in shock, "You convinced Wanda to come to church with you? Girl, how you do that?"

Kora said, "I just invited her, and we had a little girl talk. You know, woman to woman."

Debbie responded by saying, "If you got Wanda to come, I guess I will come also."

Kora said, "I knew you would say that. You should invite your gentleman caller. What's his name?"

Debbie replied, "His name is Frank, but I ain't bring him. I don't like him like that. I can see him tomorrow."

Kora replied by saying, "You don't like him like that? He comes over every night after dinner to court you. I was expecting wedding bells soon."

Debbie made a disagreeing face and shook her head from side to side.

She then said, "I just see Frank cause he buys me nice things. Like this blouse. It is so soft, it feels good on my skin. See, feel it."

Kora walked over the Debbie and felt her blouse. She told Debbie, "It is a nice soft blouse. But if you don't like Frank, why do you let him buy you things?"

Debbie replied, "I didn't ask him for the stuff, he just keep giving it to me."

Kora paused a moment then said, "Wait a minute, where is Frank getting money to buy you gifts?"

Debbie replied, "Frank works for the downtown undertakers. Girl, they give him two dollars a day!"

Kora raised her eyebrows and said, "That is good money."

Kora then sighed, looked Debbie straight in the eyes and said, "Debbie, if you spend your free time with a man you don't love, you are taking time away from meeting the man you can love."

Debbie was quiet for a moment. She then sat down at the servants' table. Kora joined her. Kora could tell that Debbie was thinking about what she had said, and gave her a minute to contemplate what she just told her.

After a minute of silence, Kora asked Debbie, "If you don't mind me asking, how old are you?"

Debbie replied, "Twenty-two."

Kora asked, "Did you have any children on your plantation?"

Tears came into Debbie's eyes and she said, "No, but Wanda and I had a very hard life on our plantation. Our master and overseer had their way with us whenever they wanted."

Debbie hung her head and started crying more intensely.

Kora comforted her by holding Debbie and said, "Its OK, you're not on that farm any more. You're safe now."

Debbie held her head up and wiped the tears from her eyes. She told Kora, "That's why I like Frank. He buys me things that take me far, far away from where we came."

Kora told Debbie, "You don't need a man for that. God can provide you with peace of mind. I want you to come to church with us tonight without Frank. Overnight, I want you to think about what I said about taking time away from meeting the right man. Tomorrow, you will know what to do."

Debbie nodded her head, indicating that she understood.

Kora then said, "Come on, girl. Helen will have our hides if we don't get started on lunch."

Debbie and Kora stood up. Debbie smiled and hugged Kora tightly. The two women embraced each other briefly and started preparing lunch.

The day dragged on as usual. Samuel waited on the economically deprived white citizens that had been treated like second-class citizens all their lives. They had no one to oppress except, the only people that these whites considered to be beneath them, Negroes. Samuel played his butler roll very well. He hated being the hotel butler and he did not see any way out. Samuel was becoming more and more bitter. Kora was stilled concerned about Samuel. She knew why her man was angry. She knew she had to help him, but she did not know how. Kora prayed for the Lord to provide a better life for her and her family. Kora felt good about her conversations with Wanda and Debbie. She knew she had dug up some old wounds that had to be dealt with for the two women to move on.

Chapter Fifteen
How to Love your Man

Kora and her recruits were all at the servants' table for dinner. After everyone finished eating, they left for church. To Kora's surprise, four other people were waiting outside for them. Kora greeted everyone and learned that Debbie and Wanda had told two of their friends, and one of those friends had told a married couple about the church. Everyone was very enthusiastic about going to church. They had all had an introduction to religion at some point in their lives. Once they were removed from God, it left a void in their existence.

Samuel carried Samuel Jr. Kora wrapped their son in a blanket to keep him warm. Junior was almost eighteen months now, he was walking and talking. The ten of them entered the church doors. They walked into the sanctuary. The room was still dimly lit with candles and it was cold. The fireplace was going but there was not enough firewood to keep the fire burning. The reverend greeted everyone. He asked them to come to the pulpit for a moment. Once in the pulpit, the Reverend Lovejoy took center stage. He opened his mouth and the words of the Lord came out.

He said, "I want to thank each and every one of you for coming out tonight. No no no, I really want to thank you because I know you had several reasons not to come. Sista Kora told me about the long, hard hours you work. I know you're tired. I know it's cold outside. I know it's cold in here. The fact that, despite all these circumstances, you still showed up tells me that you all really want the Lord in your lives. Well, you will not be disappointed. Our church is not in the best condition, but with your help we can fix it up in no time. The first thing on our agenda is educating Negroes. That's right, I said educating Negroes! I know that, where you come from, that statement could be deadly, but guess what, ya ain't where you was no mo'! You're here now in Philadelphia, Pennsylvania, the city of brotherly love. Now let me ask you, who in here is tired of being overworked and underpaid?"

149

Everyone said, "I am."

The reverend quickly responded by saying, "How do you know you're being under paid if you cain't count? With the help of Sista Kora, we're going to teach you how to read, write and count. "

Kora led everyone upstairs to the prepared teaching room. Once upstairs, they entered a dim, candlelit room with several student desks in it. Everyone took a seat. Kora sat in the middle of the desks and said, "Everyone sit around me, and turn your desk to me."

The class did as they were instructed.

Kora then said, "I was not expecting this many people but that's OK. You all can share paper and pencil. Now class will begin. If anyone has a question, they must raise their hand and wait to be called on."

Kora struggled getting her lesson plan together with her bandaged-up hand and reflected back on her days as a child in the big house. Playing school with Anna had taught Kora everything she needed know to teach elementary education. Kora reminisced on the times Anna would come home from school and reenact every lesson that she had learned in school. Kora was an excellent student. She remembered everything Anna had taught her and the way she taught it. As Kora reflected on her and Anna's good times, she noticed Wanda's hand up. She had not started teaching the class yet, and her biggest adversary had a question. Kora knew this couldn't be a good question. Kora saw Wanda's hand and briefly ignored her by pretending not to see her as she stacked her papers on her desk. Wanda waited patiently.

Kora looked at Wanda and said, "Yes Wanda, what is it?"

Wanda said, "After we get school'n, do that mean we have to talk white like you?"

The class laughed and waited to hear Kora's response. Kora had to come up with something, but she could not go off on Wanda like she wanted to. She had to maintain her composure and class demeanor.

Kora looked at Wanda and said, "Why miss Wanda, y'alls can talk howeva y'alls want. But I promise, you will know the proper way to speak English. What you choose to do with that knowledge is up to you. Now let's get started."

Kora wrote the letter A in large print on a single piece of paper. She held it up and showed the A to everyone. She then said, "This is the upper case letter A. Everyone take your pencil and draw this letter on your paper in front of you. If you don't have paper in front of you, use the back side of the person's next to you after they finish."

Everyone drew their A and held it up to show it to Kora. Kora looked at everyone's As and said, "That's a good A, everyone. Now, the A makes an *aaa* sound. Everyone say it with me."

Everyone went, "Aaa."

Kora responded by saying, "That's very good. Now this is a B."

Kora drew a B on her paper and showed it to everyone. Kora repeated this procedure until the class had completed the entire alphabet.

After the class made the *Zzzee* sound Kora said, "That's good, very good class. Congratulations, you all just completed you first class. Now, leave your paper and pencil on your desk and tomorrow we will start putting words together."

Everyone smiled with a sense of accomplishment as they left the room.
As Kora put her papers together she looked at Wanda and said, "Wanda, can I see you for a minute?"

Wanda waited until everyone left. Wanda and Kora were alone in the room and Kora said the her, "Wanda, did you see the way the reverend kept looking at you in the pulpit?"

Wanda hesitated a moment because she was not expecting Kora to say that. She finally said, "Kora please, he was looking at everyone."

Kora said, "Huh-hun girl, not like he was looking at you."

Wanda said, "You really think he was looking at me?"

Kora responded, "Why wouldn't he look at you? You're his age. He is widowed, you're not married. Why wouldn't he look at you?"

Wanda replied, "Kora, there is no way he knew all that about me unless you told him."

Kora smiled and said, "I did no such thing. Now you should join the others on their walk home."

Wanda smiled and said, "Aren't you coming with us, Kora?"

Kora replied, "I need to go over tomorrow's lessons with the reverend. I'll see you at the hotel."

Wanda left with everyone else. Samuel knew that his wife was going to talk to the reverend and he was not happy about leaving without Kora. Samuel Jr. was asleep. Samuel carried him home with the rest of his coworkers and their guests. Kora went downstairs and reviewed the next lesson with the reverend. He agreed on everything Kora wanted to go over.

As they finished going through the lesson Kora said, "Reverend, I am worried about Samuel. He has not been himself lately. He is so uptight these days, I don't know what's wrong with him."

The reverend listened and said, "I think I know what's wrong with him. Back on your plantation, what did Samuel do?"

Kora replied, "He was a plow slave."

The reverend then said, "Plow slave. That is a very physical job. That job allowed him to deal with the pressure that your slave master put him under. Didn't you tell me Samuel learned the trade of blacksmithing in Marcus Hook?"

Kora said, "Yes. He was very happy then."

The reverend replied, "Samuel is frustrated because he is a blacksmith that is forced to be a butler. He needs some kind of physical outlet."

Kora said, "I have been kind of tired lately. We have not made love in a while."

The reverend smiled and said, "He needs love'n too, but I was referring to some type of exercise. Something to replace the outlet his plow gave him."

Kora said, "OK, I'll come up with something. On another note, Reverend, ya know Wanda is not married. She is not too old to have children either."

The reverend said, "Kora, are you trying to fix me up?"

Kora quickly replied, "Yes. Do you like Wanda?"

The reverend replied, "She seems nice but I don't know her."

Kora said, "Well get to know her!"

The reverend said, "OK, OK. So what do I do? Ask her out?"

Kora laughed and said, "Reverend, will you do me the honor of walking me home?"

The reverend smiled and said, "Of course I will, Sista Kora, but before we go, I have something for you."

The reverend took one of the few lanterns that the church had and gave it to Kora.

He said to Kora, "I was told you had a little accident in your room the other night and now you have no light. The church has a few lanterns. We can spare one for you."

Kora took the lantern and said, "Thank you, Reverend."

The two walked to the Bartram Hotel together.

When they reached the porch steps, Kora said, "Come inside, Reverend. I need to check on my family and go over one more item on my agenda with you."

The reverend entered the hotel with Kora. She walked him into the kitchen and sat the reverend at the servants' table. Kora left the reverend at the table and went upstairs to see her family. She entered their room and saw Samuel Jr. asleep in the drawer he was quickly outgrowing. Samuel was sitting on the bed waiting for Kora.

Kora looked at him and said, "Hey baby, you ready for bed?"

Samuel snapped at his wife and said, "I been ready for bed. Where you been, woman?"

Kora replied, "I am working with the reverend. He is downstairs now. Baby, I am sorry I have been so busy. Just give me one minute and I'm all yours."

Kora placed the lantern on the dresser. Samuel asked, "Where that lantern come from?"

Kora quickly responded, "Church."

Samuel just looked at his wife as she walked out of the room. Kora went to Wanda and Debbie's room and knocked on their door.

Wanda opened the door and said, "Yes Kora?"

Kora said to Wanda, "You have a gentleman caller downstairs in the kitchen."

Wanda asked in a high-pitched voice, "Who Kora? Not the Reverend?"

Kora smiled and quickly nodded her head up and down.

Wanda was wearing a green bathrobe and her hair was out of its French braids and all over her head.

She said, "Tell him to go away. I look a mess!"

Debbie heard everything and said, "Girl, you got a man wait'n fo' you and you gon' send him away? Kora, come on in here and help me find sometin' fo' ha to wear."

Kora needed to get back to her husband, but she wanted to finish helping Wanda. Kora entered Wanda and Debbie's room.

She said, "Wanda can keep the robe on. It's late, he will understand. You got a scarf for your hair?"

Debbie opened her drawer and said, "Here, girl. Wear this one."

The scarf was green and matched Wanda's robe. Wanda looked in the mirror and put the green scarf on her head. She then went downstairs and into the kitchen.

When she entered the room, the reverend stood up and said, "Good evening again, Sista Wanda."

Wanda walked over to the reverend and said, "Hello again to you to, Reverend. Can I get you a cup of tea?"

The reverend said, "Yes, if it's not too much trouble."

Wanda said, "No trouble, Reverend."

Wanda went outside to get some firewood. She returned and started a small fire under one of the eyes then placed the teapot on top of it. Wanda then joined the reverend at the servants' table.

The reverend asked Wanda, "How was class, Sista Wanda?"

Wanda responded by singing the ABCs.

The reverend smiled and said, "You're a fast learner and a good singer. You should help me start a church choir."

Wanda chuckled and said, "Sure, Reverend. Whatever you need help with, I'll help you."

The teapot started whistling and Wanda got up from the table to fix two cups of tea. She placed a cup in front of the reverend and returned to her seat.

The reverend said, "Thank you, Sista Wanda."

Wanda replied, "You're welcome, Reverend. Reverend, do you mind if I ask you a question?"

The reverend said, "Not at all."

Wanda said, "I heard your wife passed unexpectedly a few months ago. I'm worried about you. I mean, who takes care of you?"

The reverend responded by saying, "They put a fair amount of being direct in the water of this hotel. If you must know, Sista Wanda, I am quiet capable of taking care of myself."

Wanda said to the reverend, "I don't buy that. What did you have for dinner, Reverend?"

The reverend said, "Soup."

Wanda replied, "Soup? That ain't no proper meal."

Wanda stood up and walked around the kitchen for a moment. The reverend watched her and liked the way she filled out her robe. Wanda saw the reverend looking at her through the corner of her eye.

She returned to the table, stood a few inches away from his side and said, "Reverend, I can whip you up some fried chicken, rice and green beans."

Wanda's large chest was directly to the right of the reverend's head. The reverend started sitting with his head down, looking at his cup of tea once Wanda stood next to him. The reverend looked up and turned his head, facing Wanda's breasts.

With his face inches away from Wanda's robust chest and his eyes looking over them at her he said, "Sista Wanda, do I have a choice?"

Wanda smiled and said, "No."

Then she started his late dinner.

Kora had returned to her own room as soon as Wanda placed the scarf on her head. As Kora entered, Samuel was standing in the middle of the room. His shirt was off and he was standing there with his hands on his waist.

He looked at Kora and said, "You ain't leave'n again!"

Kora said, "I'm in for the night, baby. I am sorry I have been so busy lately."

Samuel started pacing around the room. Kora could see that he was very upset. She walked toward the bed and unbuttoned her blouse. She dropped it on the floor and sat on the bed, topless.

She looked at Samuel and said, "Come here, baby and help me take my skirt and boots off."

Then she leaned back on the bed with her feet still on the ground.
Samuel stopped pacing and looked at his wife. He saw her beautiful topless figure, with her hair down. She was leaning back on her elbows looking at her husband with her firm perky breasts looking at him also.

As he stared at her, Kora said, "You gon' stand there in the middle of the floor all night or you coming to bed?"

Samuel snapped out of his trance. He smiled and walked over to the bed. He stood in front of Kora with his shirt off and Kora unbuttoned the belt Helen had given her husband.

Kora said to Samuel, "Did I tell you how good you look in your uniform, baby?"

Samuel did not say anything. He just smiled and looked forward to making love to his wife. Kora bent down and untied the shoes Helen had given Samuel. As she bent down, Samuel looked at her bare back. It was still defined from years of carrying water to Samuel and the other slaves. When Kora bent down, her long brown hair parted and covered her face, then hit the ground. Kora moved her hair off of the ground and off of her face with one hand, but needed two hands to untie Samuel's shoes. Samuel bent down and removed the hair on the other side of his wife's head from the ground and her face. At the same time, he used his other hand to remove the hair from Kora's hand. In one motion, Samuel transferred Kora's hair from both hands to one hand and stood up, extending his massive arm with his wife's hair in his fist. Kora untied Samuel's shoes and sat up. Samuel stepped out of his shoes and put both hands on Kora's head and started rubbing his hands through Kora's hair. Kora unbuttoned Samuel's pants and they hit the ground. Samuel stopped rubbing his wife's hair and bent down to take his pants off of his legs. Samuel stood up naked with a semi erection. Kora was leaning back on her elbows again. She looked at her husband's slightly hard, large black penis as it hung below his shredded abdominal muscles. Kora put Samuel's penis in her hand and started rubbing it. Samuel's penis reached its maximum capacity immediately. Kora continued rubbing Samuel's manhood and kissed his stomach. She kissed his navel and put her tongue in it.

Samuel moved back, looked down at Kora and said, "You know I don't like that."

159

Samuel's penis was in one of Kora's hands while Kora's face was against Samuel's rippling abdomen. She was still moving her hand back and forth. Her thumb was extended and stroking the tip of his erection every time Kora moved her hand toward the back of her head. Kora continued stroking Samuel and looked up at him. Samuel was massaging Kora's hair again. Kora looked up at Samuel and said, "I know, I was just mess'n with you!"

Kora then kissed Samuel's abs again and stuck her tongue out. She put her other hand with the bandage on it on Samuel's back to support herself. Kora slowly stood up with her tongue pressed against Samuel's abdominal muscles. As Kora moved up Samuel's torso, she continued rubbing his penis slowly. She felt his penis's throbbing pulse in her hand and knew her husband was ready to enter her. Rubbing his penis also made Kora's vaginal juices start flowing. Kora's head reached Samuel's large chest and she stopped licking his torso and kissed his chest. She then stood up with his penis still in her hand and moved her other hand to the back of Samuel's head. Samuel moved both of his hands to Kora's firm, round hips. Samuel kissed his wife passionately and rubbed her hips. The two placed their tongues in each other's mouths and moved them around in a clockwise and counterclockwise motion.

Kora stopped rubbing Samuel's penis and, with the same hand, she lifted her skirt up. She pushed herself slightly away from Samuel's muscular body and held her head back. This gesture went back to the body language that the two had developed on the plantation. Samuel knew that his wife wanted him to lick her neck and breasts. He moved down her body fulfilling her silent request. He licked her neck and moved down to her breasts. Samuel then moved his tongue in a circular motion around the erect nipple of Kora's firm, voluptuous breast. Kora's skirt was up and her hand was on her vagina. She slightly bent her legs and started rubbing her erect clitoris with her middle finger.

Samuel pushed her away from him and aggressively turned her around at the same time. Kora followed his motion and turned her back to him. She then put both her knees on the bed. The bed squeaked when Kora put her weight on it. Samuel lifted Kora's skirt up and bent his wife's body into a ninety-degree angle. The angle pushed Kora's wet, pink labia out from her hips and into Samuel's view. Samuel put his hand on the back of his erect penis and spread his legs to lower his pelvic area to Kora's hips. He placed the tip of his penis between Kora's thighs and against the front/bottom of Kora's vagina. He then moved his penis toward the back/top of her vagina. Kora's legs were slightly spread and her vagina was very moist. As Samuel moved his erect penis up against Kora's labia, the tip of his penis entered Kora. Samuel slowly pushed his pelvis forward and his erect, black penis started to disappear inside of Kora. Samuel moved his pelvis back slowly, then slowly forward again. His hand was still on his penis. Kora closed her mouth and moaned quietly so she would not wake their son up. Samuel removed his hand from his penis and pushed his pelvic flesh against his wife's hips. This pushed his penis all the way inside of Kora, just like she liked it. Kora started to move her hips up and down and Samuel moved his pelvis back and forth. The two made love passionately and gently. They were careful not to make the bed squeak because they did not want to wake Junior up or disturb their neighbors.

They continued to make love quietly and passionately for several minutes. Samuel loved the way his penis looked when he pressed against his wife's hips and it was gone then reappeared again. Samuel started pushing his pelvis a little harder toward Kora's hips. Kora was on her hands and knees on the bed. Her mouth was closed, but as her husband entered her harder, his penis began going a little deeper. Kora thoroughly enjoyed Samuel's increase in pelvic pressure. It felt good when Samuel took his penis out to the tip and all the way back into his wife. The feeling got better and better to both of them and Samuel kept increasing his stroke. The bed started squeaking, but Samuel did not stop and Kora did not want him to. Samuel placed both of his hands on Kora's hips started increasing his stroke. Samuel's pelvis was now clapping against his wife's round, full-bodied hips. The bed was squeaking louder and Kora's mouth was now open as Samuel drove his penis deeper into Kora's vaginal cavity. Samuel grabbed

161

Kora's long hair with one hand and intensified his stroke even more. The bed was now squeaking very loudly and Kora was no longer quiet. She was now passionately telling him she loved every move of his motion.

With Samuel slamming into the back of her, Kora said, "Samuel, Samuel Samuel, Ohhhh Samuel! Yes yes yes! Baby you feel sooo good!"

Samuel pulled his wife's hair harder and slapped her on the firm cheek of her buttocks then said, "Shut the fuck up, woman!"

He smacked her again and said, "You gon' bring yo' ass home from now on, ain't ya!"

With Samuel pelvic still smacking Kora and the bed squeaking Kora said, "Yes baby, yes! I'll do whatever you say! Ohhhh, don't stop baby, don't stop!"

Samuel moaned and said, "MMMMMM, SSSSSSHH, Yeah baby! MMMM!"

As Samuel felt his penis reach its hardest peak, Kora started to move away from Samuel. He dropped her hair and grabbed Kora on her waist, where her hips started. This stopped Kora from moving and caused her to feel the tip of Samuel's erection deeper in her vaginal cavity.

Kora passionately screamed out, "Oh Oh Oh Oh Samuel, please don't go no deeper, baby!"

Samuel did not stop slamming his pelvis against his wife's hips. He realized that the two of them were making a lot of noise. Now Kora was screaming uncontrollably. Samuel looked over his shoulder to look at Junior. He confirmed that their son was still asleep and looked back down at his wife. He continued his vicious movement and said to Kora, "Be quiet, woman, you gon' wake Junior up!"

Samuel reaching the deep part of Kora's cavity hurt Kora slightly but at the same time felt very good. Kora felt herself about to burst. Just as Samuel told her to be quiet Kora, released herself.

Kora orgasmically replied, "I cain't help it! You slam'n in so hard and deep Samuel. Oh Jesus, oh Jesus! Oh Jesus, ahhh, ahhh!"

Samuel pressed his pelvis against Kora's hips and stayed there. His motion briefly paused, Samuel grabbed a pillow, threw it in front of Kora and pushed Kora's head toward the pillow.

As he started his stroke again he said, "Put your head down and keep quiet!"

Kora did as her husband ordered. She relaxed her arms and buried her face in the pillow in front of her. Samuel started his clapping, bed-rocking motion again. When Kora moved her face into the pillow to muffle her echoes of orgasmic delight, her clitoris was pushed back against Samuel's penis and Samuel was going even deeper into her vagina at a forty-five degree angle. Kora screamed into the pillow and tried to move away from Samuel. Samuel increased his grip on her hips and continued his clapping motion. Kora screamed loudly into the pillow and felt herself about to release herself again. Kora stretched both her arms forward against the wall adjacent to the bed and passionately screamed into the pillow again. Samuel was driving his penis deeper and harder into Kora then he ever had. Kora couldn't take it anymore so she reached back and moved Samuel's hand off of her hip. She then tried to roll her body in the direction of her freed hip, but Samuel caught her by the hip again and tried to straighten her up on her knees again. Kora quickly moved her hips forward, causing her to push the pillow forward with her face and lie flat on her stomach. Samuel kept his penis in her and moved on top of his wife. Samuel was now in the missionary position, slamming his erect penis into the back of his wife's vagina. The clapping continued and the bed rocked and squeaked louder from the direct pressure Samuel was applying. Kora pressed her arms against the wall. She could not straighten them because now her face was against the pillow, which was against the wall. Kora's vagina was now in a vertical position and Samuel's penis was just as hard but not going as deep. Kora thoroughly enjoyed this position. She released herself again and Samuel locked his legs and straightened his arms. Samuel was no longer slamming himself into his loving wife. With his arms and legs locked, he elevated himself above his wife and bent his back to move his penis in and out of the back of Kora's vagina. Samuel felt himself about to reach his point of ecstasy.

When he exploded into his wife he erotically said, "OHH YEAH, MMMMM DAMN BABY!"

He then relaxed his body on top of Kora's. Samuel was sweating and breathing hard. His face was buried in Kora's hair. Samuel lifted himself up so that Kora could get out from under him. She did, and the two of them both moved to the head of the bed and lay on their backs beside each other.

Kora looked at Samuel and said, "Wow, baby. Where did all that come from?"

Samuel replied, "You been too tired to give me love'n I guess I was a little backed up."

Kora said, "Baby, I am sorry if I neglected you. I promise you that will not happen again."

Samuel smiled and said, "OK, baby. You know everyone heard you."

Kora replied, "Heard me! You're the one banging in me like you ain't never had none before!"

The two laughed and Kora said, "I'm so glad we did not wake Junior up."

Samuel replied, "That boy would sleep through anything."

Kora looked at Samuel and climbed on top of him. She then said, "Samuel I want you to do something for us."

Samuel responded, "Whatever it is, I'm not going to like it."

Kora spread her legs and straddled her husband. She kissed Samuel and said, "Now how do you know that? I haven't asked you yet."

Samuel said, "Cause you only ask me things you know I'm not going to like when you're kissing on me."

Kora smiled and said, "Do I do that?"

Samuel quickly replied, "Yes. Go on and ask me so we can get some sleep."

Kora kissed Samuel again and said, "Baby, I want you to get up an hour early in the morning and go chop firewood for the church."

Samuel was stroking his wife's hair down her back while she was talking to him. Samuel quickly stopped stroking her hair and said, "I cain't give you no hard love'n no mo'. You done lost your damn mind woman!"

Kora gently hit Samuel in his mouth and said, "Watch your mouth, Samuel. I have not lost my mind. Baby, I know it is frustrating being a blacksmith in butler uniform. I know you get sick of doing all the degrading things the white folk have you doing. Back on the plantation you had an outlet, your plow. Now you just frustrated with no outlet. It is affecting you, your personality and our marriage. So please, baby. Chop the firewood for us baby, please."

Samuel said, "You are amazing, woman. So you think if I get up and chop firewood in the morning I won't be so uptight?"

Kora lifted her hips off Samuel and took her skirt off. She then laid her naked body on top of her husband and said, "It's worth a try. Just try it for one week and see how you feel. Also, you will be providing heat for our classes."

Samuel said, "OK OK Kora, I'll go get some firewood in the morning."

Kora smiled and kissed Samuel. Samuel interrupted the kiss and asked Kora, "How am I supposed to get up in the morning?"

Kora said, "How do you get up every morning?'

Samuel replied, "You wake me up."

Kora smiled kissed Samuel again and said, "You can start chopping the day after tomorrow."

Samuel asked, "Why not tomorrow?"

Kora said, "Cause I ain't sleepy."

Kora kissed Samuel and lifted her hips. She then placed his semi-erect penis inside herself and felt Samuel getting harder. She said, "See, you ain't sleepy either."

Kora kissed Samuel and bounced on top of him until the two of them were exhausted from their lovemaking and fell asleep.

While Kora was upstairs working on her marriage, Wanda was downstairs trying to arrange one. Wanda fixed the reverend a fine meal. The two ate, drank tea, talked and laughed.

The reverend looked at Wanda and said, "It's getting late. I was waiting for Sista Kora."

Wanda said, "Kora? Why are you waiting for her?"

The reverend said, "I walked her home and she asked me to come inside and wait for her. She said she needed to go over more lessons with me."

Wanda smiled and said, "Don't get mad, Reverend, but I think we are the lesson."

The reverend replied, "What do you mean Wanda?"

Wanda said, "Kora came to my room and told me I had a gentleman caller in the kitchen."

The reverend laughed and said, "Why Wanda, I think we have been fixed up."

Wanda replied, "I guess we have, Reverend. I guess we have."

The reverend then said, "It's getting late. I need to get going."

As they stood up and headed for the front door, Wanda said, "I can serve you breakfast on my break around nine."

The reverend smiled and replied, "I wouldn't want to miss that. I'll see you then."

The reverend looked Wanda deep in her eyes and walked out the door.

Chapter Sixteen

The Planted Seed Grows its Roots

The following morning, Kora was in the kitchen scrambling eggs while Debbie prepared pancake batter. Wanda stuck her head in the kitchen and said, "Morn'n Kora."

Kora looked at Wanda and said, "Good morning Wanda. How are you today?"

With a large smile on her face Wanda replied, "I'm a little tired. I went to bed kinda late. How 'bout you? How did you sleep?"

Kora looked at Wanda as she stuck her head in the doorway smiling. Debbie stopped mixing the pancake mix and looked toward Kora, waiting for her response.

She responded to Wanda by saying, "I didn't sleep much either. I was up all night too, girl."

The three women laughed and went back to the chores that they were working on. Kora still did not like the thin walls in their living environment, but she was glad that her and Wanda could joke about what they heard instead of almost having a physical confrontation.

Debbie continued making the pancakes and said, "I thought about it, Kora. I think you're right, I'm going to tell Frank I cain't see him no mo."

Kora replied, "That's good Debbie. I'm sure you will find a good man in no time."

Debbie flipped the pancakes and put them on a plate. She put the plate on a carrying tray along with a plate of Kora's eggs and bacon. She then carried the tray filled with food into the dining area.

When she returned she said to Kora, "I don't know about that, Kora."

Kora replied, "Sure you will. You are a beautiful young woman. Any man would be lucky to have you."

Debbie sat at the table and said, "I don't know, Kora. See, I ain't never willingly been with a man before."

Kora stopped washing dishes and sat at the table with Debbie. Debbie then said, "My master started having his way with me when I was only thirteen. Me and Wanda left when I was eighteen. I been here since then and Frank is the first man I met I wasn't afraid of."

Kora listened and then asked, "Why weren't you afraid of Frank?"

Debbie said, "I just got to know him. He use to eat here every morn'n. He sat at my table one day and started telling me dumb jokes while I was work'n. I couldn't help but laugh. After that, he sat at my table every morning making me laugh. Then one night he showed up here on the porch with flowers and candy."

With a puzzled look on her face, Kora looked at Debbie for a moment and then asked, "Girl, you sure you don't like Frank?"

Debbie replied, "Kora, Frank is married."

Kora took a deep breath and said, "I think you're doing the right thing by leaving Frank alone. You can find you a good, available man."

Debbie than asked Kora a question that she was not ready for.

She asked, "Kora, have you ever dated a married man?"

Kora was silent. She didn't know what to say. Debbie went on to say, "I like Frank, but I'm not try'n to take no other woman's man. Kora, is it wrong to see a married man if you think he could be the one for you?"

Kora thought about her and Samuel and how her answer would affect Debbie. She then took a deep breath and said, "Samuel was married when he started courting me. Not a day goes by that I regret being with him. I cannot tell you how much I love that man. I used to tell myself that I didn't take him from his wife, she gave him to me. If he was getting what he needed at home, he wouldn't be with me. I realize now that is just an excuse to court a married man. To answer your question Debbie, yes, it is wrong to court a married man."

Debbie looked at Kora and asked, "How did you know Samuel was the right man for you?"

Kora replied, "I just knew. I never had any doubt. Heck, I knew he was the man for me long before he did. I started dreaming about us being together when I started bringing him water, which was years before he got married. Look Debbie, my situation was different than yours. I was still a slave. You are a free woman now. As free women, we have to maintain a certain dignity. A high level of morals and values. Leave Frank, you will find the right man. You just have to take it slow with him and him with you."

Kora looked at Debbie and took hold of her hands on top of the table. Debbie said, "Thank you Kora."

Kora said, "No Debbie, thank you. Now come on, we got work to do."

The days in December went by fast. Kora watched and observed her new friends as they went about their everyday routines. The reverend started courting Wanda. Debbie stopped seeing Frank. Frank kept coming to see Debbie after she told him she did not want to see him anymore. Kora told Debbie to tell Frank if he came by there again Debbie would tell his wife. Debbie never saw Frank again after that.

The church grew faster than anyone could have imagined. Every night, more and more people showed up. Kora had to adjust the format of the classroom to accommodate everyone. She broke the classroom into three sections. Beginners, Intermediates and Seniors. She walked by each group and made sure that they understood their lesson plan. She also started another classroom for new students that had just started. They needed a little more attention than the others. Once she taught them the basics, they moved to the Beginners section in the next room. The class grew so fast that Kora had to expand the time from one hour to one and a half hours. No one complained. The Negroes had a thirst for knowledge. When they started reading, it opened up a whole new world to them. Kora also took up small donations from everyone and purchased lanterns and school supplies. The church now had heat because Samuel was bringing firewood every morning. Samuel's attitude did improve. He still hated his job, but chopping firewood and making love to Kora helped him to deal with the stress from his butler duties.

A few days before Christmas, Kora told the reverend that she didn't think her students were getting enough sleep. She witnessed several of her attentive pupils sleeping in class. Kora and the reverend agreed that, starting on the first of the new year, they would change that class schedule to Tuesday, Thursday and Sunday evenings. The classes would be two hours long. On Sunday, the reverend would preach and they would not have class. Kora started assigning homework to keep the students learning at a fast pace.

On Christmas day, everyone was off work by six p.m. They went straight to church after work. Everyone congregated in the sanctuary and conversed in a happy and jolly mood. The church had purchased a few lanterns, but not enough to light up the entire sanctuary. The reverend placed several lanterns around the perimeter of the stage to make sure that everyone could see him. The rest of the congregation stood in dim light looking, at the stage in bright light. The reverend walked onto the stage and the congregation silenced itself instantly. The congregation looked onstage and saw a large, husky dark complexion man over six feet tall on the stage. Through the bright, flickering lantern flames they could see his black suit, white shirt and black tie.

The Reverend Lovejoy looked at his fellow worshippers and had to take a moment to contain himself. He could not believe that, in less than a month, a small group of ten grew to over fifty faithful parishioners. With his Bible in hand and a black robe on over his suit, the reverend started preaching.

He said, "Here at The African Methodist Episcopal Church of Our Lord, the first thing we always do is acknowledge your presence. We thank you for coming. I know most of you cooked Christmas dinner and may be a little weary. Your feet may be a little sore, but you showed up, in the middle of winter, to worship with us on Christmas day. As I look out onto this congregation, I see a lot of new faces. Yes, this is truly a blessing. You know, we as human beings have a tendency to take people for granted. What I mean by that is, as we move about our busy day, we constantly come across others that help us and most of us don't even notice them. We don't take the time to say two little words; thank you. Let me hear you all say 'thank you.'"

The congregation all said, "Thank you."

The reverend continued by saying, "Yes. That felt good, didn't it? One month ago. – to be exact, it was the last Sunday of the month - I met ten people eager to receive the teachings of our Lord. It made me feel good to teach those ten individuals. Now I want to take a moment to thank them. So when I call your name, please stand up. Debbie Johnson, she is in charge of our collection. One month ago, she could not count. Thank you Debbie. God is good. Mr. and Mrs. Jones, this couple has set a fine example of a strong, healthy marriage. Thank you Mr. and Mrs. Jones. Michael Robertson, this young fella has quickly mastered reading and writing. He has recruited several of his young friends to come study with us. Thank you Michael. Deacon Smith,

172

Mr. Smith informed me he was a pastor on his southern home. He told me that was many years ago. He has assisted me in resurrecting the African Methodist Episcopal Church of our Lord. Thank you Deacon Smith. Sista Mary Ann Jackson, Sista Jackson came to me that day in November and told me she USED to attend church in the south many years ago. Then she thanked me for resurrecting The...y'all say it with me..."

The entire captivated crowd said, "The African Methodist Episcopal Church of our Lord."

The reverend went on by saying, "Sista Jackson, I cannot resurrect our church home alone. It takes fine people like yourselves to uplift any church. So I thank you for your knowledge and wisdom. Now, Sista Jackson, just to give you a heads up, you better watch out for Deacon Smith. I see the way he looks at you... (the congregation laughs). Sista Wanda Gertrude Manning. This sista has excelled in the classroom, has a BEAUTIFUL voice and makes some very good fried chicken, which we will be selling every Tuesday and Thursday evening. Thank you Sista Wanda. Now, would Sista Kora Freeman please stand up. I cannot say enough about this sista. She recruited most of the people I just thanked. She is in charge of our education ministry. Sista, from the bottom of my heart, I thank you! You young brothers better not even think about it... Brother Samuel Freeman. See why I told you not to think about it? I thank you, Brother Freeman, for the heat! Yes Lord, thank you for going into the woods every morning and chopping us some firewood. Now last, but certainly not least, I want to thank Samuel Freeman Jr. You see, he is why I do this. I see little Negro babies and know we have a chance and an obligation to make this land a better place than the one we grew up in. So, I thank you Samuel Freeman Jr. for inspiring us all. Let the church say 'Amen.'"

The congregation repeated the reverend's word and said, "Amen."

The reverend then said, "Now I have thanked all of you, I have thanked the people that have been very special to the resurrection of this church, why do I feel like I am missing someone?"

The reverend paused, took a step back, then straightened his arms by his side and loudly said, "JESUS! I thank God almighty for giving us his only son! When you wake up everyday you should give thanks to the Lord, but especially on this day, because most of us take the Lord for granted. If you are like most people, you need to take a moment to thank God for allowing his only son to sacrifice himself for us."

The crowd bowed their heads.

Reverend Lovejoy started praying, "Lord we thank you for providing for us. We thank you for the sun, the moon and the stars. We thank you for helping us get through the day because we know there are some days when we feel like we just can't make it. Now we are not just thanking you for the blessing you have already bestowed upon us, but we thank you for the blessings we are about to receive. Let the church say, 'Thank you, Lord.'"

The congregation all said, "Thank you, Lord."

The reverend was sweating and wiping his forehead with a handkerchief. While he was perspiring, he looked out onto his fellow worshippers and said, "Good job on the heat, Samuel. Good job."

The reverend paused again as he continued to wipe the sweat from his forehead. He resumed by saying, "Now, praising God is free. You can do it anytime, anywhere. But if you want to do it here, you need to donate a tithe to the church, because the church home ain't free! Can I get an Amen?"

Everyone said, "Amen."

The reverend then said, "Yes Lord, we have bills too. For those of you that don't know how to tithe, I will tell you how. You need to give ten percent of you weekly earnings to God. OK, I'll make it simple for you. Most of us make about fifty cent a day. If you set

174

aside five cents a day for the Lord, you will see this church grow into a fine church we can all be proud of. Five cents. That just a nickel. If you cannot give ten percent, give what you can. If you are not sure how much you make or how much to give, see Sista Kora. Once again, I want to thank you all for coming out. I have truly enjoyed spending my Christmas evening with all of you. Thank you. Now, Sista Wanda will come up and lead us in the Christmas song, 'Silent Night.'"

Wanda walked up to the stage as the reverend requested. She sang "Silent Night" just as her and Reverend Lovejoy had rehearsed it. The reverend played the piano while Sista Wanda sang. Wanda had a strong but smooth-sounding powerful voice. As she sang the favorite gospel Christmas carol, her voice relaxed everyone in the sanctuary. Wanda finished the song and stepped down off the stage. The reverend got off the piano bench and took center stage again. He then asked everyone in his congregation to prepare their tithe.

The reverend gave everyone a moment to get their tithe ready then said, "Oh Lord, please accept our humble offering and watch over us as we fix up our place of worship to make it the center of stability in our community. Amen."

Everyone said, "Amen."

Debbie took a pail from behind the stage and a lantern from the front of the stage. With her lantern in one hand and a collection bucket in the other, Debbie passed the bucket down the front pew for the congregation in the row to place their offerings. Sista Jackson was on the other side of the pew with her lantern, waiting to collect the collection pail and send it down the next pew. After the two women finished the collection, Debbie brought the bucket on stage and placed it behind the stage on the ground. The two women returned the lanterns to the spotlight place that they had removed them from and took their seats.

175

The reverend took center stage again and said, "Yes, God is good. Thank you everyone for your offering. I want you all to know that good Christians help each other. We have some good Christians in here today that have an abundance of food. They have enough food to share to make sure that families that may not have eaten a decent meal on Christmas will eat one with us tonight. Tonight we have set up a table in the northern corner to serve everyone here."

The reverend lifted a lantern and held it in the direction of the table.

"No need to rush. There is plenty for everyone. Just line up in a single file line. We have servers waiting to fix your plates. I know I cannot wait to get some of Sista Wanda's fried chicken!"

Everyone followed the reverend's instructions and got in line. The lanterns were moved from the stage to several tables against the wall that were filled with food. When the lanterns provided the light, everyone could see three turkeys, lots of fried chicken and two roasted pigs. There were also sweet potatoes, macaroni and cheese and string beans. Their plates were fixed and they all ate and laughed and enjoyed each other's company on Christmas Day.

After dinner, Kora recruited several people to assist with cleaning up the dinner dishes. It did not take long because Kora and Wanda had cooked the food and they both cleaned as they cooked. After the eating area and kitchen were clean again, everyone hugged and thanked each other and went to their own homes to continue celebrating Christmas with their families. Everyone except the reverend and Wanda.

After everyone left, the reverend looked around the sanctuary and said to Wanda, "That was a nice dinner. Everyone cleaned up so fast. Come on Wanda, let's count the church blessings."

The reverend put the lanterns lights on the table, Wanda secured the collection bucket and proceeded upstairs. The reverend followed with two lanterns in his hands. Wanda poured the coins on a table in one of the classrooms that was not being used. The reverend placed the lanterns on the table to provide light to count by, and the two separated the coins into four piles. The four piles consisted of pennies, dimes, nickels and quarters. Each one took two piles and started counting. The reverend and Wanda counted the offerings every night and followed this same collection process before closing the church door and the reverend walking Wanda home. Tonight, the bucket was much heavier than usual. Wanda and the reverend sat quietly in the flickering candlelight and silently counted the offering.

After a few minutes, Wanda said, "I got three dollars and seventy-four cents, Reverend. What you got?"

The reverend replied, "I have five dollars and eighty-two cents, Wanda. How much is that altogether?'

Wanda looked up toward the ceiling and whispered to herself as she motioned with her index finger as if she was writing on an imaginary blackboard.

After thinking out loud and muttering for a moment, in a loud clear voice she said, "Nine dollars and fifty-six cents."

The reverend said, "Yes. That's the same answer I have."

Every week, the reverend and Wanda counted the offerings and the reverend asked Wanda to count the currency. Every week, the congregation grew by one or two people. Every week there was a little more to count in the offerings than the week before. Wanda was afraid at first, but with the reverend encouraging her and Kora's teachings, she learned how to count money at an accelerated pace. The reverend and Wanda then pulled four pails filled with alike currency and placed them on the floor near the table. They then placed each pile of currency in the bucket on the floor with the identical currency. The reverend then placed the buckets back in the back of the closet. No one knew the location of the church offerings accept Wanda and the reverend. After the reverend placed the last bucket in the closet, he sat down on the floor next to the doorway and breathed a sigh of relief. Wanda blew out one of the lanterns and joined him.

In her Sunday dress, she sat next to him and asked the reverend, "Tired, Reverend? You have had a long day."

The reverend replied, "Yes, Wanda. Today has been long. It may have been longer if it were not for you. You relaxed the crowd with your soothing voice, you have learned how to read and count at a phenomenal pace and your fried chicken, mmm-mmm, you have truly been a blessing!"

Wanda looked into the reverend's eyes and moved her head closer to his. The reverend accepted the invitation and the two exchanged oral pleasures with each other. The two kissed and the reverend put his hand on the back of Wanda's head. Wanda then shifted her body and straddled the reverend. In her blue Sunday dress, Wanda straddled and kissed the reverend adoringly. Through her underwear, Wanda felt the reverend getting an erection. As the reverend's erection grew, so did Wanda's level of excitement. Wanda pressed her face closer to the reverend and spread her legs farther apart. She felt the cotton on her underwear covering her labia against the cotton of the reverend's black suit pants, covering his erection. Wanda continued kissing the reverend. She pressed her full-figured hips down and rose up on her knees while at the same time moving back and forth against the bulge in the reverend's suit pants. The reverend enjoyed feeling Wanda's hips pressed against him. He placed his hands on the back of her hips and squeezed her as she rocked back and forth. Wanda then removed her hands from the reverend's head and face, unbuttoned the top of her dress and removed both of her breasts. When the reverend saw Wanda's beautiful breasts he pushed Wanda off of him and jumped up.

178

With his back to Wanda, he said, "I am sorry, Sista Wanda, but we cannot do this. Not here, not now."

Wanda sat on the floor with her dress open, devastated. The reverend looked down at her and said, "Button your dress up, Sista."

Then he turned his back to Wanda again to wait for her to become presentable. Wanda got dressed and stood up. She said, "What's wrong, Reverend? Don't you want me?"

The reverend turned around and said, "Wanda, I have not felt this way since my wife died. I like you a lot Wanda, but we cannot fornicate in the house of the Lord on the day we celebrate our savior's birthday."

Wanda stepped toward the reverend, smiled and said, "I understand, Reverend. I can wait until tomorrow night."

The reverend immediately replied, "That's not what I meant, Wanda. I am a man of the cloth. I cannot go around fornicating with members of my congregation! Look, Wanda. Let's just continue what we have been doing. Let's continue to spend time getting to know each other."

Frustrated, Wanda said, "OK, I understand, Reverend."

The reverend then said to Wanda, "Don't sound so down, Wanda. I still want us to spend time together after class. I just cannot have a sexual relationship with a woman that is not my wife. Now, come on, I'll walk you home."

The two walked out of the room and started down the stairs. Wanda had the lit lantern in her hand and noticed a nickel on the steps.

She picked it up, smiled and said, "Looks like this little fella didn't make it to the closet with his friends. I'll be right back, Reverend."

Wanda walked back into the room and opened the closet door. She leaned forward to reach the back of the closet and extended her arm holding the lantern so she could see the nickel bucket. She found the pail filled with nickels and something else.

The reverend was waiting for Wanda on the steps. Wanda walked out of the room and approached the reverend. The reverend could see that Wanda was holding the lantern in her left hand and something else in the right, but he could not see what it was.

Before he could ask, Wanda held out her right arm and said, "Reverend, why do you need this?"

In Wanda's right hand was a gun. Wanda stood about five feet from the reverend, holding out her hand and waiting for an answer. The reverend slowly reached out and took his pistol from Wanda.

Then he said, "This is my safe."

Wanda asked, "What you say'n, Reverend?"

The reverend replied, "Until I have a safe to keep the church offerings in, this gun makes me feel safe."

Wanda then said, "I don't know, Reverend. I don't like guns."

The reverend responded by saying, "Look Sista Wanda, I live here alone. We are collecting a lot of money. So far, we have collected over one hundred dollars. I need to, no I *have* to, protect myself in case someone tries to rob us."

Wanda asked, "Who gon' rob a church?"

The reverend walked back into the room to put the gun back in the offering closet. On his way into the room, he shook the gun in his hand and said, "No one will rob this church. No one."

After he put the safe back, he returned to the steps with a black folder in his hand. He said to Wanda, "Sista, can you please shine your light on me for a moment?"

Wanda held the lantern in his direction. The reverend opened the black folder and started writing in it. He then said, "I almost forgot the record this evening's offerings."

Wanda asked him, "You mean you write down how much money we take in?"

The reverend looked at Wanda and said, "Come closer, Wanda. I want to show you something."

Wanda moved closer and the reverend showed Wanda the contents of the black folder. In the folder, there were dates with dollar amounts by them and a store receipt. Wanda held the lantern over the ledger and the reverend said, "Wanda, I have to document every penny we take in. I also have to record how I spend the church's money. You see that receipt?"

Wanda nodded her head up and down.

"That is from the lanterns I purchased a few days ago. There are other receipts from the food and tables we bought. Everything we do with the money goes in this book."

Wanda looked at the reverend and asked him, "Reverend, where you learn so much 'bout preach'n and count'n?"

The reverend replied, "My father taught me."

Wanda said, "He taught you good."

The reverend looked at Wanda and said, "Yes, he did. And it's *well*, Wanda, he taught you well."

Wanda replied, "What you say'n? I don't even know yo' daddy. He ain't teach me nut'n!"

The reverend laughed and took the lantern out of Wanda's hand and placed it on the ground. He then kissed Wanda and said to her, "You know Wanda, the church is growing very fast. I am going to be an inspirational and central figure in the community. I cannot do this alone. I would like very much to meet a woman I can trust to carry herself as a fine preacher's wife should. I expect her to be able to read, write, count and speak proper English."

Wanda kissed the reverend and said, "OK, Reverend, if you wants me ta talk white fo' you, I will. I mean, if you want me to speak proper English for you, I will."

The reverend looked at Wanda in surprise and said, "You mean you could speak properly all the time and you didn't. Why not?"

Wanda said, "I have been around Kora a lot lately. She's half white and speaks very good English. I remember how my master and other white folks use to talk to me. I know how to use proper English. I just never had a reason to, until now."

Wanda kissed the reverend again. The reverend then said, "You know, Wanda. Kora being half white has nothing to do with her speaking properly. Look at me, I am not half white and I use proper English."

Wanda removed her hands from the reverend and placed them on her hips and said, "You were never a slave! The fact Kora is half white has everything to do with her talking properly and knowing her schooling so well. See, Kora was a slave but not like me. Kora is half white and lived in the big house where she learned her schooling and how to speak properly. I use to think she was so smart. Now I know, it ain't much to this schooling stuff. She ain't so smart. At least I know she ain't smarter then me."

The reverend looked at Wanda with her hands on her hips in her sassy mood and grinned and said, "Then *I*, Wanda, smarter than I."

Wanda rolled her eyes at the reverend and replied, "Whatever!"

The reverend just laughed and said, "Calm down, mama. I'm just mess'n with you."

He then stepped toward Wanda and moved in to kiss her again. Wanda moved back and said, "It's *messing,* Reverend. And don't be messing with me!"

The reverend chuckled and said, "Yes ma'am. Now have you calmed down enough to kiss me again?"

Wanda smiled the laughed and said, "I was a little uptight, wasn't I?"

The reverend replied, "Yes you were."

The two kissed and the reverend walked Wanda home. When they arrived at the front of the hotel steps, the reverend said to Wanda, "Wanda, did I ever tell you that I like courting you and I am not interested in courting no one else?"

Wanda replied, "No, Reverend. You never told me that. It is nice to hear."

The reverend then asked Wanda, "Are you interested in being courted by anyone else?"

Wanda smiled and said, "You know I'm not interested in no one else but you, Reverend."

The reverend responded by saying, "I know, but it is nice to hear."

The reverend then moved close to Wanda and kissed her on the cheek. He said, "Goodnight, Wanda."

Wanda smiled and said, "Goodnight Reverend."

When the Reverend Lovejoy returned to the church on Christmas evening, the first thing he did was sit down and compose a letter to his younger brother Edgar Lovejoy. The letter read:

Hello Edgar,

I hope this letter finds you in good health. I also hope you can forgive me for not writing you sooner. I have been very busy. The church has grown in measures you would never believe. We are establishing a solid foundation in a small South Philadelphia neighborhood. I met an educated Negro woman that is a fantastic teacher. Her teaching style reminds me of mother. We have managed to recruit new members at an alarming rate. The freed Negroes are so eager to learn.

I am writing you now because I foresee myself in need of an assistant pastor this summer. I do not want the demands of the church to overcome the influential members of the congregation. I have a plan to ordain several ministers and expand the education ministry significantly. I am going to establish a leadership hierarchy in the church this summer. A hierarchy that trains the associates on the foundation's base. We will teach them from the ground up how to run the church. This way, there will always be a solid center of guidance in the house of the Lord. This will be a difficult task. It requires a lot of planning and hard work. I cannot think of anyone I would rather enter this venture with then you.

Edgar, there are no words to express how much I miss my Mary. As you can imagine, the death of my wife and newborn child devastated me! I went into a downward spiral of depression and self-pity. I was at my lowest when the Lord sent an angel. He sent the young Negro educator and she was seeking my assistance. She introduced me to a new world of freed slaves thirsty for knowledge. The Negroes work all day then still manage to come to church to learn and do the Lord's work. Yes, I miss Mary but I have met a beautiful, strong, intelligent sista. She is an ex-slave with a no-nonsense attitude and has become an excellent educator also. I hope you can meet her this summer and accept the position of assistant pastor of the South Philadelphia branch of The African Methodist Episcopal Church of our Lord. I look forward to seeing you soon.

The Reverend Marcus Lovejoy

Chapter Seventeen
All Work and No Play

For the rest of the winter, life in South Philly progressed in a very positive way. The church continued to grow, the reverend continued to court Wanda and Samuel and Kora continued to work hard for the church. By the spring, the growth of the congregation created a demand for another classroom. Wanda and Debbie were Kora's best students. Kora made both of them her teaching assistants to help her handle the increase in Negro students. In June, Kora discussed a plan with the reverend to make Wanda and Debbie qualified church educators by July. Kora agreed to spend an hour every evening with Debbie and Wanda until she was convinced that they were ready to teach unsupervised.

Debbie and Wanda were excited about their opportunity. The three women were still working fifteen hours a day in the hotel. They were also in the classroom or sanctuary for two hours, three evenings a week. Debbie and Wanda had been edified by Kora's teachings enough to have education class sessions with Kora in place of homework. The women spent hours every evening learning how to communicate elementary education in a classroom environment. By the end of June, the two ladies were ready to lead individual classes in the African Methodist Episcopal Church of our Lord.

In July, Wanda and Debbie were content about leading their own classrooms. The two women were also tired. The long working hours and time in the church were taking their toll on everyone. Kora was concerned about her family. She felt she did not see Samuel enough. One evening after work, when they did not have church or class, the three teachers sat at the servants' table relaxing after a hard day's work.

Wanda looked at Kora and Debbie and said, "I don't know about you ladies, but my feet are killing me."

Kora agreed by saying, "Mine too. I am so tired I can't even get up to go to bed."

186

Debbie looked at the two women and in a serious tone said, "You know, ladies, we work too hard. Have you two ever thought about how much money we make for this hotel? Kora, since you came here, business has more than doubled. I'm tired of bustin' my butt with nothing to show for it!"

Kora looked at Debbie and smiled as she said, "Lord, your mind has been hard at work."

Debbie replied, "I remember the reverend telling us, we would not know we were being overworked and underpaid if we could not count. Well we can count now, so now I know we're being overworked and underpaid!"

Wanda asked, "You're right Debbie, but what can we do about it?"

Debbie responded by saying, "That's a good question, Wanda. I have given it some thought. You could talk to the reverend about us moving into the church."

Kora and Wanda looked at Debbie like she was crazy. They both shook their heads and said, "No."

Wanda went on to say, "Debbie, have you lost your damn mind?"

Debbie looked at Wanda and said, "No, I haven't lost my mind. My mind is perfectly fine, thank you. Look ladies, the church is big enough for all of us. We can stay there and stop working until Helen agrees to give us more money or less hours."

Wanda and Kora looked at Debbie in silence for a moment, then laughed loudly for a few minutes.

Kora was still laughing slightly as she slowly stood up and said, "Lord knows, some people get educated and just don't know how to act. I'm going to bed."

Kora slowly climbed up the stairs. Her feet hurt so bad that she could barely walk to her room. She made it to the room and opened the door. Samuel Jr. was sitting on some pillows covered by blankets on the floor. He had outgrown the drawer.

Samuel Jr. looked at Kora as she opened the door and said, "Hi Mommy."
Kora looked at their son then she looked at her husband and asked, "Why is he still up?"

Samuel replied, "He isn't sleepy."

Kora looked at her husband out the corner of her eye with a sarcastic look on her face. On her way into the bathroom she said, "He would have gone to sleep if you weren't talking him to death."

She walked into the bathroom, then looked back and asked Samuel, "Baby, would you fix me some bathwater please?"

Samuel didn't say a word. He just got up and went downstairs to warm up the water for his wife. When he walked into the kitchen, Debbie and Wanda were still talking at the table. Samuel acknowledged the ladies and prepared his wife's bathwater. He knew just how she liked it. Not too hot, not too cold. Samuel put a bucket of water on the stove and sat at the table with Wanda and Debbie.

Wanda looked at Samuel and said, "Samuel, are you ready to move?"

With a puzzled look on his face Samuel said, "Move? Move where?"

Wanda then looked at Debbie and said, "Tell him, Debbie."

Debbie snapped at Wanda and said, "Shut up, Wanda!"

Wanda smiled and walked out of the kitchen. Samuel removed Kora's bathwater and placed another bucketful of water on the stove. He went upstairs and entered his family's room. Samuel Jr. was asleep. Samuel walked past him and entered the bathroom. Kora was lying in the tub with nothing on. Samuel slowly poured the warm water over his wife's head, just like she liked it. Samuel loved pouring water on Kora. He poured it on her head and watched it get absorbed by her hair and run down her body. After he emptied the bucket on Kora, Samuel returned to the kitchen to retrieve the other bucket. He replaced the warm bucket with another bucket full of cold water. Samuel returned to Kora and poured water on his wife again. He continued pouring water on Kora's naked body until the top of the water reached the midlevel point in the tub. Samuel then returned downstairs for the last bucket of water. He put the stove fire out and returned to his wife with warm water in hand. Samuel placed the bucket on the bathroom floor close to the tub and he was careful not to spill one drop. He then quickly removed all his clothes.

A few times a week, Kora and Samuel went through this bath ritual. Kora had created their bath night to help them cope with the everyday pressures of the unjust world that they lived in. Kora knew that she was overworked and underpaid. She also knew that Samuel was dissatisfied as a butler. Kora loved their bath nights because the bath felt great after a long, hard day's work. Also, she got Samuel to take a bath before he made love to her. While Kora relaxed in the tub, Samuel's warm water stimulated her sexually. She watched her man strip in front of her and became even more aroused. Kora sat up and Samuel moved his torso to the small space that she created between her and the back of the tub. As he sat down in the water, Kora pressed her body against his. Samuel secured himself on the bottom of the tub and hugged his wife from behind. With one arm, Samuel took hold of the last bucket of warm water and held it over himself and Kora. He placed his other arm on the bottom of the bucket. With Samuel's beautiful massive defined black arms extended directly over Kora, she looked up, reached back with both of her arms, grabbed Samuel by his upper triceps, held her head back so the top of her head was in Samuel's chest and opened her mouth.

189

Samuel looked up at the bucket and pushed the bottom forward causing the water to fall head first all over the two of them. Being in the tub with Samuel and the sensation of the warm water stimulated her clitoris. Kora squirmed and pushed her head back further into her husband's chest. Once she had a mouth full of water she closed her mouth. The bucket emptied and Samuel placed it on the floor. Samuel placed his arms on his wife's stomach and held her. Kora moved her arms off her husband and onto the top of the tub. When Samuel held her, the two enjoyed a moment of silence as they relaxed. The top of Kora's head was still against Samuel's chest and her mouth was still full of warm water. Kora puckered her lips, exhaled from her diaphragm and pushed a small fountain directly above the relaxing couple. The two laughed a comfortable calming outlet of relief.

Samuel said, "You never did that before."

Kora replied, "It just hit me."

In his serious voice Samuel said, "What do you think about moving?"

Kora turned her head to make eye contact with Samuel and asked, "Have you been talking to Debbie?"

Samuel replied, "Actually, Wanda mentioned it."

Kora turned her head and leaned back so her mouth was in Samuel's ear. She put her hands on the back of Samuel's head and said, "Let talk about it later, baby."

Kora kissed his ear and twisted her body one hundred and eighty degrees in the direction of Samuel's ear that she was whispering in. The cast iron tub was large enough to hold the two of them comfortably. Kora straddled Samuel and kissed him passionately. She started stroking his submerged penis and increased his erection. Kora proceeded to rub her thumb over the tip of Samuel's penis and Samuel responded

190

to his wife by putting his hand on her lower back and pulling her hips closer to him. Kora elevated her hips and placed the tip of Samuel's hard penis inside her. She moved her hips down slowly and Samuel's erected manhood entered his wife underwater. The warm water entered Kora as her husband did. This sensation was very soothing to Kora. Kora and Samuel had never made love in the tub before. She was enjoying their first underwater experience. She moved down a little more, slowly taking Samuel deeper inside her. Then she lifted her hips and slowly came down again. Kora continued this slow motion lovemaking pace while she kissed Samuel. She kissed him and, as they slowly gyrated, the warm water and Samuel's penis massaged her vaginal cavity. Lately, Kora and Samuel had made love often and aggressively. The night Samuel made love to her from behind and she begged him to stop, she noticed that her husband had slept peacefully. Kora knew that their lovemaking helped her husband deal with his butler frustrations.

While they kissed and Kora slowly gyrated underwater. Samuel ran his hands through Kora's long thick curly hair and kissed his wife obsessively. He pulled Kora's hair down her back exposing her neck. Samuel gently pinched his wife's nipples and savored the skin on her neck. Kora moaned and Samuel pushed his beautiful wife off of him.

Kora looked at him and asked, "What's wrong, baby? I'm making too much noise?"

Samuel smiled at his wife and aggressively grabbed Kora's hips. He turned Kora's torso toward her backside. Kora followed her husband's motion. She placed her hands on the side of the tub and allowed Samuel to guide her into a submissive, animalistic lovemaking position. Samuel looked at his wife bent over in front of him, waiting for him. He observed her for a moment. Samuel was still overtaken by Kora's beauty. There she was, bent over in front of him, the surface of the bathwater was touching Kora's vagina. Her round hips sat above the water like a sun waiting to set.

Samuel kneeled behind his wife and put his hand on his penis. He placed its tip into his wife again. Samuel held Kora by her hips with one hand and held his penis with the other. He moved his hips closer to his wife and penetrated her deeper. Samuel removed his hand and moved forward and backward slowly. He placed both hands on Kora's waist and increased his movement. Kora started moaning again and Samuel became more aroused. He took hold of his wife's hair again and intensified his stroke. Now, Samuel was slamming into the back of his wife. The waves were splashing out of the tub. Samuel and Kora's clapping echoed throughout the bathroom and beyond. Erotically, Kora responded to Samuel's mannish gyrations by moaning louder and telling her husband to be quiet.

She said, "You make'n too much noise baby! You make'n too much noise! Ohhhh! Samuel! Samuel! Oh God Samuel!"

Just then, in the middle of their water splashing, pelvic clapping, erotic moans, the bathroom door opened. Junior walked into the bathroom and saw his father pounding his mother from behind. Samuel saw his son enter the room and did not stop making love to his wife. He motioned with his arm for his son to leave the room and said, "Get out of here, Junior! Go back to bed!"

Samuel Jr. stood in the bathroom doorway rubbing his eyes and staring at his parents making love. After a few seconds, Kora realized that Junior was not leaving, so she pulled away from her husband. Samuel also realized that Junior was not leaving, and let his wife pull away. Samuel sat back in the tub while Kora got her towel and stepped out of the tub. With the bathwater dripping on the floor, Kora left little wet footprints on the floor as she escorted her son into the other room with her towel wrapped around her. Kora led their son to his pile of pillows and blankets and put him back in the bed.

Once in bed, Junior asked his mother, "Mommy, why was daddy spanking you? Did you do something bad?"

Kora smiled and said, "No, Little Samuel. Mommy didn't do anything wrong. If I did, Daddy would not spank me. Men do not spank women. Daddy and Mommy were playing an adult game. A game that only adults are allowed to play. The next time you hear Mommy and Daddy playing, you just go back to sleep, OK?"

Their two-year-old son replied, "OK, Mommy. Will you tell me a bed time story?"

Before Kora could answer, Junior's father yelled from the bathroom, "Junior, go to bed! Now!"

Kora said to their son, "You heard your father. Goodnight, son."

Kora kissed their son on his forehead, walked back into the bathroom and closed the door behind her. Samuel was still in the tub. He was leaning back, waiting for Kora to rejoin him. Kora dropped the towel on the floor and climbed into the tub, straddling her husband again. She kissed Samuel and massaged Samuel's penis underwater again. Once again, Kora lifted her hips, placed the erect tip of her husband inside her and slowly moved down toward her husband. The bathwater was significantly cooler now. The room-temperature water entering Kora was still stimulating. The two made love quietly and passionately, kissing, licking, sucking, rubbing and gyrating in the dim, moonlit bathroom. Kora felt her husband's penis get extremely hard. She knew he was ready to reach his orgasm. Kora knew when her husband was ready to release himself by the depth of his penis. When Samuel was about to ejaculate, his penis would be its hardest and he would ram it in her for several minutes before his massive body would tense up and explode. It was these few minutes before Samuel's climax that Kora enjoyed the most because Samuel's penis would thump a place deep in her vaginal cavity that he had not been reaching before. Samuel's erection and vicious stroke would cause him to strike Kora's spot several times before he released himself inside of her and collapsed on top of her. These intense minutes usually caused a loud, passionate dual climatic experience.

This time, Kora was on top. Kora was in control of their pace. When Samuel reached his peak, he tried to turn his wife around but she resisted by grabbing his shoulders hard with both hands. Kora kissed her husband and said, "I got this, baby."

She then started raising her hips up as high as she could with her husband inside of her. When she felt the tip of his penis on her clitoris she would slam back down, ramming Samuel deep into her and hitting her spot. Kora repeated her stress-relieving gyrations over and over and over. As her hips moved up and down in the tub, the water started splashing again. Samuel felt himself about to release himself inside of Kora and he grabbed her hair and pulled it hard down her back. The intense feeling of having her hair pulled, Samuel hitting her spot, the bathwater and knowing she was in control of her strong powerful man made Kora have the best orgasm she had ever had! Kora dug her nails deep into Samuel's shoulders and, with her head back, screamed as she came.

She screamed, "I'm coming Samuel! Oh my! Oh God! Oh God! Shiiiiittt! Samuel!"

Kora collapsed on top of her husband, sank down in the tub and rested her head on Samuel's chest. The two relaxed for several moments. They caught their breath and enjoyed the peace they now had as freed slaves. On the plantation, Samuel was always leaving after their erotic silent outburst concluded. Now they were free to relax and enjoy each other's company. This is one of the things Kora enjoyed most about being free. She could enjoy her time with Samuel. Kora lay on her husband, listening to his heartbeat.

After a few moments, she heard him say, "Baby, You were loud. I've never heard you be that loud."

Kora replied, "I wasn't that loud, was I?"

194

Samuel looked down at his wife's head on his chest. She was looking up at him, waiting for an answer.

Samuel replied, "Yes you were and you cursed also."

Kora quickly replied, "Stop play'n, Samuel. You know I don't curse."

Samuel laughed and said, "You did then."

Kora asked him, "Did I? Really?"

Samuel replied, "Yes. Come on let's ask Junior if you don't believe me. I know he heard you."

Kora smiled and kissed Samuel. The two climbed out the tub and dried each other off. They opened the bathroom door and noticed Junior asleep on his bed. The two went to bed that evening feeling relaxed and relieved.

The next morning, Kora entered the kitchen with Samuel Jr., ready to great her co-worker Debbie. Debbie was in the kitchen getting breakfast started.

Kora Looked at Debbie and said, "Good morning, Debbie."

Debbie replied, "Hello Kora. Hi Little Samuel."

Samuel Jr. waved to Debbie and sat at the servants table. Kora joined Debbie in preparing breakfast. The two women worked through their daily routine silently for several minutes. Debbie gave Samuel Jr. a plate of eggs and bacon.

Junior responded by saying, "Thank you."

Debbie replied, "Oh, you're welcome, little man."

Debbie was fixing several plates for the breakfast customers in the dining room. She left the kitchen with four plates on a tray. She was carrying the tray on her shoulder with one hand and the tray stand in the other. Debbie returned a few minutes later with the empty tray and stand. She had several other orders she was beginning to prepare. Kora started preparing the orders that were ready to serve. She took the tray and loaded it up with the guests' orders and exited the kitchen. When she returned she also had more orders to prepare. The two women worked in this fast nonstop pace during the breakfast lunch and dinner rush. In between the meals, they were preparing dishes that took a long time to cook, like baked potatoes or their signature meal, a slow cooked broiled steak.

When Kora first arrived at the hotel, she tasted the steak. It was tough and dry. Kora observed how the ladies cooked it. She noticed that they prepared it when it was ordered. They cooked it over a high fire to prepare it as quickly as possible. One of the first changes Kora made was teaching the women how to properly prepare a steak. The first thing she did was soak the meat overnight in iced lemon juice with a little salt. After the breakfast rush, she rubbed pepper into the salt and lemon-soaked meat. She then placed it on a very slow fire on the outside grill. She then placed several potatoes in the oven and started backing them. When the lunch and dinner crowd arrived, all the ladies had to do was make a salad and vegetables. Kora also precooked her famous fried chicken. The chicken did not take long to cook, but it was one of the most inexpensive meals on the menu and in high demand. Kora's implementation of slave plantation efficiency showed the ladies how to make the best steak in town at a fast pace. Kora's years in the big house taught her everything she would need to make it as a freed Negro in America.

The two women worked at a fast pace for the rest of the morning, waiting on customers. After the morning crowd left, Debbie started the dishes and Kora started the steaks.

The women were able to work at a slower pace now because there were no customers waiting for their plates.

As Kora seasoned the meat she did not make eye contact with Debbie but said to her, "Debbie, I think we need to talk to Wanda about your plan again."

Debbie looked at Kora and asked, "Wow, last night I was a joke to you two. What happen between last night and this morning?"

Kora said, "Let's just say I had a chance to sleep on it."

Debbie stopped washing the dishes and turned around to face Kora.
She asked her, "This wouldn't have anything to do with Junior interrupting your adult games last night would it?"

Kora stopped seasoning the meat, looked at Debbie and said, "Damn Debbie, did you have your ear to our wall last night?"

Debbie laughed slightly and replied, "Kora, please. Everyone hears everything you two do every night. These walls are thin and y'all ain't the quietest couple in the world."

Kora replied, "Yeah, we have to move. My family has out grown our living conditions."

Debbie then said, "My living conditions are fine but my feet hurt. I guess we all have our own reasons."

Kora asked, "How do you think we can convince Wanda to talk her man into letting us move into the church?"

Debbie thought for a moment then said, "I think you and I should talk to her tonight after church. Now that we are both on the same page and the two of y'all ain't laughing at me, we should be able to convince her."

Kora quickly replied, "OK, then. Tonight it is."

They paused and went back to work for several minutes, then Kora said, "Debbie."

Debbie said, "Yes Kora."

Kora said, "I'm sorry I laughed at you."

Debbie responded, "Its OK, Kora. Just don't let it happen again."

The two women smiled and continued working on the slow-cooked lunch items. Samuel entered the kitchen and sat at the table with his son. He acknowledged his wife and Debbie by saying, "Morning ladies."

Debbie replied, "Good morning Samuel."

Kora fixed her husband a plate and placed it in front of him. Samuel looked at his wife and said, "Thank you baby."

Kora placed a quick lip-touching kiss on her husband and removed their son's plate. Junior looked up at his mother and said, "Thank you, baby."

Then he puckered his lips waiting for a kiss like his father received. Samuel heard his son's remark and quickly scolded Junior by saying, "She is Mommy to you, not baby. Do you understand?'

Junior asked, "How come you can call her baby?"

His father then said, "Because I am an adult and you are a child."

Kora returned to seasoning the meat after she fed her husband. She was on the other side of the kitchen when her husband told their son he was an adult. She quickly looked in the direction of her husband and son anticipating what their son would say next.

Junior looked at his father and asked, "When I get to be an adult, can I spank Mommy?"

Kora started walking toward the two of them before Junior asked his question. She grabbed Junior immediately after he asked the question that almost got him a backhand across his face.

Samuel looked at his wife and child as they stood over him and said, "That boy's mouth is too damn smart."

Kora took Junior to the table she was seasoning the meat on and showed him how to rub pepper into the meat. She then returned to the table with her husband and told him in a low voice, "His mouth is smart because he is smart. Last night when Junior saw us he asked me why you were spanking me. I told him we were playing adult games. That's why he asked you if he could spank me when he becomes an adult."

Samuel stopped eating, looked at his wife and said, "Your son is funny."

Kora responded, "Oh, now he is my son. Man, finish your eggs. We all have work to do."

Samuel finished his breakfast and returned to his butler duties.

Lunch and dinner went as planned. The evening educational service in the church went well also. Wanda and Debbie started teaching their own classes. On the way home all the two women could talk about was their first day teaching.

Debbie asked Wanda, "Girl did you ever think we would be teachers?"

Wanda replied, "Teach? I never thought I would be able to read myself. Now here I am teaching."

The women talked and walked all the way home. Once in the hotel, Kora told Samuel that she wanted to talk to the ladies for a few minutes. Samuel went upstairs and Kora went into the kitchen with Junior, Wanda and Debbie. They all sat at the servants' table and continued talking.

Debbie said, "I cannot believe on my first day I taught the entire class how to count to twenty. Ladies let me tell you. This one gentleman in the first row was sooo cute, I could hardly keep my eyes off him."

Kora responded by saying, "You are there to teach, not man hunt."

Debbie replied, "That's easy for you to say, you have a man. Besides, he looked so good as he counted one, two, three..."

All of a sudden, Junior joined Debbie in counting. The twenty-month-old child said, "Four, five, six, seven eight nine ten."

The women look at each other in shook. Kora said, "I'm not surprised. Junior is with me in class all the time. He is just repeating what he hears."

With a witty grin, Wanda said, "You better hope that's all he repeats."

Debbie and Wanda laughed. Kora did not find the two of them amusing. As the two ladies laughed, Kora looked at them and said, "Which reminds me, ladies. Today was a long day. Our feet hurt and we are tired. We are being overworked and underpaid and it is time we did something about it."

Wanda stopped laughing and said, "OK Kora, you are right. So what do you want to do about being overworked and underpaid?"

Kora replied, "I think Debbie had a good idea last night. We need to move out and negotiate better hours and better pay."

Wanda looked at Kora and asked, "Just where you plan on moving to?"

Debbie and Kora looked at Wanda and smiled. When Wanda realized what Debbie and Kora wanted she quickly said, "Ohh no. I told you last night, I'm not jeopardizing my relationship with my man by asking him can we all move into the church just because you can't get yo' love'n in private."

Kora quickly replied, "Wanda, this isn't just for me. It is for all of us. We can demand Helen give us more money and less hours. If we are not living here, we can stop working here until she gives us what we want. Aren't you tired of cleaning up after white people all day, Wanda?"

Wanda responded to Kora by saying, "I been cleaning up after them all my life. It doesn't bother me."

Debbie joined in by saying, "Wanda, you're being selfish. No one is trying to damage your relationship. We just want a better life for all of us."

Wanda sat still, contemplating her next statement. While she was thinking, Kora said, "Wanda, you don't have to talk to him alone. The three of will talk to him together. We just all have to be on the same page. We have to stick together and see this through to the end."

Wanda asked, "What are we about to go through, Kora?"

Kora responded by saying, "Ladies, we are about to threaten Helen's profits. She is not going to want to pay us or cut our hours. She will be stubborn. It may take some time to convince Helen to pay us and give us less hours."

The three ladies were quiet for a moment.

Debbie then said, "I'm in."

Wanda replied, "If you two think we can pull this off, I'll help you."

Kora quickly said, "Don't do this for us, do it for yourself."

Wanda nodded her head and the three women agreed to discuss moving into the church with the reverend and organizing a work stoppage until their demands were met.

The next evening after work, the three women went to the church on their out-of-class night to talk to the reverend. Reverend Lovejoy invited them in and they all sat in the church's large kitchen, sipping tea.

After everyone was comfortable, the reverend asked, "So, what can I do for you ladies?"

Wanda started the ladies' request by saying, "Reverend, we have a problem and we think you can help us."

The reverend replied, "If I can, I will. How can I help you?"

Debbie said, "We want to organize a work stoppage with all the hotel workers. We are tired of being overworked and underpaid. The problem is all the hotel employees live in the hotel. We need a place to stay until we go back to work."

The reverend then replied, "It is amazing to me how an education can make you strive for a better life so quickly. So, you all want to stay here?"

Debbie replied, "Yes, temporarily."

The reverend then asked, "How many of you need to stay here?"

Debbie replied, "Myself, Wanda, Kora, Samuel and Samuel Jr. That makes five."

The reverend replied, "You know, usually the church would not take in boarders. However, this is for a good cause. I also think you all have a good chance of having your demands met. You all can stay here, temporarily."

The three ladies were very excited. The reverend then went on to say, "You know ladies, I have experience in the labor negotiation field. I could help you."

The ladies were overwhelmed with excitement. Not only had they secured a place to move into temporarily, but now they had a leader. Everyone went back to the hotel anxious to get started on the work stoppage plan.

Chapter Eighteen
We Have Rights Too

When they arrived at the hotel, everyone went into the servants' quarters to come up with a strategy that would catch Helen's interest and make her pay attention to the hotel workers. Samuel joined the group and they all sat at the servants' table with their mouths shut and ears open. They were waiting for the reverend to advise them.

Reverend Lovejoy began the first union meeting by saying, "The first thing we need to do is elect a spokesperson to represent all of us when we talk to Helen."

Debbie asked, "Why can't you talk to her, Reverend?"

The reverend responded by saying, "It should be someone Helen works with and respects."

Wanda said, "That's easy, Kora can represent us."

Everyone agreed and nodded their heads. The reverend then said, "We also need to establish the union bylaws."

Wanda asked, "Reverend, what are bylaws?"

The reverend answered Wanda by saying, "Bylaws are the laws we establish to govern the union. The first bylaw we should have is the voting bylaw."

Wanda quickly said, "Vote? Reverend, you know we can't vote."

The reverend replied to Wanda by saying, "You can vote in this union. I propose we establish a three-fourths majority vote bylaw. That means any motion would have to have three-fourths of the union's approval to get accepted."

Samuel asked the reverend, "Do you get a vote, Reverend?"

The reverend replied, "No. Only union members vote. I am a consultant, not a member."

Samuel replied to the reverend by saying, "Right now there are only four of us. Two-thirds or three-fourths will not make much of a difference. If one person objects, that would be three-fourths of a majority. If two people object, that will be one-half and the motion will not be passed. I think we should consider the future of our union. We are small now, but if we expand three-fourths or two-thirds will make a difference. I think we should establish bylaws that will not need to be amended in the future. Therefore, I think we should have a two-thirds motion approval vote in the bylaws."

Everyone looked at Samuel and did not say a word. Samuel attended class with everyone else. He did not participate in the class discussions. He did his homework and kept quiet during class. Everyone assumed that Samuel did not like school. Samuel did like school. it just was not his nature to speak up in class. He usually maintained his quiet demeanor and kept to himself.

After everyone got over the shock of Samuel speaking up, the reverend said, "If you agree with Samuel, show your hands."

All hands were raised. The reverend then asked, "There is still a motion on the floor to elect Kora as the spokesperson. Who thinks Kora would make a good spokesperson?" Three hands went up. The one hand that did not go up was Samuel's.

Reverend Lovejoy then said, "The motion has three fourths acceptance and Kora is accepted as the spokesperson for this negotiation."

Samuel raised his hand and said, "I make a motion that we have a silent anonymous vote. Voters have the right to make their vote in private. If everyone knows who is voting yes or no it could affect the decision of the voter."

The reverend then asked, "We have a motion on the floor for anonymous voting. How many of you support anonymous voting?"

All hands went up. Reverend Lovejoy asked Wanda to pass out paper and pencils to everyone. While Wanda passed out the writing materials the reverend said, "From now on, we will vote on paper. I will count the votes. That reminds me, we should be keeping minutes for this meeting. We need a secretary. I make a motion that we elect Wanda for secretary."

Wanda quickly responded by saying, "Me, oh no, Reverend, I don't even own a watch."

The reverend smiled and said, "Wanda, keeping minutes means taking notes of the meeting."

Wanda replied, "Oh, well why didn't you say that? OK, I'll keep the minutes. That is if the committee votes yes on your motion."

The reverend replied, "Now you are getting the hang of it. Everyone please write yes or no on the paper in front of you and pass it to me."

The reverend collected the papers and counted them. He then said, "It is unanimous, Wanda is our secretary."

The meeting ended and Kora stayed behind to discuss the negotiation strategy with the reverend. Kora and the reverend conversed about their negotiation tactics for almost thirty minutes and then Kora went upstairs to go to bed. Kora walked into their room and noticed Samuel Jr. asleep on the floor near the bathroom.

Kora looked at her husband and asked him, "Samuel, why didn't you vote for me to be the spokesperson?"

Samuel replied, "Because I rarely see you as it is. I know if you take on another role, I will never see you."

Kora responded to her husband's comment by saying, "Baby, I know I haven't been here for you and I am sorry. I am just trying to help us all have a better life. I see how frustrated you are being a butler. I know you should be a blacksmith. I just need you to be patient with me."

Samuel looked at his wife and went to bed. Kora joined her husband in bed and said to him, "Be prepared to move out tomorrow. I am going to talk to Helen. I do not think she is going to give in to our demands right away. We may need to apply some pressure with a work stoppage to let her know we are serious."

Samuel yawned and said, "If you need me to do anything, just let me know."

Kora kissed Samuel gently on the lips and said, "Thank you, baby. Goodnight."

In the morning, Kora joined Debbie in the kitchen for their morning breakfast-serving ritual. After breakfast Kora found Helen in her office. Kora walked into Helen's office and said, "I need to talk to you. It is important."

Helen said, "OK, Kora. Have a seat."

Kora sat on the other side of Helen's desk. Helen asked, "So what is so important?"

Kora said, "Listen Helen, the other workers and I think we are being taken advantage of. We are tired of working fifteen hours a day."

Helen looked are Kora with a surprised look on her face.

After several moments of silence, Helen said, "Tired? Kora, do you realize how fortunate you all are to be working here. You are getting paid to do what you all used to do for free."

Kora responded by saying, "We were slaves when we did it for free. We are free now and the fifty cents a day you pay us is not enough. We want to work fewer hours and we want a raise."

Helen angrily said, "A raise? Kora, have you gone mad? What makes you think you can work less and make more?"

Kora replied, "Helen, I see how crowded this place is every day. It is our hard work that runs this place and keeps the customers coming back."

Helen raised her voice and said, "Kora, I am not giving you all a raise or shortening your hours and if you do not get back to work now, you may find yourself looking for another job!"

Kora then replied to Helen by saying, "You know Helen, I was hoping you would be reasonable. Since you are not willing to negotiate a better labor agreement, you leave us no choice but to walk out immediately."

Kora stood up and proceeded toward the door. Angrily, Helen said, "Not willing to negotiate? Better labor agreement? That sounds like union talk to me. Who have you been talking to?"

Kora walked out of Helen's office and went into the kitchen where the other workers were waiting for her. Kora said, "Let's go. Helen is not taking us seriously."

Everyone went to their room and secured their pre-packed bags. Helen watched as everyone walked out of the hotel together. They all walked to the church where the reverend was expecting them. He showed everyone to their room. Kora and Samuel had their own room and Samuel Jr. had a connecting room next to his parents. Debbie and Wanda each had their own rooms also. Everyone unpacked and met in one of the classrooms to go over the plan for their next move.

The reverend started the meeting by saying, "I purchased groceries to make meals to sell like we talked about. Remember, the church is not in the business of making loans. This is a rare occasion. It will not happen again."

Kora, Wanda and Debbie all went into the church kitchen to prepare the plates they planned on selling. They all knew that if they walked out of their jobs they needed another source of income to survive. Living in the church and selling breakfast, lunch and dinner meals was the perfect strategy for a substitute income. The church members sold the plates out of the back door of the church and did not allow anyone to eat in the church. Most of the Negroes ate on the vacant yard across the street from the church. This was free advertising for the Negro working staff's fight for rights. Everyone witnessed the people around the church enjoying their breakfast, lunch and dinner.

It took Helen a week to get a staff in place at the hotel. During that time, the word spread about the Bartram Hotel's former staff working out of the church. The majority of the hotel customers were lower class European Americans. During the week, the hotel was not serving meals and the hotel regulars found diverse places to eat them. All of the Bartram Hotel's regular guests knew that the hotel's former staff was working down the street at The African Methodist Episcopal Church of Our Lord. None of the European Americans patronized the former slave's religious foundation. Despite the fact the food at the Negro church was much better than anything else around, the loyal European American Bartram Hotel customers refused to support the, "Educated uppity Negroes'" cause.

The reverend anticipated the change in market base. He knew they would have to sell the plates to other Negroes in the neighborhood. Most of the Negroes in the neighborhood could not afford to eat in the hotel. The reverend knew he could lower the price of the plates because the overhead from preparing the plates in the church was much lower than the overhead in the hotel. The lower price allowed the church to create a market segment in the heart of the Negro community. Occasionally, late in the evening, a European American citizen would make a late-night dinner call to the hotel. The late-night dinner caller could slink up to the back door of the church and pay the reduced price for their overly satisfying meal. The reverend instructed Kora and the staff to include extra portions in the late-night caller's plates. The reverend was relying on word of mouth to increase the late-night European customer base.

Helen hired and trained her new staff and reopened the hotel kitchen within a week of the former staff's walking out. The food the new staff prepared was not nearly as tasty as the former staff's cuisine. The kitchen was not as efficient either. The plates took much longer to prepare. The European customer base returned to the hotel immediately after it reopened, only to be disappointed and return to their former temporary eating venues. With the hotel sales down and no resolution to the problems, Helen knew it was only a matter of time before she would have to swallow her pride, seek out her former staff and negotiate their return to work.

One rainy mid-June morning, a well-dressed stranger walked into the church kitchen. Kora, Debbie and Wanda were in the kitchen preparing breakfast plates. The three women looked up and saw the man standing in the kitchen. The gentleman was a well-dressed Negro. He was about six feet tall, two hundred and fifteen pounds and he was wearing a grey suit and had his matching hat in his hand. The man was dripping wet as he stood in the kitchen doorway, watching the ladies work.

Kora noticed the drenched stranger first and said, "Hello, breakfast well be ready any minute now. What would you like?"

The man replied, "This kitchen sure smells good. I'd like some eggs, grits and bacon please."

Kora continued scrambling her eggs and said, "Coming right up. You must be new in town. We usually don't let people eat in the church, but since you are alone and it is pouring outside, you can have a seat at the kitchen table."

The man smiled and said, "Why, thank you. That is very kind of you."

The gentleman removed his coat and placed it on the back of the kitchen chair he sat in. With his raincoat off, the ladies could see that the stranger was wearing a white shirt and black tie. Kora looked at Debbie and motioned for her to come fix the man's plate. Debbie fixed a plate and carried it to the gentleman.

Debbie placed the plate on the table and asked the stranger, "Are you a preacher?"

The man replied, "Why yes, yes I am. Did my suit give me away?"

Debbie laughed and said, "It sure did."

The stranger started to eat and Debbie asked him, "What's you name, preacher?"

Wanda said to Debbie, "Let the man eat, Debbie. We can get to know him later."

The stranger chewed with his mouth full and swallowed. He then said, "Oh, she is not bothering me. In fact, I am enjoying her company."

The stranger then wiped his hands on a napkin and said, "I am Reverend Edgar Lovejoy."

Wanda and Kora stopped working. They looked at the young reverend in silence.

Before anyone could say anything else, Debbie said, "Well, hello Reverend Lovejoy. I am Debbie, that is Kora and Wanda. We all live and work here with the Reverend Marcus Lovejoy. You must be related to him?"

Edgar replied, "Yes, he is my brother."

Debbie sat down at the table with the reverend. As she sat, Wanda said, "Debbie, for God sake child, let the man eat."

Edgar looked at Debbie and replied, "No, no, please stay. I would enjoy your company."

Debbie stayed and the reverend continued to eat his breakfast. Edgar ate slow and held a conversation with Debbie.

He asked her, "Where are you from Debbie?"

Debbie replied, "Virginia."

Edgar continued eating and finished his breakfast. He complimented the ladies by saying, "That was a very good meal. Thank you, all of you. How much do I owe you all?"

Kora smiled and said, "Now, Reverend. Your money is no good here."

Debbie took the Reverend Edgar's plate to the sink and proceeded to wash it. Edgar stayed in his chair and turned around to face all the ladies. He studied them for a moment and said, "Excuse me, Debbie, did I hear you say you all live here?"

Kora and Wanda looked at Debbie as she said, "Yes, we live here, temporarily."

While the women worked, there was a knock on the back door. Debbie answered it and handed the man a plate of food in exchange for ten cents. The same plate cost fifty cent when the former slaves worked in the hotel kitchen. Edgar watched while the ladies cooked, sold plates and cleaned up the kitchen in a very efficient manner. Edgar kept his eye on Debbie. He admired her small frame, pleasant demeanor and her ability to work so proficiently. While Edgar was admiring Debbie, he heard a familiar voice say, "Edgar, is that you?"

Edgar turned around and saw his brother Marcus standing in the kitchen doorway with Samuel. Edgar stood up to greet his brother that he had not seen in almost a year. Marcus walked toward Edgar and Samuel Jr. ran to his father. The two long-lost reverends embraced each other in a happy-to-see-each-other hug. It was obvious that the two brothers were close.

The two broke off the hug and Marcus said, "Man, let me look at you. You look good Edgar. I see you haven't missed any meals."

Edgar laughed and said, "You aren't doing so bad yourself. You have three lovely ladies in the kitchen cooking for you."

Marcus smiled and said, "Watch out, man. They aren't cooking for me. They are cooking for themselves. I take it you have met everyone."

Edgar replied, "Everyone but this gentleman."

Edgar motioned to Samuel. Samuel then walked over to the two reverends with Samuel Jr. in his arms. Marcus said, "Edgar, this is Samuel and his son Samuel Jr. Samuel is Kora's husband."

Edgar looked at Samuel and said, "It's nice to meet you two."

Samuel shifted his son to the left side of his body and extended his right hand. The two men shook hands and Samuel said, "It's nice to meet you too, Reverend."

Edgar replied, "Please, call me Edgar. If you all call me Reverend, things can get a little confusing around here."

Marcus looked at his little brother and said, "Come on, man. Let's go upstairs so I can show you your room and we can catch up."

The two men walked upstairs and Marcus led his brother to the last empty room in the church. The two men walked in and Marcus said, "I am so glad you're here Edgar. When I didn't hear from you, I began to get worried. How was your trip?"

Edgar replied, "It was long, but it is good to see you. You look good. I have been very concerned about you since Mary passed. I am sorry I was not here for you in your time of need."

Marcus smiled at Edgar and said, "Yes, it was a very tough time for me. I thought about coming back to Boston. I was down here alone and I was not doing anything in the church or in this community. I was feeling sorry for myself. I even began to question my faith. Just as I was about to give up and come home, I met Kora and her friends. They have truly been a blessing to me, the church and this community."

Edgar listened to Marcus and said, "You mentioned in the letter that you met someone?"

214

Marcus replied with a smile on his face and said, "Her name is Wanda. She was in the kitchen with you. All the people you met in the kitchen have really helped me get over my tragedy. Meeting Wanda has also been a blessing. Edgar, she is smart, strong and tough. Her strong will is just what I need to help me make this church the center of this community."

Edgar was happy to hear that his brother was doing well after such a horrible experience. He still had questions about all the people living in the church. Both brothers were raised by an African Methodist Episcopal church reverend, their father The Reverend Marcus Lovejoy Senior. Marcus and Edger knew their father would not approve of Marcus's current living arrangements.

With concern in his voice Edgar asked, "So, what is the story on the church boarders?"

Marcus replied, "They are not boarders. They are laborers in the middle of a negotiation. They live where they work, so I let them stay here while they settle their disagreements. I know it is not a common move for the church to allow citizens to move in, but these people are special. They are all responsible for the resurrection of the church and myself. They have recruited and educated this community. When they came to me and asked me if they could stay here, I did not hesitate to say yes."

Edgar replied, "Labor negotiations can get dangerous, Marcus. Are you sure you did the right thing when you put the church in the middle their fight?"

Marcus replied, "Their fight is our fight. Because of what they have meant to this church and me, I feel obligated to assist them in any way I can."

Edgar then asked, "The woman you met, Wanda. Is she staying here also?"
Marcus replied, "Yes."

215

Edgar then said, "Marcus, I know you are not fornicating with her in the church."

Marcus angrily replied, "Don't be ridiculous! Unlike you, I am not fornicating with her or anyone else outside of marriage. Which is another reason I wanted you to come down here. I wanted you to know I was OK, I also need you to help me establish the hierarchy in the church and I want you to marry Wanda and myself."

Edgar looked at his brother and said, "I am happy to see you are OK. You always have been strong. When do you want to marry Wanda?"

Marcus replied, "As soon as possible. I don't want to keep her waiting. I will propose tonight at dinner. We can get married over the weekend. Then next week you and we will start ordaining and training everyone you met in the kitchen."

Edgar asked his brother, "You don't think it is too soon, Marcus? Mary hasn't been gone a year."

Marcus responded to his brother's question by saying, "Too soon? How do you know when to get remarried after your previous mate died? There is no statute of limitations on how long one should wait. I need a wife. I want a family. I am lonely. I think Wanda can meet all of my needs and she will be good for the church."

Edgar replied by saying, "You know, older brother, I listen to you talk and I hear everything you're saying, but I have not heard you say you love her. Do you?"

Marcus took a deep breath and said, "I don't know. I have asked myself that question over and over again. I just don't know."

Edgar advised his brother by saying, "Marcus, don't ask that woman to marry you if you do not love her."

Marcus then said to his brother, "You are wise beyond your years, Edgar."

Edgar then yawned and said, "Well, you and Dad taught me well. Now, if you don't mind, I am tired from my trip. Can I take a bath and a nap before dinner?"

Marcus replied, "Sure you can, little brother. I'll put some hot water on for you."

Marcus walked out the door. Before he exited the room, Edgar asked him one more thing.

He asked, "Marcus, is Debbie spoken for?"

Marcus replied, "Look at you, you haven't changed at all. You haven't been here for an hour and already you are picking out your next victim. No, she is not spoken for. I'll tell her you asked."

Edgar laughed and said, "No no no, don't do that. I got it from here, big brother."

Marcus smiled, left the room and closed the door behind him. While Edgar rested, Marcus added going over the ordainment and leadership hierarchy to his agenda. He was very excited about Edgar making it to South Philadelphia safely. Marcus planned several projects to complete over the summer. Marcus knew that he needed his brother's assistance with the expansion of the church. He also knew his that little brother was right when he advised him not to marry Wanda unless he was sure he was ready. Now, after talking to Edgar, Marcus was confused about marring Wanda. He was so apprehensive about marring Wanda that he found it hard to concentrate on his paperwork. Despite his mental preoccupation, Marcus was able to push Wanda out of his mind and focus on his outline for his hierarchy.

When dinner hour arrived, Marcus went into Edgar's room to wake up his younger brother. To his surprise, Edgar was awake and reading the Bible.

Marcus looked at his younger brother and said, "Dinner is ready. You hungry?"

Edgar responded by saying, "Yes."

Edgar closed the Bible and left it on the side of his bed. He then followed his brother and the aroma of dinner into the kitchen. By now, it had stopped raining. Edgar witnessed the ladies hard at work. There was a line outside the kitchen door and the ladies were selling dinner plates as quickly as they prepared them. Marcus and Edgar sat down and joined Samuel and Samuel Jr. at the dinner table. Debbie quickly placed their prepared plates in front of them. After Debbie placed their plates on the table, everyone stopped working and joined hands as they thanked the Lord for their blessings.

Reverend Edgar Lovejoy said, "Lord, we thank you for this fine meal you have blessed us with. We thank you for giving us the strength to fight for what we believe in. We thank you for reuniting my brother and me. We thank you for giving us all these fine customers to support us. Lord, we thank you for the blessing you have already provided us with and we ask that you continue to watch over and protect us, Lord. In Jesus' name we pray, Amen."

The ladies cooked baked salmon, string beans, baked potatoes and a fresh garden salad. There was also a chocolate cake for dessert. Reverend Marcus Lovejoy, Reverend Edgar Lovejoy, Samuel and Samuel Jr. started eating while the ladies went back to work. After the dinner line was severed, the ladies had a chance to eat. They joined the men at the dinner table. The men were finished eating and having an after-dinner conversation about Helen and her new staff.

When Kora joined the dinner table and conversation Reverend Marcus said, "Kora, I think we can expect Helen down here to negotiate any day now."

Kora replied, "I agree, Reverend. I heard things aren't going so well in the hotel without us working there. They say the food is bland and the service is slow."

Debbie ate her food and joined in by saying, "The Negroes will not be happy when we go back to work in the hotel. This is the best food some of them have ever had."

Reverend Edgar replied to Debbie by saying, "You know, you all do not have to stop selling plates out of this kitchen when you go back to work. You can still come down here a few times a week to sell dinners for the church."

Reverend Marcus then said, "That's a good idea Edgar. You all can help the community and the church by volunteering a few times a week."

Kora replied to the reverend's responses by saying, "We can talk about volunteering after we go back to work."

Marcus agreed with Kora and said, "You're right, Kora. We are getting a bit ahead of ourselves. Kora, you and I should meet tonight to make sure we are on the same page. You will be talking to Helen any day now."

Kora and the rest of the women got up from the kitchen table to finish cleaning up the kitchen. Kora replied to Reverend Marcus's request by saying, "OK, Reverend. As soon as we finish cleaning up the kitchen."

Immediately after Kora agreed to meet with the Reverend Marcus, Samuel got up and left the dinner table and abruptly walked out of the kitchen. Kora said, "Excuse me please."

She followed her husband upstairs.

Once the couple were in their room, Kora said to Samuel, "What is wrong with you? Why are you being rude in front of our guest?"

Samuel irritatedly replied, "I am tired of you spending all of our family time with the reverend!"

Kora sighed and said, "Baby, I told you, this is only temporary. I need you to continue being patient during our negotiation period."

Samuel responded to his wife by saying, "I have been patient. My patience is wearing thin. You are spending too much time away from your family. Damn it Kora, you are staying with us tonight!"

Samuel's demands made Kora livid. Enraged, Kora raised her voice and said, "Who are you giving orders to, Samuel Freeman? Need I remind you that I have followed you from bondage to Marcus Hook and then to South Philadelphia without question? I have let you guide and provide for our family and you have done a fine job. You cannot do it alone. Now, it is my chance to help our family and friends and you want to stand in my way. I am going back downstairs to talk to the reverend about Helen. We will continue this conversation when I return."

Samuel was still upset with his wife, but after she reminded him how she supported him, he felt guilty and selfish. He did not say a word as his wife walked out the door and returned to the kitchen. While Kora and Samuel were talking, the ladies finished washing the few dishes from dinner. When Kora walked into the kitchen, Reverend Edgar and Debbie were on the way outside to take a walk and Wanda was sitting at the dinner table with Reverend Marcus and Samuel Jr.

Kora joined them and asked the reverend, "Are you ready to discuss our strategy, Reverend?"

The reverend responded by saying, "Yes, I am. Wanda has been talking to several of the local Negroes we serve. They have informed her that the hotel's European customer base has left because the food and service is very poor. This leads me to believe that Helen will be down here to ask you all to return to work very soon. We are in a very good negotiating position. Helen needs us to keep the hotel open. I want to know what you believe it would take for you all to return to work."

Without hesitation, Kora said, "We want our work hours decreased to twelve hours a day and we want a fifteen cent per day pay increase."

Reverend Marcus replied by saying, "Then you have to ask for more than you want and negotiate until Helen agrees to your terms. For example, tell Helen you want to work eight hours a day and you want a twenty-five cent per day raise. Helen will not agree to your terms. Then you make it appear as if you are giving up some things you want by agreeing to less money and more hours. This should make Helen feel like she is getting something out of this negotiation."

Kora responded by saying, "I understand, Reverend. I am ready for Helen."

After her brief talk with Reverend Marcus, Kora and Samuel Jr. returned to her upset husband. Samuel was lying on the bed in his favorite thinking position. He was on his back with his hand under his head. He was deep in thought and didn't move when his family came into the room. Kora told Samuel Jr. to say goodnight to his father. Junior walked over to his father and did as he was told.

He said, "Goodnight, Daddy."

Samuel responded by hugging his son and saying, "Goodnight, son."
Kora walked Junior to the room next to their room and put their son in the bed. She then returned to their bedroom to talk to Samuel. She sat on the bed with her husband on it and said, "Baby, I don't like it when we fight."

Samuel replied, "I don't like it either. Look Kora, I was wrong for getting mad at you. I know you are only trying to help our family and friends. It's just, I get so frustrated when you are not with us."

Kora leaned over and kissed her husband. She got undressed and climbed into bed and reminded her husband how much she loved him.

The next morning, Samuel was up at sunrise working on the roof. Kora and her kitchen crew were in the kitchen organizing the serving line for breakfast. Just as Reverend Marcus predicted, Helen walked down to the church to talk to Kora about returning to work. While approaching the church, Helen observed the Negroes sitting outside eating their breakfast in a joyful, ecstatic mood. She also noticed Samuel hard at work on the roof. Samuel's shirt was off and the rising sun's rays felt good on his back. Samuel was humming while he worked. Helen heard him humming and realized she had not heard Samuel hum in quite some time. Helen walked into the church sanctuary. No one noticed her. She heard the familiar sound of an industrial kitchen hard at work and walked into the kitchen. When she entered, Debbie noticed her first. Debbie was standing at the back door selling the plates. She stepped away from the back door and stared at Helen. Kora and Wanda noticed Debbie focusing on the kitchen door and looked to see what she was staring at.

Debbie and Wanda worked for Helen for years before Kora came to the hotel. Helen gave them their first job after they ran away to Philadelphia. Debbie and Wanda suddenly felt guilty when Helen walked into the church kitchen and watched them doing in the church what they did for her for years. Once Kora noticed Helen, she immediately implemented the plan her and the Reverend Marcus discussed. Kora greeted Helen and walked her back into the empty sanctuary.

Kora asked Helen, "What are you doing here?"

Helen responded by saying, "You know what I am doing here. Don't make me say it."

Kora directed Helen to one of the pews and said, "Have a seat. We can talk here."

Helen sat down and Kora asked her, "Do you want us to return to work?"

Helen replied, "Do you want to come back to work?"

Kora said, "I don't know. We like working in the church."

Helen raised her voice a little and said, "OK Kora, stop it. Let's not play games. Just tell me what it will take to get you all back at the hotel."

Kora quickly replied, "We want to work eight hours a day, a twenty-five cent per day raise and you need to do something about the rats."

Helen didn't think long about Kora's demands. She quickly replied, "Don't be ridiculous! I am not cutting your hours in half and doubling your salary! Come up with a more reasonable offer."

Kora said, "Well, what do you think is reasonable?"

Helen replied, "You continue to work sixteen hours a day and I will give and five cent raise."

Kora immediately stood up and started to walk away and Helen said, "Wait, Kora. Don't walk away from me again."

Kora sat back down and replied, "You need to come better than that Helen."
Helen then said, "Kora, I need you to work the sixteen hours because I cannot afford to hire more staff."

Kora replied to Helen by saying, "Helen, I know how good business was when we were there. You can afford it."

Helen thought for a moment and said, "Will you train them?"

Kora replied by saying, "I trained everyone else, didn't I?"

Helen then said, "OK, but Kora, you have to work more than eight hours and I cannot double your pay."

Kora responded by saying, "OK, but you can afford to cut our hours down to twelve and give us a fifteen cent per day pay raise."

Helen pondered over Kora's proposal and said, "OK. But I need you all back tonight."

Kora responded by saying, "That is not a problem, but I need you to meet one more condition. I need you to hire a butler and make Samuel a handyman."

Helen thought about Kora's request and said, "Kora, if I have to hire another butler I cannot afford to give you all a fifteen-cent raise. I can only give you a twelve-cent raise."

Kora responded by saying, "Let me think about this for a moment."

Kora went into a deep brief meditation. She knew that if Samuel went back to being a butler again it would tear him up inside. Kora desperately wanted her strong loving confident happy husband back. She felt like she was selling out her friends but she looked at Helen and said, "OK, but no one can know about this."

Helen cheerfully said, "Then it is settled. I will see you all tonight."

Kora responded by saying, "Don't forget about the rats. What are you going to do about them?"

Helen replied, "Oh right, the rats are gone. The temporary staff put out rat traps and we have a few cats in the kitchen and back yard."

Helen left the church and walked back to the hotel to prepare for her efficient staff's return. Kora gleefully walked into the kitchen with the good news. Everyone was in the kitchen waiting for her report.

Kora beamingly said, "We are going back to the hotel today!"

Anxiously Debbie asked, "What did we get, Kora? What did we get?"

Everyone was excited about going back to work in the hotel and waited for Kora's response. Kora answered Debbie by saying, "Our hours are cut from fifteen down to twelve. We are also getting a twelve cent per day raise."

Everyone including the reverend brothers exhaled with relief and enthusiasm. Their two-week fight was over and they had won. Their victory felt good. They had earned the respect of Helen and the Negro community. After celebrating, everyone went to their rooms to pack and prepare for their return to the hotel. Samuel and Kora were alone in their room.

Kora said to Samuel, "Samuel, I have something to tell you."

Samuel looked at his wife and said, "I'm listening."

Kora proudly said, "I have good news. You are no longer the butler, you are the handyman."

Kora paused, waiting for her husband's response. Samuel did not understand what Kora meant when she said he was no longer the butler. He asked his wife to clarify by saying, "What do you mean, I am no longer the butler?"

Kora, still proud of her accomplishment said, "I negotiated a handyman position for you upon our return."

Samuel approached Kora smiling from ear to ear and said, "You did that for me, baby?"

Kora also smiled and said, "Auh-hun."

Samuel gave his wife a big hug and picked her up off the ground. They hugged and kissed. Samuel put his wife down and said, "Thank you baby! Thank you!"

Kora replied, "You're welcome."

The two finished packing and moved back into the hotel with the rest of the Negro hotel staff.

Chapter Nineteen
You Can Run But You Can't Hide

In Wilmington, Delaware, life went on without Kora, Samuel and Harold. Tom's brother Mike sold him two male field slaves for a reasonable price and gave him a female house slave as a favor. Mike felt bad about his brother losing three of his most valuable workers. After the great escape, life changed for everyone on Tom's plantation. Maggie and Mandy still felt isolated from the other slaves. They worked with the others during the day and Maggie was Charles's wife in the evening. Charles was now drinking more and working less. On more than one occasion, he could be found asleep in the middle of the day in Maggie's shack. With no one to supervise them, the Negroes' work productivity decreased dramatically. The two new field slaves, George and Jack, did not know how vicious Charles could be. They viewed him as a drunk that they could take advantage of. The other workers remembered the sober Charles that beat little John to death. Drunk or not, they were still afraid of Charles. The lifestyle that Charles forced on Maggie caused her to be consistently bitter and incensed. Maggie became disinterested in men. She was also no longer afraid to speak her mind to the other Negro males on the plantation. Maggie had several confrontations with George and Jack. She was the only Negro woman that ever talked back to the men of color that she worked with.

Jack and George were young and very immature. On their other plantation, there had been no elders to teach them how to behave. George and Jack did not know how to express their fondness for a young lady in the proper manner. They consistently called the women out of their names, groped the women, and on more than one occasion they exposed themselves to the female Negro workers.

Jack and George were younger and stronger than the other male slaves on Tom's plantation. When the other males approached them about disrespecting their women, the two outsiders simply replied with, "Shut up, ol' man!"

One time they also said, "Nigga, I'll talk to anyone a these bitches any way I want! What you gon' do about it? Huh? Huh?"

With no one to protect her and Mandy from their own kind, Maggie knew that she had to protect them herself. One day while Charles was sleeping off his alcohol consumption, the workers were working in the middle of the tobacco field at midday. Jack made the mistake of confronting Mandy in his usual vulgar manner. Mandy was bent over picking tobacco and Jack walked up behind her.

Jacked smacked Mandy on her behind and said, "That's just how I want you when we fuck'n, baby. Yeah, I likes to get it from da back!"

Mandy was furious! She stood up quickly, turned around and tried to slap Jack. Jack grabbed her arm and overpowered her. He forced her to the ground and climbed on top of her. Jack was on his knees, straddling Mandy and pinning her to the ground.

With a devilish look on his face, he said, "Yeah, I like my bitch to have a little fight in her! You gon' be my bitch tonight!"

At that moment, Maggie walked up behind Jack, grabbed a handful of his thick, black hair and pulled his head back. She then put the sharp edge of her knife against Jack's exposed throat. Jack immediately removed his hands from Mandy and put them on Maggie's arms to try to free himself. Maggie applied pressure to her hand with the knife in it and her blade broke the skin on Jack's throat. When Jack felt the knife break his skin, he realized that he had been subdued, and put his hands up to indicate that he was surrendering.

Maggie then told Jack, "You picked da wrong woman ta fuck wit! If you eva fuck wit her again, I'll kill ya! We clear?"

Jack quickly replied, "We clear."

Maggie backed up with her knife still on Jack's throat and his hair still in her hand. As she backed up, her knife moved back also. Jack moved with the knife, to prevent it from breaking his skin again. When Maggie backed up, taking him with her, she put Jack in a very vulnerable position. Jack was on his feet with his knees bent back and Maggie supporting his weight. Mandy watched Maggie move Jack off of her and saw the outline of Jack's genitals. His shabby pants were still covering them, but Mandy noticed them right away. She quickly picked herself up off the ground and lifted her foot in between Jack's legs, toward his testicles. Mandy put every ounce of frustration and fear into her kick. Her foot landed squarely on Jack's genitals! Jack let out a high-pitched scream and moved his hands and body weight down toward his midsection. This caused Maggie's knife to cut Jack's neck again. The knife missed his jugular vein by inches. Maggie let Jack go and he fell to the ground in a fetal position, moaning in pain.

George was relaxing in another cabin after having sex with another slave when he heard his friend scream. He came running to see what had happened. George saw Maggie and Mandy embracing each other and his friend next to them on the ground in pain, bleeding from his neck. George started to move toward Maggie and Mandy and the two women broke their embrace. Maggie stood in front of George about ten feet away from him. She made sure that George saw the knife in her hand, with Jack's blood still on it. George stopped in his tracks.

Calmly but firmly Maggie said, "You come any closer and dey gon' be two niggas on the ground instead of one."

George didn't say or do anything. He just stared at Maggie in disbelief. No woman had ever stood up to him like that before.

While George stared at Maggie, the woman that George was having sex with, Bridget, came running up to George and said, "What happen? George, you OK?"

Without breaking his gawp George softly replied, "Yeah baby. I'm fine."

Mandy approached Maggie again and Maggie put her arm around her without taking her eyes off George.

Mandy said, "Come on, Maggie. Let's go to our spot."

Maggie took her eyes off of George and looked at Bridget and said, "You a dumb bitch."

Then Maggie wiped her knife on her skirt and tucked it between her skirt and her hip. The two walked to their favorite place on the plantation, the old oak tree. Maggie and Mandy would often go to the oak tree in the middle of the day while Charles slept. They knew that Maggie could handle Charles and they were in no danger. George and Jack would often take one of the female slaves and have sex with them while Charles was sleeping off his alcohol consumption. Most of the field slaves still feared Charles and didn't even think about not working while Charles slept.

Maggie and Mandy arrived under the oak tree and Mandy was very grateful. Immediately after they were in the old tree's shade, Mandy turned and kissed Maggie.

The two broke their kiss and Mandy said, "Thank you, Maggie. Thank you for being dare fa me."

Maggie replied, "I will always be dare fa you."

Mandy laughed out loud and said, "You made sure Jack and George won't even tink about messin' wit' us no mo'."

Maggie laughed with her girlfriend and said, "Shit, girl. What 'bout you? You surprised me wit' yo' kick. I didn't know you had it in you!"

Mandy stopped laughing and said, "He made me mad. I saw his ting get'n hard when he was on top of me. I wanted to make sure he wouldn't even tink 'bout come'n back to finish what he started."

Maggie replied by saying, "Yeah, I tink you made yo' point. Come on, let's go back to the tobacco field befo' Charles wakes up."

Mandy agreed and the two ladies returned to their workstations. When they returned, they noticed that Jack and George were not with the rest of the group. Someone told Maggie and Mandy that George had taken Jack back to the shack because Jack could not walk on his own.

Bridget said, "I hope Jack is OK. He was hurt'n real bad."

Maggie snapped at Bridget and said, "Fuck dat Nigga! He gots what he deserve. Come on, y'all. We got tobacca to pick befo' Charles gets up."

The crew finished picking their tobacco and Charles never showed up. Maggie and Mandy knew that when Charles slept all day, he was up all night. They knew that the two of them would not be seeing each other that evening.

Several nights a week, Charles would drink himself into a deep sleep. On these evenings, Maggie would not hesitate to find her true love Mandy. Maggie's love for Mandy was too strong to hide from their Negro companions. All of the people of color on the farm felt that Maggie enjoyed being with Charles because he gave her preferential treatment over the other workers. They had no idea that this could not be further from the truth. Maggie hated Charles. Maggie knew that she was drinking too much again. She drank to cope with the fact that she was forced to be with the most repulsive man, inside and out, that she knew. Several nights a week, Maggie was forced to have an unsatisfying sexual experience with a man that didn't take a bath and reeked of alcohol and tobacco. Charles's teeth were also rotten, and the combination of his dinner, cigar, evening cocktail and decaying teeth caused the worse halitosis Maggie had ever smelled in her life. Charles was always kissing Maggie. On more than one occasion, Maggie ran outside and vomited while Charles sat on the bed with her after dinner and attempted to make love to his beautiful black slave.

This was Maggie's life. She was an outcast amongst her peers, and forced to play the role of the loving wife with a man she despised. After two years of this vicious circle routine, Maggie decided that she would rather be dead than remain a slave. Maggie was no longer afraid of being caught. Now she knew that the day would come when her and Mandy could run away to freedom like her husband had. She had no idea that that day was closer than she thought.

The hot summer days passed and fall moved in. The slaves moved from the tobacco field to the apple orchard. One weekend in September, Mandy went with Tom to Mike's place to help out with a family dinner. Mandy spent the weekend on Mike's farm and talked to Old Man Eli. When the two met, it was as if the hands of time were turned back two years. Just as Eli told Harold about Harriet Tubman coming two years ago, that evening he said the same thing to Mandy. Mandy could hardly contain herself. She could not wait to tell Maggie. Mandy knew that she would have to wait until Charles was asleep to let her lover know their wait for freedom was becoming very short. Mandy returned to her plantation and kept her exciting good news to herself.

The first few days in the cool autumn breeze, the Negroes worked hard. On the Wednesday evening of that week, Maggie hunted her lover down after Charles had drank himself to sleep. Maggie found Mandy alone in her shack. The two women went off on their biweekly romantic rendezvous. The ladies walked to the old oak tree on top of the hill. They didn't know that this was the meeting place for Samuel and Harold two years prior.

Maggie led the way, and when they arrived under the tree, she turned around and kissed Mandy passionately. The two women held each other tightly and kissed zealously. Maggie aggressively removed Mandy's blouse. She then put her arm on the back of Mandy's knees, forcing her to bend them. Maggie supported Mandy and guided her to the soft Delaware grass. Maggie climbed on top of her lover and resumed kissing Mandy. Maggie rubbed Mandy's breast while they kissed. Maggie then moved down Mandy's chest and proceeded to lick her breast.

Mandy moaned and said, "Mmmm, Maggie wait, I have sometin' ta tell ya."

Maggie replied by saying, "Tell me later, baby."

Then Maggie moved down further on Mandy and kissed her navel. Maggie was lying in-between Mandy's legs while she caressed her. Maggie started to push Mandy's skirt up, but before Mandy's skirt was above her hips, she pushed Maggie's head away from her and said, "Maggie, stop. I mean it. I have some very good news to tell you."

Maggie replied, "Good news? Good news?! Shit woman, you better come ova hea and give me sum good love'n!"

In a serious tone, Mandy replied, "No! Now, I tol' you, I gots to tell you sumtin'. And no it cain't wait!"

Maggie realized that Mandy was not going to allow her to make love to her until she listened to her good news.
She moved alongside Mandy and said, "OK, OK, OK, baby, what is dis, 'Good news' you got fo' me?"

Mandy lay on her back, looked up at the stars and said, "We gon' be free!"

Maggie looked at her and impatiently said, "Dat it? Dat yo' good news?"

Mandy sat up and surprisingly asked, "Is dat it? What you mean, 'Is dat it' Don't you want to be free? Lately all you talk 'bout is kill'n Charles and be'n free."

Maggie saw the seriousness in Mandy's eyes. Her hormones began to die down and logic prevailed. Maggie asked Mandy, "You mean we gon' be free, soon?"

Mandy simply replied, "Yep, real soon."

Maggie began to get excited. She asked Mandy, "How? How we gon' be free?"

Mandy replied, "Ova the weekend, Ol' Man Eli told me Harriet Tubman is coming and she gon' lead us to freedom!"

Maggie threw herself to the ground on her back, lifted her hands in the air and said, "Freedom, I can taste ya! Yes, yes, yes. When, Mandy? When Harriet come'n?"

Mandy replied, "Don't know. Eli just said be ready."

Maggie was quiet for a moment then asked Mandy, "You tink dis how Samuel escaped?"

Without hesitation, Mandy replied, "I'm sure it iz. Eli tol' me he tol' Harold Harriet was come'n two years ago."

Maggie replied, "Good. If Harriet helped them escape, she must know where they iz."

Mandy asked Maggie, "Why do you want to find dem so bad? You still love Samuel?"

Maggie quickly said, "Hell naw! I love you an only you, baby. I just want to find that high yella bitch Kora! I gots sumtin' fo' ha!"

Mandy laid back down and asked Maggie, "You think you can forget about Kora long enough to continya give'n me some love'n?"

Maggie smiled and climbed back on top of her lover. The two made love to each other and returned to their cabins. Mandy lived alone in her cabin because Maggie asked Charles not to allow any other slave to move in with her.

When Tom asked Charles why he was not trying to breed Mandy, Charles lied and said, "Mandy is crazy. She tries to kill every slave he puts in her cabin."

Tom had thoughts of having his way with Mandy. When Charles told Tom his lie, Tom decided to stay away from Mandy. He knew he was too old to be fighting with one of his feisty Negro females. This was only one of the ways that Maggie continued to use Charles to protect her and her girlfriend. Maggie also told Charles that Jack and George were not working when he was sleep during the day. Maggie told Charles this after Jack and George indicated that they may attack her and Mandy again. Maggie decided that she needed to make sure that George and Jack knew not to mess with her and her woman ever again. This is the reason that the other slaves did not like Maggie. They knew that she was the overseer's woman and, on more than one occasion, Maggie used her influence over Charles to get what she wanted. Maggie didn't care about the other slaves. She only cared about her and Mandy.

Soon after, Maggie told Charles about Jack and George not working, the field slaves heard the awful, resonating sound a slave being beaten. The noise came from the barn. Everyone ran to the barn. All the Negroes knew it was either Jack or George being whipped because they were not in the fields with the other workers. As the Negroes got closer to the barn, they heard the cries more clearly. The screams of agony were high-pitched and sounded like they were coming from a child again. The slaves arrived in the barn doorway and looked inside. Once again, they were horrified. Instantly, their mental prison was reinforced by what they were watching.

Inside the barn, Charles had his gun to Jack's head. George was hog tied up on the ground next to Charles and Jack. Jack had a whip in his hands and lashed it forward. Everyone watched the whip to see its target. Everyone was devastated when they saw Bridget strung up in the whip's path, with her feet dangling a few feet off the ground. Female slaves were rarely beaten. Their masters knew that beating a female could damage their reproductive system or cause them to miscarry if they were pregnant. Young Negro children were a valuable commodity in the south. They were slaves that the master did not have to buy, and he could sell them for a nice price. The master knew that Negro woman were strong enough to work in the fields until they gave birth, and be back in the fields with their infants a few days after giving birth. Slave owners also knew that Negro woman were tough enough to give them a multitude of free labor, but not strong enough to take the lashings of a cow hide whip.

Everyone watched in horror while Charles made Jack whip George's girlfriend. From the ground, George pleaded with Charles.

He said, "Please masa, don't hit ha no mo'! She didn't mean it. I made ha do it. She wanted to work. I made ha go to da cabin wit' me. Masa, please stop!"

When George said this, everyone knew that Charles had caught George and Bridget in the cabin making love in the middle of the day when they should have been picking apples. George and Bridget always made love in the middle of the day. George didn't force Bridget either. Bridget was in the audience the day that Charles killed Little John. She was just a child and maybe she had forgotten the lesson that Charles was teaching that day, but she would not forget this lesson.

George's pleas for mercy fueled Charles's efforts. Charles loved it when his Negroes begged. Especially the big strong Negroes. This made Charles feel superior.

Charles replied, "Shut up, Nigga! You animals need to learn, they is a time to work and a time to breed! You don't breed while you suppose to be working!"

Charles then looked at Jack and said, "What the fuck you wait'n fo', boy?! Did I say stop? Hit her again!"

As Charles said this, Bridget said, "No, masa Charles. I be a good Nigga! I be real good! Please, masa. No mo'!"

When the whip whistled through the air and cracked open another part of Bridget's skin, a field slave named Kimberley ran toward Maggie to confront her. While Bridget screamed in agony, one of the elders held Kimberley back as she said, "This is all yo' fault, you sellout!"

Maggie turned to face Kim and showed her the knife, reminding Kimberley that she did not give a damn about anyone except Mandy.

After a few more lashes, Charles decided that Bridget had had enough. He cut her down and her body fell to the ground, motionless. Bridget was not dead, but she was exhausted from pain. She could not move a muscle.

After Charles cut Bridget down, he said, "All y'all need to know, when I ain't here, Maggie's in charge. Now get back to work!"

The next few days, Charles wasn't in the apple orchard with the workers. Maggie saw to it that everyone did their job. George and Jack also worked hard while Charles wasn't there. While the slaves worked, the animosity toward Maggie and Mandy grew. Maggie sensed the field slaves' attitude, but it did not bother her. Mandy noticed the uneasy feeling in the field also. It didn't bother her either. Both Mandy and Maggie were used to being outcasts. As far as they were concerned, Charles put Maggie in a position that would allow her to get back at the people that had ostracized them.

The next few days after Bridget's beating, Charles slept during the day and was up with Maggie all night. Maggie told Charles that she could not stay up with him all night and watch the workers all day also. He had to let her get some sleep. Charles agreed and returned to work in the fields after his short vacation. One evening, Eli brought Michael to see Tom. That same evening, Charles drank himself to sleep again and Maggie went looking for her girlfriend. She went to Mandy's cabin. When she opened the door, Eli was on the other side. He was walking out as Maggie came in.

Eli said, "Even'n, ma'am," then closed the door behind him.

Maggie looked at Mandy in disbelief. She could not believe what her eyes revealed to her. There was Mandy on the bed, under the covers with no clothes on. Maggie angrily asked Mandy, "What da hell was go'n on in here?"

Mandy replied, "Relax Maggie. That wasn't noth'n. I just like ta be wit' a man every now an' then."

Maggie then asked, "How long you been fuck'n him?"

Mandy smiled and replied, "Oh, a while. Don't tell me you thought you the only one of us dat could get sum love'n from a man, did you?"

Maggie quickly replied, "What I get from Charles ain't hardly love'n, and I wouldn't call Charles no man. But never mind about me, I still cain't believe you was fuck'n dat ol' man!"

Mandy smiled and said, "Girl, please. That ol' man knows how to please a woman! He be put'n his manhood in me and slide'n it in and out and he feels so GOOD!"

Maggie then quietly asked, "Would you rather be with him than me?"

Right away, Mandy said, "No baby, I love you and we run'n away together. We gon' get as far away from this place as possible. Eli told me Harriet's plan. He said Harriet will send a messenger soon. He said I should put a candle in da window so da messenger will know which cabin is mine. When the messenger comes fo' me, I gets you and we leave this place forever."

Maggie then asked, "Dat why you gave him some love'n? So he would tell you how to leave wit' Harriet?"

Mandy replied, "No, girl. He told me dat befo' we got started. I told you, I gave him some love'n because I like sum man love'n every now and then."

Maggie then said, "I don't like the way dat man smelled. You need to wash him off you."

Mandy smiled and replied, "You know how to make my bathwater."

Maggie also grinned, then walked into the kitchen to fulfill Mandy's request. While she was up, Mandy asked, "Maggie, will you also put a lit candle in the window please?"

Maggie gladly lit the candle and placed it in Mandy's window. Maggie and Mandy were in a joyful mood because they knew that the number of days to their freedom was getting smaller and smaller. Mandy watched Maggie while she placed the lit candle on the windowsill and prepared Mandy's bathwater. After admiring her aficionada for several minutes, Mandy got out of bed and into the bathwater that Maggie had prepared for her. Then, Maggie slowly and sexually put soap on Mandy and removed it with warm water until she was satisfied that Eli's scent was no longer associated with her devotee. Mandy then completed the same task for Maggie. Once the two ladies were engulfed in their homemade soap's scent, they climbed into bed and continued to express their love for one another to each other. The flickering candle caused a lovely illumination-changing shadow of their bodies intertwined together in several passionate, sexually satisfying positions.

In the morning, Maggie met Charles in the apple orchard and stood alongside his horse while he barked out orders to the other Negro workers. Maggie looked up at the man on his horse and wondered how much longer, how much longer would she have to let this man take advantage of her. How much longer would she have to fake her sexual satisfaction to please this man that she despised? How much longer would she have to sneak her saliva and urine into this man's dinner to give her some sense of redemption? Maggie knew that the answers to these questions were coming soon. The fact that she did not know the answers and that Charles was forcing her to ask herself these questions every evening made her numbered days as a slave seem to go from the present to infinity.

After the candle sat in the window for several evenings, the wax melted and would not allow another match to light its short wick. Maggie and Mandy were very paranoid. They did not want to inquire about another candle. They did not want to take the chance of having anyone question the candle in Mandy's window. The ladies knew that they had to replace the candle as soon as possible or their chance at freedom may pass over them. After several conversations, the ladies decided to ask Donna, the master's new house slave, for a candle. Mandy told Donna that she had very bad nightmares of their master coming into her cabin when she was young and raping her. She said that the candle let her sleep better. Donna sympathized with Mandy and gave her a few candles.

On the first evening that Mandy lit one of her new candles, there was a knock on her door in the middle of the night. Mandy immediately got out of bed. As she walked to the door, she wondered if it was Harriet's messenger to freedom, or maybe that Donna had figured out what the candle was really for and told Charles. Then she thought that if Charles knew what the ladies had planned, he would not knock. He would just bust in yelling and cussing like he always did. Mandy's door was twenty feet from her bed and those were the thoughts that circled her mind in the short time that it took her to reach her door. She opened it and was standing face to face with a young, teenage African slave.

He looked at Mandy and whispered to her, "Harriet sent me."

Mandy smiled and hugged the boy. She closed the door behind her for the last time. The boy said, "Come on, freedom is dis way."

Mandy told him, "Wait, we have to gets one mo' person."

Maggie took the lead and they quickly and silently ran to Maggie's cabin. Mandy gave Maggie the sign by knocking on her door three times. Maggie was awakened immediately. Mandy opened the door and her greatest fear was in front of her. Mandy and the boy saw Charles in the bed with Maggie. Charles also woke up from Mandy's knock. Once he awakened and focused on Mandy and the boy, he jumped out of bed with no clothes on. He moved toward his gun belt that was on a chair in the middle of the room. Maggie was prepared for her escape. She that knew Charles would be in her room when Mandy showed up on the freedom train. Maggie anticipated Charles getting up and going for his gun, so she made sure that he slept on the side of the bed closest to the door. Once Mandy started lighting her candle, Maggie started sleeping with a ten-inch long carving knife under her side of the bed.

Mandy was not aware of Maggie's plan. She and the boy watched in horror at what happened next. While Charles went for his gun, Maggie reached under the mattress and grabbed her knife. She moved quickly, and when Charles reached his belt, Maggie's naked body was right behind him. Maggie grabbed his dirty blond hair, secured his head in a chin up position, reached around Charles's head with the knife and in one smooth violin stroke, Maggie unzipped Charles's jugular.

Severing Charles's jugular prevented him from screaming. Charles moved both of his hands to his throat and, acting in survival instinct, he tried to keep his blood in his body. Charles's hands were no match for his pulse. His heart continued to pump and the blood continued to flow out of his neck. Maggie released her death grip and Charles fell to his knees, gasping for air, and then fell face first to the ground. Mandy and the boy watched Maggie move like a cat in the night executing its prey. They saw Maggie's naked body standing over Charles. Charles's brain stopped sending the involuntary signal for his heart to beat. His heart stopped and his blood slowly formed a pool around his head. The puddle grew and outlined the circumference of Charles's body.

Maggie watched Charles's body fall and bleed. She stood over him admiring her work. Maggie felt relieved while she watched the life flow out of her oppressor. Mandy and the young messenger witnessed the entire slaying from a close doorway view. Mandy looked at Maggie staring at Charles and said, "Maggie, Maggie, come on, girl. We gots to go."

Maggie came to her senses and quickly moved her naked body over Charles's body and through his pooled blood. Maggie went to the other side of the small shack that she had shared with Charles for the last two years to get dressed. She quickly put on her skirt, blouse and boots. Maggie walked to the door, prepared to leave with her temporary guide and companion. The young messenger Harriet sent had just witnessed a brutal slaying. He just stood in the doorway, looking at Charles's body.

Maggie said, "Come on, boy. We gots to go!"

The young man still did not move. Maggie then slapped their front runner to bring him back to reality. The young teenager shook his head and looked at Maggie.

Maggie said, "What's wrong? Ain't you seen a dead body befo'?"

Harriet's messenger shook his head from side to side, indicating that he had never witnessed a dead body before.

Maggie watched his head and said, "Well na ya have! Come on, let's go."

After the young teenager was slapped back to reality, he led the three of them across the plantation and into the waiting forest. The escaping slaves disappeared into the moonlight-cast shadows of the trees. The young field hand led Maggie and Mandy to the middle of the woods where Harriet was waiting.

Mandy was excited about meeting Harriet Tubman. Maggie still had Charles's blood on her hands, skirt and boots.

When Harriet approached the two new comers she asked Maggie, "What yo' name, girl?"

Maggie replied, "Maggie."

Harriet looked her up and down and said, "Where that blood come from?"

Maggie replied, "I killed da head masta."

Harriet looked at Maggie and Mandy, then motioned with her arm toward the other runaways and said, "You two join da others."

Maggie and Mandy did as they were told and listened as Harriet gave her speech. This time, the marathon started soon after Harriet finished her speech. A month ago, on her way down south, Harriet had stopped at Thomas Garrett's farm and asked him to bury the supplies at a particular tree and mark it with rocks to make it look like a grave. Thomas did as Harriet asked. Harriet and Thomas knew that she could not come by his place again. Thomas could not explain two groups of runaway slaves showing up at his place. Harriet moved the escaping workers further north and found the marked tree in the woods. Harriet had the young field hand dig up the ground around the tree. Within a foot of the surface, the boy hit the top of a trunk. Some others helped him pull the trunk out and opened it. Inside were boots, fall clothes, water containers and bags of black pepper. Harriet had bags of fruit with her. She made sure everyone had eaten and put on their new boots to prepare them for their twenty-five mile run. Everyone ate, got dressed and off they went.

The group ran their marathon to freedom to the river, then upstream to Marcus Hook. Once on shore, Harriet took her Canadian-bound former free labors to Quincy Manley's farm again. Quincy was happy to see Harriet. He had not seen her since she had brought Samuel and Kora to the farm two years ago. Harriet didn't like going to the same safe house every year. She had several different routes that she traveled to get to Canada. Harriet knew that if she went the same way every time, it increased her chances of getting caught.

While everyone was recovering in Quincy's barn, Harriet assigned two freedom runners to keep watch all night. Then she went into the house to talk to Quincy. The two sat in his kitchen drinking tea and bringing each other up to date on their lives.

Harriet asked Quincy, "So how you been, Quincy?"

Quincy replied, "I've been fine, and you?"

Harriet replied, "Fine, fine. Is Samuel and Kora still ha?"

Quincy was quiet for a moment then replied, "No. Samuel is wanted for murder. He left in the middle of the night with his family and we have not seen him since."

Harriet replied in surprise, "Murder! Da must be some mistake. Samuel ain't no killer."

Quincy then informed Harriet of the details by saying, "He is accused of killing a slave catcher. He was in Marcus Hook late one night getting supplies for me. We have not seen him or his family since. We believe the slave catcher approached Samuel and tried to take him back to the south and Samuel resisted. After their confrontation, he must have come back here and took his wife and son with him out of town because he knew the sheriff would hang him if he caught him."

Harriet was sipping her tea and looked at Quincy and said, "So, Kora had a little boy, hun?"

Quincy replied, "Yeap. Samuel Jr. Amanda was the midwife."

Harriet finished her tea and said, "Thanks for the tea. I think I needs to rest now. We can talks mo' in the morning."

Quincy agreed and Harriet went to the barn with the other Negroes to get some rest. While Harriet was gone, Maggie told Mandy to ask Harriet where Samuel was. Maggie knew that Mandy had a better chance of obtaining Samuel's location because of her pleasant demeanor.

In the morning after breakfast, Mandy approached Harriet and said, "Excuse me, ma'am, but my brother Samuel ran away with you two years ago. I was hoping you would know where he is? I miss him dearly."

Harriet replied, "Yes, I remember Samuel. I married him and his wife two years ago right ha in dis barn. Don't know where he be now. Quincy said he and his family just up and left one night."

Mandy went back to Maggie and informed her of what Harriet said. When Mandy told Maggie that Harriet had married Kora and Samuel, Maggie angrily replied, "So she married my man! I'm gon' kills dat bitch!"

Mandy asked Maggie, "Why you so upset about Kora and Samuel get'n married? Just lets dem be. Let's stay with Harriet and move to Canada."

Maggie looked at her lover and explained to her why she hated Kora so much. She said, "Kora took my protector. After Samuel left, Charles started having his way with me again. Dat's when my life became a liv'n hell. It should have been me leaving wit' Samuel. Not the fuck'n yellow-ass spoiled house bitch!"

Mandy then asked, "So you gon' kill Kora when you finds her?"

Maggie responded to Mandy by saying, "I sure is. But first we gots to find dem. Tomorrow I wants you to go to the house and ask the missis where they is. I bet she know. The missis always knows sumtin'."

Harriet informed all the former slaves that they would be leaving for Canada in two days. The two women didn't have much time to find Samuel and Kora. The next day around lunchtime, Mandy walked to the house and entered the kitchen where Amanda was preparing lunch for everyone.

Mandy walked into the kitchen and said, "'Cuse me ma'am, but do you mind if I help?"

Amanda looked up and said, "No child, I appreciate you offering, but I can handle lunch."

Mandy replied by saying, "I just feels real bad, you fix'n fo' us all by yo' self. I would feels much better if you would allows me to help ya."

Amanda hesitated because Quincy had a firm rule: No Negros in the house except Harriet.

Quincy was in Marcus Hook and Amanda could use the help so she said, "OK, child. Come on in and put an apron on."

Mandy smiled and entered the kitchen. While she entered, Amanda asked, "So child, what's your name?"

Mandy replied, "Mandy."

Amanda said, "That's a pretty name. I'm Amanda. Lunch is almost ready, so you can help me clean up."

Mandy simply replied by saying, "Yes ma'am."

Mandy had not come to the house to work. She had an ulterior motivation. Mandy's plan was to go to the house, befriend Amanda and get the information that Maggie had requested. Amanda finished the sandwiches and started to take them to Harriet and her escaping clan. Mandy saw this as an opportunity to bond with Amanda by showing what a hard worker she was and said, "I can do that, ma'am."

Then Mandy picked up the large serving plate with the sandwiches on it and carried it to the well where the other ex-slaves were congregating. Harriet looked at Mandy and asked, "Child, what you dewn in the house?"

Mandy replied by saying, "Just help'n out."

Then Mandy returned to the house. Mandy's illusion of a grateful hard-working woman fooled everyone, even Harriet. Mandy returned to the kitchen and when she entered Amanda said, "Thank you Mandy. That was very nice of you."

Mandy replied, "No problem, ma'am. Can I helps with the dishes?"

Amanda was tired and welcomed the help. She said, "Sure Mandy, and thank you."

Mandy started washing dishes and said, "You know, this is very nice of you and your husband. How long y'all been help'n runaways like us?"

Amanda replied, "Ohh, only a few years."

Mandy then said, "My brother ran away with Harriet two years ago. He was sa'pose to come back fo' me. I'z all the family he gotz. Our brother an' sister were sold and we was taken from our folks when we was little. I fear he may be dead. Dat the only reason he would not get word to me let'n me know where he is."

Amanda felt bad for all the southern migrants. She knew that they had a hard life and a long journey ahead of them.

Curiously she asked, "What's your brother's name?"

Mandy could tell by the way Amanda asked that she was feeling sympathetic. She continued to play on Amanda's emotions by saying in a sad state, "Samuel."

That name went around in Amanda's mind over and over when Mandy said it. Samuel had left a very strong impression with the Manleys. He won Quincy over with his hard work and Amanda truly loved Kora. Quincy and Amanda knew that Samuel had been accused of killing the slave catcher and they believed that he had done it. However, they understood why he did it and left. They wished they could find him again just to know that him and his wife and son were alright.

When Amanda heard Mandy say Samuel's name, she calmly said, "I know your brother."

Mandy looked at her and said, "You do?"

Amanda said, "Yes, he and his wife lived here for about a year. I delivered their son two summers ago."

Mandy enthusiastically asked, "They have a son?"

Amanda replied, "Yes. His name is Samuel Freeman Jr."

Mandy then asked the question she originally came to the house to ask. She stopped washing the dishes and looked Amanda in her eyes, and with excitement in her voice she asked, "Do you know where they is now?"

Amanda was torn. She knew that she should not tell Mandy what she knew because Mandy would most likely leave the group to look for her brother. Amanda also felt bad because she knew that slaves were often separated from their families. She felt obligated to help Mandy find her long-lost brother. She felt that slaves should not be forced to run all the way to Canada. Amanda thought that if a slave wanted to lead a free life in northeast America, that was their God-given right. Amanda was not a leader of the Underground Railroad. She was simply a one-stop-shop. She did not understand Harriet's strict rules. Harriet understood that if a slave left the group and was caught, they would be tortured until they revealed secrets that would assist slave catchers in capturing Harriet and her runaways.

Because Amanda believed Mandy's convincing lie and did not understand Harriet's rules she said to Mandy, "One day the Marcus Hook sheriff came looking for your brother. A slave catcher was dead and Samuel and his family were gone. Quincy and I think the slave catcher tried to take Samuel back down south and Samuel killed him then left town."

Mandy put her hand over her mouth and gasped for air then asked, "So where they now?"

Amanda replied by saying, "We told the sheriff we had no idea where Samuel was. That is not true. Harriet told my husband she told Samuel if he got into any trouble to go to Philadelphia. We believe he is in South Philadelphia."

Mandy was staring at Amanda and tears started running her face. When Amanda saw Mandy crying, she was convinced that Mandy really missed her brother. Without hesitating, she gave Mandy directions to Philadelphia. "Walk to the river and follow it upstream for about two days. It will take you to South Philadelphia."

Mandy walked out of the kitchen and thanked Amanda without finishing the dishes. As she left, Amanda said, "When you find your brother, will you please tell him my husband and I understand why he did what he did and we are not upset with him?"

Mandy did not respond to Amanda. She wiped her fake tears from her face and rushed to tell Maggie her exciting news. Mandy truly loved Maggie and loved pleasing her not only sexually but also mentally. Mandy loved to give Maggie good news. She was now feeling the same way she felt when she told Maggie that Harriet was coming. Mandy found Maggie in the barn, finishing her lunch. She made eye contact with Maggie and walked to a corner in the barn.

Maggie followed Mandy to the corner and asked, "Did you find out where they is?"

Mandy smiled and while nodding her head and said, "Yes. He in South Philadelphia. It a two-day walk from here."

Maggie responded to Mandy's news by saying, "Girl, I could kiss you. Good job. We leave'n here tonight."

Mandy asked Maggie, "What about the guards?"

Maggie replied, "If they gets in my way, I'll kill them two."

Sounding surprised, Maggie said, "Kill the guards? Why you want to do that? They was slaves just like us."

Maggie angrily replied, "If they gets in my way, I'll kill em. Nothing's gon' to keep me away from Samuel and Kora."

Maggie anticipated her and Mandy leaving the group. She made sure that the two women slept near the front door of the barn.

The same evening that Amanda told Mandy where Samuel was, Maggie and Mandy left for Philadelphia. When they left the barn, they knew they had to get past the two night watch workers. Mandy was extremely concerned about the wellbeing of Harriet's young recruits. When they approached the place on the farm with nothing between them and Philadelphia except the night watchmen, Maggie took her knife out. Mandy stopped her and whispered, "How you gon' kill both of them without one getting away or screaming?"

Maggie quietly said, "I been watch'n dem fo' a night or two. Every night, one goes to the outhouse and one stays put. I kills the one that stays and wait fo' the other one."

Mandy replied by saying, "I don't like you do'n all this kill'n, Maggie."

Maggie replied to Mandy by saying, "Stay here, baby. I'll be right back."

Maggie left to find the lookouts. When she came around a large bush, she saw the two guards together. They were sleeping on the ground about fifty yards ahead of her. Maggie knew that they were sleep and decided to kill them anyway to prevent them from waking up while she and Mandy were leaving Quincy's farm. With her knife in her hand, she quietly walked toward the slumbering bodies. When Maggie was within twenty-five feet, she prepared to rush the asleep-on-the-job lookouts. Just then, she heard something step on a stick behind her.

Maggie turned around without saying a word. She stood with her knees slightly bent and her arms extended. Maggie was in her fighting stance. She heard another noise that was closer to her, but she could not see anything in the night's blackness. Maggie was getting nervous. Her palms were starting to sweat. Maggie moved her head from side to side, quickly trying to spot her follower. Finally, from behind a tree, Mandy revealed herself. When Maggie realized that it was Mandy following her, she was relieved upon first sight.

Then she got angry and said, "What you dewn here? I told you to stay back there while I secure our freedom."

Mandy replied, "I know what you said, but I am not go'n let you kill some innocent ex-slaves just cuz you feels like it."

Maggie looked over Mandy's shoulder and said, "Besides, they 'sleep anyway. Come on. We don't need to kill 'em. Let's just go to Philadelphia"

Maggie agreed and the two women left for Philadelphia. For two nights, the women traveled just as Samuel and his family had traveled two years prior. Harriet's escapees moved at night because this was the first thing that they had learned from Harriet; to move in the night undetected and rest during the day. The two ladies followed the river upstream for two days and found South Philadelphia waiting for them.

Maggie and Mandy arrived in South Philadelphia very early in the morning before sunrise on their second day of walking. The ladies were hungry. They did catch some fish the first day of their travels but they did not have any luck with the fish in the cold river the next day. They had not eaten in over twenty-four hours. When the two approached South Philadelphia, the city was still asleep. They walked from block to block looking for someone to ask where could they get a good hot meal and a nice warm bed. The ladies walked past Bartram St. and on the next block over they found

252

the Last Stop Tavern. This was the only place they noticed with any activity in it this early in the morning. They walked to the porch of the tavern and heard live music being played. They had not heard this type of music before. The music sounded alive. It had a nice, smooth, upbeat sound. The two ladies walked up the porch steps just as Donald came out of the tavern's double doors. Donald watched Maggie and Mandy come up the steps. He was intoxicated and said, "Damn, where you two big booty country-ass ladies come from?"

Maggie recognized his drunken smell and look. She knew that this man was intoxicated and she strongly desired a drink of whisky. She replied to Donald by saying, "Don't worry abouts where we from, Nigga. Take us inside and buys us some food and a drink."

Maggie then took Donald by the arm and led him back inside the tavern. Mandy followed the two inside. Once inside the smoke-filled room, Donald led the two ladies to a table and ordered drinks for the three of them. Mandy sat down and looked around the room. She observed the waitresses working in their revealing outfits and promiscuous attitudes. She also studied the band on the stage. There was a banjo player, a drummer and a piano player. The three musicians were playing at a nice up-tempo pace that set the mood for the entire room. Maggie enjoyed the atmosphere in this tavern a lot. She had never witnessed anything like it before. As she continued to observe the room, her stomach reminded her that she had not eaten in over a day.

Maggie then asked Donald, "Where can we get a good hot meal and a nice warm bed?"

Before Donald could answer, Deloris brought three glasses of whisky to the table. She placed one glass of whisky in front of each of the three people occupying the table. When she placed the drinks on the table, she glared at Mandy in an intimidating manner. Mandy and Maggie were the only women in the tavern that did not work there.

Donald drank the whisky in his shot glass, stared at Mandy and said, "Damn, woman. I got a warm bed. I can feed y'all."

Maggie drank her shot, reached out and put her hand on Donald's chin. She moved it toward her so that Donald was no longer looking at Mandy but staring at Maggie. Maggie then asked, "What yo name, Nigga?"

Donald replied, "Donald, and yours?"

Maggie took Mandy's drink and drank it. She then said, "I'm Maggie and this is Mandy. Don't talk to ha. You just deals wit' me. Now looks, Donald. We hungry and tired. Can you help us or not?"

Without taking his eyes off Maggie, Donald said, "Feed'n y'all. Find'n y'all a bed. That's a tall order fo' someone I just met. What's in it fo' me?"

Without hesitating, Maggie said, "I'm in it fo' you, Nigga. Now gets us sometin' to eats. We hungry!"

Just as Maggie made her demands to Donald, Deloris returned to the table and said, "Look, the only girls allowed in here are work'n girls. Y'all ain't work'n, so y'all gots to go!"

Mandy saw Maggie reaching for her knife and said, "We willing to work."

Deloris looked at Mandy and said, "Oh, y'all are? Y'all look like some dirty-ass country hoes. I don't know if y'alls can work here."

Mandy saw Maggie getting very agitated. She knew that her girlfriend was about to stab the woman who had no idea that she was standing next to a cold blooded killer. Mandy reached over and grabbed Deloris by the hand and pulled her away from

Maggie. Mandy then sat in her seat with Deloris standing over her, rubbed her hand and said, "Oh, we cleans up real nice."

Deloris looked down at Mandy, smiled and said, "Yeah, I bet you do."

Mandy moved Deloris away from Maggie, removing her from the danger she had no idea she was in. Mandy acted in the only way she knew how. Mandy always used her God-given beauty to influence people to get what she wanted. Deloris did not know that Mandy was only trying to move her out of harm's way. Deloris thought that Mandy was flirting with her. When Deloris responded to what she thought was Mandy's invitation to an intimate conversation, Maggie became infuriated. Just as she started to withdraw her knife, a large white woman walked in front of Maggie and said, "What the fuck you hoes dewn in my place?"

Maggie looked up and saw a large white woman standing directly in front of her. The woman was wearing a black skirt, a red blouse and black boots. This large white woman also had a revolver in her hand. Maggie saw the gun and eased her hand off of her knife. Mandy released Deloris's hand and said, "We just look'n fo' work. We been travel'n and we hungry."

The white lady then said, "Y'alls hungry, huhn? Donald, you know these hoes?"

Donald replied, "I just met them, ma'am."

The woman then asked, "Would you pay for one of them if they worked for me?"

Deloris looked at Donald when the woman asked him that question, because Donald was Deloris's best costumer.

With Deloris gazing at him, Donald replied, "Yes, ma'am."

The woman then said, "Deloris, take these girls upstairs and get them a bath. Donald, go to the Bartram Hotel and get us some breakfast."

Mandy and Maggie stood up and followed Deloris upstairs. Donald did as he was told and went to the hotel for breakfast plates from Kora's kitchen. Once upstairs, Deloris took the two women into a large bedroom with two beds in it. The room had one bed against two of the adjacent walls. There was also one dresser and one bathroom. Deloris walked into the bathroom and pointed to a wood-burning stove against the far wall in the bathroom.

She said, "Y'all can fix yo' hot water right here in the bathroom. You have to go to the kitchen to gets the water."

Maggie took the large metal basin that was on top of the stove and said, "Show me where the kitchen is."

Deloris guided Maggie to the kitchen and the two women left the room. Mandy stayed behind and started a fire in the stove. Maggie returned with the basin filled with water. She put it on top of the stove. Maggie then took the other basin on the side of the tub and left the room again. When she left this time, Mandy went into the bedroom and sat on the bed. Mandy was tired, hungry and her feet hurt. She took off her boots and lay down on her back with her bare feet on the hardwood floor. Maggie returned with more water and poured it into the tub. Maggie repeated the act several times until the tub was filled with hot bathwater.

When the bathwater was ready, Maggie said to Mandy, "Yo' bath is ready, baby."

Maggie was in the bathroom and did not hear a response from Mandy. She walked into the bedroom and saw Mandy asleep on the bed. She walked over to Mandy, gently touched her on her stomach and said, "Baby."

256

Mandy opened her eyes and Maggie repeated, "Yo' bath is ready, baby."

Mandy smiled and said, "Thank you, Maggie."

Mandy sat up and removed her blouse. She then removed her skirt and walked naked across the room and into the bathroom. Maggie also removed her clothes and entered the bathroom. Maggie brought a chair with her and sat on the side of the tub. She bathed her girlfriend just as they did back on their plantation. While Maggie bathed Mandy she said, "This is the best bath you ever gave me. It feels soooo gooood, Maggie."

When she finished her sentence she bent her knees and submerged her entire body and head in the bathwater. She stayed down for a few seconds and surfaced with soap on her face. Maggie softly wiped it off and said, "You happy as hell this morn', baby."

Mandy replied, "Ain't you happy, girl?"

Maggie said, "No. I'm hungry and I don't like you flirt'n with hoes right in front of me!"

Mandy laughed and said, "Is that what you think? I was not flirt'n with Deloris. I was try'n to gets her away from you befo' you stabbed her."

Maggie replied, "You mean you don't likes ha?"

Mandy said, "No, baby. I love you and no one else."

The two women kissed and Mandy got out of the tub. Maggie dried Mandy off and got in the tub herself.

While Mandy bathed Maggie she said, "Don't it feel good, Maggie?"

Maggie replied, "Yo' bath always feels good."

Mandy then said, "I mean, don't it feel good know'n we ain't got to deal with Charles ol' stink'n ass after we gets all nice and clean!?"

Maggie laughed and said, "Yeah that do feels good. But I do have to deal with Donald."

Mandy asked, "What you mean, Maggie?"

Maggie replied, "Donald went to get us breakfast, right?"

Mandy said, "Right."

Maggie then said, "Well we ain't gots no money. I gots to pay him back wit' sumtin'. I'm gon' fuck that Nigga so good he gon' be buy'n us breakfast, lunch and dinner every day."

Mandy didn't say anything. She just continued to bathe Maggie. While the two women bathed each other, Deloris returned to the room with the large white woman with her. The two women had the breakfast that Donald had purchased for Mandy and Maggie with them. Deloris and the other woman walked into the bathroom and saw Mandy bathing Maggie.

The white woman said, "Y'alls stop play'n wit' each other and come out here. Don't put yo' clothes on. Hurry up, I ain't gots all day!"

Maggie got out the tub and Mandy dried her off. The two naked ladies walked into the bedroom with the white woman and Deloris standing waiting for them. The white woman said, "Come here. Stand right here."

The woman motioned for the two to stand next to each other in front of herself and Deloris. Maggie and Mandy did as they were told. The woman walked back and forth in front of and behind Mandy and Maggie. She looked them up and down. She observed their small but firm breasts. She also admired their small waistlines and firm, robust hips. She studied both ladies' hourglass figures in admiration.

She then said, "My name is Gertrude. I own this place and I like what I see in y'all. If y'alls wants to work here y'alls can. But this ain't just no ordinary bar. We fucks our guests also. If y'alls think you can handle that, you can start on yo' breakfast and then get to work."

Maggie said, "I gots no problem wit the job, but I'm da only one dat will be work'n."

Maggie motioned toward Mandy, "She will just stay in here wit' me."

Gertrude angrily said, "Bitch, who you give'n orders to?"

Without hesitation, Maggie looked at Gertrude, opened her mouth and started singing. She sang, *I been on my plantation, all of my life.*

My master done beat me and made me his wife.

He always make'n me cook fo' him, love'n him and clean up after him.

All I ever dream about is run'n away to be free.

I got the blues, I got the low down plantation blues.

Ya see, all I have is my dreams and my master try'n to take that too.

Then Maggie talked the next portion to her audience. She said, "Hey gal, pick that tobacco, clean up the house, make my children some clothes, fix me sumtin' to eat."

Then she sang again, *Ohh, I got the blues. This is why I got the low down...*

Plantaaaaaation...

Bluuuuuuuuuuuuuuuuuuuuuuues.

Maggie then stopped singing and looked at Gertrude. Gertrude was quiet for a moment then said, "You two can eat now. I gots yall some clean clothes and nightwear in these boxes."

Gertrude then pointed at Maggie and said, "You needs to take care of Donald after you eat. He bought this food fo' y'all. After that, get some rest and be ready to rehearse with the band tonight."

Maggie and Mandy put on their nightgowns and ate their breakfast. Gertrude and Deloris walked out into the hall where Donald was waiting. Gertrude said to him, "Give them a few minutes to eat, then go in."

Donald nodded his head up and down indicating he understood.

Deloris looked at Gertrude and said, "I cain't believe you gon' let her girlfriend stay here fo' free."

Gertrude replied by saying, "Girl, please. Ain't noth'n free in this word. You don't need to worry about them two. I got plans for them."

Donald patiently waited several minutes outside of Maggie and Mandy's door. Soon the door opened and Maggie stepped into the doorway and said, "You ready to come in?"

Donald stood up and walked into the room. Mandy had fallen asleep in her bed. Maggie was wearing a cream-colored cotton nightgown that ended at her knees. When Donald walked into the room, Maggie walked to her bed and climbed in. She left the cover on the far side of the bed turned down to invite Donald to join her. Donald sat on the edge of the bed and took his clothes off. He then accepted his invitation and got under the covers with Maggie. Once in the bed. Donald turned and faced Maggie.

Maggie said, "I wanta thank ya fo' the breakfast. It was very good."

Donald replied, "Yeah, the Bartram is known fo' its cook'n."

Several minutes later, Mandy was awakened by Maggie's bed squeaking. Mandy turned over and observed her lover sexually satisfying Donald under the covers. Mandy watched as Maggie's covers moved in a steady, sexual, gyrating motion. After several minutes passed, Donald moaned loudly and released himself. He then moved off Maggie and the three of them fell asleep. Maggie and Donald slept until late afternoon. When they woke up Donald put on his clothes and started to leave.

Maggie got out the bed with her nightgown on and said, "Thanks again fo' breakfast."

Donald replied by saying, "Yeah, Kora's dinner is also good."

In shock, Maggie asked, "Did you say 'Kora?'"

Donald replied, "Yeah, Kora is a real good cook."

Maggie gathered her composure and asked, "Where is this Bartram Hotel?"

Donald said, "It's just on the other block. You go'n there fo' dinner?"

Maggie said, "I don't know. Maybe."

Donald left and Maggie excitedly woke Mandy up.

She said, "Wake up girl. I found her! I found Kora!"

Mandy sat up and asked, "What you mean, you found Kora?"

Maggie said, "We was eatin' her breakfast. Donald said she work at the Bartram Hotel."

Mandy then asked, "How you know it our Kora?"

Maggie then asked, "How many people you know named Kora can cook a breakfast like we had?"

Mandy replied by saying, "OK. If it is Kora, what you gon' do?"

Maggie looked at Mandy in disbelief and replied, "Kill her!"

Mandy asked, "When?"

Maggie said, "Tonight. Right after band practice."

The ladies got dressed and went downstairs. Against Maggie's wishes, Mandy discussed jobs she could do around the hotel with Madam Gertrude. Maggie rehearsed with the band. Both interactions with the Last Stop Tavern's employees went very well. The band loved Maggie and Gertrude decided Mandy could be the dishwasher. Maggie and Mandy had dinner with the band and Madam Gertrude. Everyone got along very well. They all ate, drank and laughed. All except Mandy. Mandy did not drink and she felt like she did not fit in. She quietly enjoyed her dinner and kept her eye on Maggie.

Maggie was consuming a large amount of alcohol. She was becoming intoxicated. Mandy knew that when Maggie was inebriated, she had a tendency to become violent. After dusk, Maggie and Mandy went out the back of the tavern and headed toward the Bartram Hotel. Mandy accompanied Maggie silently. She did not say a word. Maggie reeked of alcohol.

When they arrived at the hotel Mandy stopped Maggie and asked her, "Are you sure you want to do this?"

Slurring her words, Maggie replied, "Fuck yeah I want this! What the fuck wrong with you, baby? You know what this bitch put me through. You was dare too."

Mandy then said, "But it ain't Kora's fault if…"

Before Mandy could finish, Maggie put her index finger on Mandy's lips and cut her off by saying, "Shhhhhhh. You stay here, baby. I'll be right back."

With that statement, Maggie went up the porch stairs. She walked into the hotel. The hotel lobby was dark and empty. Maggie saw a lantern burning in the kitchen and heard the faint sound of dishes being washed. Maggie walked toward the kitchen. As she got closer, she also heard voices in the kitchen. Maggie recognized one of the voices. She drew her knife out of her hip holster and moved quickly into the kitchen to see if her ears deceived her. Maggie burst through the kitchen door and stood in the kitchen entrance. She was energized to see that her ears were very reliable.

Chapter Twenty
When Angels Leave

For almost three years, all that Maggie had thought of was killing Kora. Now here she was, face to face with the woman she blamed for all of her problems. Maggie stood in the kitchen entrance with her knife in her right hand and in plain view for anyone to see. Kora was in the kitchen with Samantha. Samantha was one of the new hire trainees that Kora was training to work the evening shift. Samantha was short, petite and very fair skinned. Samantha looked like Kora's sister. When Maggie burst through the door, Kora and Samantha turned around immediately. Kora could not believe her eyes. She stared at Maggie in shock. Maggie gawked back at Kora with her knife out.

After several moments with their eyes locked on each other, Maggie smiled and said, "Hey girl, remember me? Yeah, you can run but you cain't hide. I found yo' ass and now I gots to kill you!"

Samantha ran out the back door when she saw Maggie's knife. There was nothing between Kora and Maggie except forty feet of hardwood floor. Kora reached behind her to grab a knife out of the drying dishes. She did not take her eyes off Maggie. When Kora blindly reached for a knife, Maggie advanced. When she charged, she felt someone grab her from behind. It was Mandy.

Mandy took hold of Maggie and said, "This is wrong, Maggie. I'm not gon' let you do it."

Maggie turned around and freed herself from Mandy's grip.

Maggie then said, "I cain't believe you gon' stop me from kill'n this bitch! You know what I been through cuz ah ha!"

Mandy said, "It ain't ha fault. You cain't keep blame'n ha. Charles was enough! Now no mo' kill'n!"

When Samantha ran out the back, she went around to the front of the hotel and upstairs to get help for Kora. Samuel, Debbie, Wanda and Samantha came rushing into the kitchen through the front door just as Mandy told Maggie there would be no more kill'n. Samuel looked at his ex-wife and hesitated. He then proceeded over to Kora to make sure she was OK. Kora had found a knife and was ready to defend herself. Mandy led Maggie past the others and out of the hotel without saying a word. Kora put the knife down and grabbed her husband's large muscular arm. She hugged his arm and pressed her face against it.

He said to her, "You OK, baby?"

Kora did not say a word. She just clung to Samuel's arm tightly and she was shaking with fear. Samuel comforted his wife by holding her tightly.

He said, "Its OK, baby. She's gone now."

Kora let Samuel's arm go and hugged her man.

She became responsive again and said with a quivering voice, "What is she doing here, Samuel? How did she find us?"

Samuel replied, "I don't know, but she is gone now."

Everyone just stared at Kora and Samuel for a moment.

Then Wanda asked, "You two know that crazy woman?"

Samuel replied, "Yes, we know her. I want to thank all of you for coming down here with me so quickly and thank you Samantha for getting help so quickly. We should be OK now. Come on, baby. I left Junior upstairs. Let's go check on him."

A strange silence entered the kitchen while Kora and Samuel went upstairs to their bedroom. When they walked into their room, Samuel Jr. was sitting on their bed, falling asleep. Samuel picked him up and placed him under his blankets and on his pillows on the floor near the bathroom. Kora was extremely nervous. She was pacing back and forth from the doorway to the opposite wall.

With her voice still cracking, Kora repeated the question to Samuel and asked, "How, Samuel. How did she find us? I never thought we would see her again."

Kora started pacing faster and breathing harder.

Samuel tried to calm her down by saying, "Calm down, baby. I don't know how she found us, but I will protect you just as I always have."

Kora began to feel nauseous. She ran into the bathroom and vomited into the commode. Samuel went into the bathroom after his wife. He stood in the doorway and watched his wife regurgitate into the commode.

He asked her, "Are you OK, baby?"

After Kora emptied her stomach, she stood up, wiped her face off and said, "I don't need this, not now."

Confused, Samuel said, "What are you talking about? You don't need what?"

Kora snapped at her husband and said, "I don't need that bitch threatening us while I'm pregnant!"

Samuel responded by saying, "Pregnant?! Are you sure, Kora?"

Kora replied in a harsh way again by saying, "I have been pregnant before Samuel, I know what it feels like."

Samuel then asked his wife, "Do you want me to make you some tea, baby?"

Kora paused and realized how rude she was being to her husband. She felt guilty about snapping at him when he was always there for her. She walked over to Samuel and hugged him.

She then said, "That would be nice, baby. Thank you."

Samuel went downstairs to the kitchen to make his wife's tea. Kora waited for him to leave then knocked on Debbie and Wanda's door to talk to Wanda. She asked Wanda to come to her room so she could talk to her. Wanda agreed and followed Kora back to her room. Once back in her room, Kora spoke quietly so that she would not awaken Samuel Jr.

She said, "I need to talk to you, but you have to swear to me that you will not tell anyone. Not Debbie or the reverend.

Wanda replied, "OK, Kora. I will not say anything."

Then Kora said, "That crazy woman that busted into the kitchen was not so crazy. Samuel and I know her. Her name is Maggie. She is Samuel's first wife."

Kora paused and looked at Wanda to gauge her response. Wanda kept the quiet tone and asked, "She was Samuel's wife back on your plantation?"

Kora calmly responded by saying, "Yes. Her and Samuel were field hands and I was the house slave. Samuel wanted to run away but Maggie didn't want to. Maggie was terrified of our overseer. She was too afraid to leave. I, on the other hand, was protected from the horrors in the field by my master father. I was not afraid to run away. I knew Samuel a long time. I remember the first day he arrived on our farm. He was long and skinny. I was young and frail also. Performing our daily duties in the field made us grow and develop into the fine physical specimens we are today. Oh I loved that man the first time I laid eyes on him. For years I thought about making Samuel my husband. I was going to ask my master father if I could marry Samuel but I was afraid to ask. The next thing I knew, Samuel was marring Maggie. I was heartbroken. Samuel's strong desire to be free and Maggie's fear of our overseer drove a wedge between them. This is when Samuel approached me at the well late one evening. He did not say a word. He just took me in his arms and had his way with me. I have been even more in love with that man ever since we consummated our love the first time. I would follow him anywhere."

Wanda did not say a word. She sat and listened to her friend pour her heart out.

Kora continued by saying, "When we left the plantation, I did not think I would ever see any of those slaves again. I'm afraid, Wanda. What should I do? This woman has a right to be furious with me. She wants to kill me. How can I protect myself?"

The door opened and Samuel walked in with his wife's tea. Kora was grateful and Wanda went back to her own room. Kora took the tea from Samuel and thanked him. She sat on the bed next to Samuel and drank her tea. Kora was deep in thought. She did not say a word. She was concerned for her and her family's safety. She knew that Samuel would be there for her, but he could not be with her twenty-four hours a day. Kora finished her tea and lay in bed next to her husband. Her mind was still racing, thinking about her safety. She did not go to sleep for hours.

In the morning, Kora washed up and prepared Junior for another day of her working preschool lessons. Kora's husband got dressed and prepared to leave. He asked Kora if she was OK being alone with their son and, against her wishes, Kora assured him that she was. Kora headed for the kitchen with Samuel Jr.'s hand in hers. When she arrived in the kitchen, Debbie was already preparing breakfast. Junior sat at the kitchen table and watched two of the women in his life work together to serve over thirty people in less than two hours. Every morning, Kora placed fresh biscuit dough in a bowl and kneaded it. She then gave it to Junior to massage. The dough did not need it, but this kept her son occupied. After the ladies finished serving breakfast, Samuel joined his current and extended family in the kitchen like he did for every meal. The four of them usually ate, talked and laughed. This was their break and moment to relax. Wanda was always in the kitchen with them but not this morning. The thoughts of Maggie's threats the previous evening, along with Wanda's absence, left everyone in a quiet, apprehensive state.

Just as they all finished breakfast, Wanda came into the kitchen. Even Samuel Jr.'s face lit up when she entered the room.

She asked, "Y'all leave any food for me?"

Kora replied, "Sure did. It's on the stove."

Wanda fixed her plate, sat at the table and ate with everyone else. Debbie asked, "Where you been, girl? We thought you wasn't coming."

Wanda jokingly replied, "Girl, please. You know I ain't miss'n no meals."

Her friends smiled and wondered where she had been. Everyone was finishing eating as Wanda had just started, and they had to get back to work. They hesitantly got up from the table to return to work.

Wanda looked up from her plate and said, "Kora, stay a while? I don't like to eat alone."

Kora was glad that Wanda had asked her to stay. This was the first time that they had a chance to continue their conversation from the other evening. Kora and Samuel Jr.

stayed at the kitchen table with Wanda. Samuel Jr. was so quiet that the others often forgot that he was in the room and discussed topics inappropriate for children. This was about to become one of those conversations.

After Wanda finished her breakfast she said, "I thought about what you said last night. You and I both know you were wrong for stealing her man. What's done is done and we cannot undo it now because you and Samuel have a child together. Maggie has every right to be mad at you. However, you are my friend and I cannot let anything happen to you without trying to help you. Here, this is all the help you will need."

Wanda reached down in-between her skirt and hip and removed a black pistol with a wooden handle. It was the same gun that the reverend kept in the church closet. The two women were so caught up in the moment that they forgot about the three year old quietly observing their every move and listening attentively.

Kora asked, "Oh my, Wanda. Where did you get this thing from?"

Wanda replied, "Don't worry about that. You just take it."

Kora replied in a curious way by saying, "I can't take that gun. I don't even know how to use it."

Wanda picked up on Kora's tone and said, "I will teach you."

In surprise, Kora said, "You will teach me? Who taught you?"

Wanda sharply replied, "Look, you ask too many questions. Do you want to learn how to defend yourself or not?"

Kora responded, "OK, Wanda. You're right. When do we start?"

Wanda replied, "Right now. This will not take long."

Wanda held her hand out and Kora gave her back the gun. Then Wanda said, "You open it like this and put the bullets in. Close it, cock it, aim and pull the trigger. See? Easy."

Wanda was demonstrating everything she was saying with the gun in her hand. She then removed the bullets and handed the gun and bullets back to Kora.

Wanda said, "Here, you try it."

Kora successfully loaded the gun and cocked it. She placed it by her side after she had cocked it.

Kora smiled and said, "See? Easy."

Wanda laughed slightly and said, "You got it, girl."

Kora tucked the gun in her waist between her skirt and hip. She tucked her blouse in over the pistol to conceal it. She hugged Wanda, thanked her and the two women returned to work.

Back at the Last Stop Tavern, Maggie was just waking up. The night before, Mandy had removed Maggie's clothes and put her nightgown on her inebriated lover just like she had done many times before. Maggie did not feel well. She had an upset stomach and headache. Mandy was awake for a few hours thinking about Maggie and what had almost happened last night.

Maggie moaned in discomfort as she tried to get out of the bed and said, "Ohhhh, my head is killing me! I feels like I got hit by a wagon!"

Mandy replied, "You know dis is what happens when you drinks too much."

Maggie slowly walked into the bathroom and vomited into the commode. Mandy heard her girlfriend regurgitating and knew that she needed some coffee. Mandy was used to Maggie's hangovers. They were so frequent that they became the norm in their relationship.

While Maggie was still bringing up her meal from the night before, Mandy jokingly said, "Would you like some coffee to go with your Earl?"

Maggie snapped back and said, "I ain't in no mood to put up with yo' dumb ass jokes! Just get the damn coffee!"

Mandy went into the kitchen to get the coffee pot. She returned and lit the wood-burning stove in the bathroom. She put the coffee pot on top of it and waited for the coffee to brew. Within a few minutes, Mandy was pouring Maggie a fresh, hot cup of coffee. Maggie was lying on her bed holding her abdominal section. Mandy handed Maggie the coffee and pulled a chair up to Maggie's bed. Maggie sat up and sipped her coffee.

Maggie looked at Mandy and asked, "We got any milk?"

Mandy replied, "Girl, please. We ain't on no farm no mo'."

Maggie chuckled and continued to drink her black coffee. After she finished half the cup she began to feel better. Maggie sat up and put her back against her wall. She stretched her legs out over the side of the bed and continued drinking her coffee. Coffee was not something that the other slaves on the plantation had access to. Mandy and Maggie's coffee on Tom's farm was compliments of Charles.

Maggie looked at Mandy and said, "I cain't believe you stopped me from kill'n that bitch last night. Why you do dat?"

Mandy replied, "Cause I ain't in love with no killer. No mo' kill'n, Maggie."

Maggie was feeling much better and she said, "Baby, please. You know I hate the bitch! Kill'n her would make me feel so much better."

Mandy then asked, "Maggie, why do you like kill'n so much?"

Maggie replied, "Cause the world been shit'n on me since I was born. No one but you gives a fuck about me and I don't give a fuck about them either."

Mandy replied, "You know Maggie, I been think'n. We free now. Dat means ain't no masa to tell us what ta do and how ta do it. We control our lives now. I know you had a rough past. I was right dare wit' you. Now dat we free, we controls our future. Somehow I saw a better life for us as free women. I didn't think you would be ho'n and me wash'n dishes fa a live'n."

Maggie quickly replied, "Wash'n dishes? You wash'n dishes?"

Mandy sighed and said, "Maggie, is that all you heard me say?"

Maggie replied, "No, baby. I hear you. But what else we gon' do?"

Mandy replied, "I been think'n about dat. You is gon' be a singer some day. You gon' sing about all the horrible tings dat happened to you. You have a beautiful voice."

Maggie got out the bed and walked into the bathroom. She poured herself another cup of coffee and stood in the bathroom doorway looking at Mandy.

She said to Mandy, "You been think'n about a lot, haven't you?"

Mandy replied, "I guess I have been. Maggie, I want you to promise me you will stop drink'n and stop try'n ta kill everyone you don't like."

Maggie smiled and said, "Shit woman, as long as I has to fuck these sorry-ass men, I'm drink'n. As far as kill'n, well I will promise if you get us outta this fucked up life, I won't kills anyone dat ain't trying to kills me."

Mandy got up from her chair and walked over to Maggie.

She gently kissed Maggie on the lips and said, "You stink'n, baby. You needs a bath."

Mandy then walked to the large pail next to the stove. She bent down to pick it up and Maggie smacked Mandy's buttocks with a fair amount of force, *SMACK!*

Mandy dropped the bucket, jumped up, started rubbing her hip and shrieked, "Ow! What was that fo'?"

Maggie replied, "Why you wash'n dishes? I told ya I don't want ya work'n."

Mandy picked up the bucket again and walked out the bathroom with pail in hand.

While she walked she said, "Girl, please. All I do is listen to you let some man hump on you. I needs my own life, ya know!"

Mandy walked out of the room with bucket in hand. Maggie stood in the bathroom doorway watching her. To Maggie, it appeared that Mandy's hips were larger than usual. Maggie watched her lover from behind. She studied the grace in her soda-pop figure swaying back and forth in her nightgown. Maggie looked forward to Mandy's return. She could not wait for Mandy to start their daily bath.

That evening at the Bartram Hotel, Kora and the other original laborers relaxed as their trained staff took over dinner. Kora was spending quality time with her family. Debbie was taking an evening walk with Reverend Edgar Lovejoy. Wanda and Reverend Marcus Lovejoy were sitting in the hotel kitchen. The two were having a conversation at the servants' table.

The Reverend Marcus said, "Sister Wanda, I am very proud of you. You have come a long way since you first joined the church."

Wanda responded by modestly saying, "Thank you, Reverend."

The Reverend went on to say, "Yes, Lord. You have become an excellent teacher, secretary, cook and you do it all with such grace and elegance. You are one heck of a woman, Wanda."

The reverend paused and Wanda blushed. She waited for the reverend to continue but he stopped talking. Wanda was anticipating a marriage proposal from the man that she loved. Wanda knew that she was older than other single women. She wanted to get married and start her family soon. When the reverend started singing her praises, she just knew that the next sentence would be a marriage proposal. When the reverend was quiet, Wanda's temper reared its ugly face.

After several awkward moments of silence Wanda said, "If I'm all that, why ain't you ask'n me to marry you?"

The reverend just looked at Wanda with an astonished expression on his face. He did not say anything. After a few more tongue-tied seconds for the reverend, Wanda realized how unsympathetic her tone was when she allowed her anger to speak for her.

Wanda took a deep breath, placed her hands on the reverend's hands and said, "Look Marcus, I know you are concerned about getting married so soon after your late wife died. You need to realize you cannot control love. We cannot pick and choose when and who we fall in love with. I truly believe God has a plan for us. Since we have met we have both embellished each other's lives. Now, I know you're afraid. I am too, but we need to overcome that fear and move to the next chapter of our lives as husband and wife."

The reverend was quiet again and Wanda began to get frustrated from his lack of communication. Despite her frustration, Wanda waited patiently.

Just as Wanda's patience grew thin, the reverend took Wanda's hand and said, "Wanda, everything you just said is correct. I could not agree with you more. Unfortunately, I am not ready to remarry yet. I may be ready soon, I do not know. I do look forward to working with and spending time with you."

Wanda replied, "Reverend you know I care for you deeply. If you want me to wait, I understand and I will wait."

The reverend replied, "Thank you for being so understanding."

Wanda quickly replied in her usual sassy tone and said, "Just don't keep me waiting too long. I do have other options, ya know!"

The reverend laughed and pulled Wanda toward him. He said, "Woman, please. You ain't going nowhere!"

The two kissed and laughed and continued to enjoy the evening together in the kitchen. Upstairs, in Samuel and Kora's room, Samuel was on the floor playing with his son while Kora mended his torn overalls. All of a sudden, Kora got up and went into the bathroom to vomit. Samuel watched her through the bathroom doorway. When Kora came out of the bathroom, she stopped in front of the bed and stood there for a moment. Samuel walked up behind his wife and hugged her. When he hugged Kora, he felt her pistol on her side. He pulled the bottom of his wife's blouse from in-between the top of her skirt and Kora's hip. Samuel then seized the gun.

With gun in hand Samuel said, "Kora, what is this?"

Kora replied, "It's a gun, Samuel."

Samuel replied, "I know it's a gun. Why do you have it?"

Kora responded by saying, "I have it because a crazy woman wants to kill me. I need to protect myself."

Samuel angrily said, "I can protect you."

Kora responded to her husband by saying, "You are not with me twenty-four hours a day. The gun is."

Samuel then said, "I don't want our son around no gun!"

Kora was getting agitated. She was very irritable and did not feel like arguing.

She said to Samuel, "Oh, Samuel. I keep that thing away from junior. Hell, he never even saw the damn thing until you started acting a fool just now! Now give me my gun back!"

Samuel then asked, "Where did you get this thing, anyway?"

Kora responded by saying, "Don't worry about all that, just give it back to me."

Kora held her stomach and sat on the bed. Samuel immediately sat next to his wife and put the gun on the floor in front of them.

He held Kora and asked her, "Baby, you OK?"

Kora dove off the bed, onto the floor, and grabbed the gun.

Samuel Jr. laughed and said, "Mommy tricked you, Daddy."

Samuel Jr. then ran over to his mother and tried to take the pistol.

Kora held it in her other hand and said, "No, baby. You cannot play with this. It is for adults only, understand?"

Samuel Jr. sadly replied, "Yes mommy."

Kora then stood up and put her gun back where her husband had removed it from. She then held her hand out for her son to take.

She said to Samuel Jr., "Come on, Junior. Let's go downstairs to the kitchen."

While Kora and her son walked out of the room, Samuel sat on the bed observing his fearful wife. He watched Kora and his son exit the room and lay on the bed with his hand under his head.

Kora and Samuel Jr. entered the kitchen with Wanda and Reverend Marcus still sitting at the table. Kora let Junior's hand go so he could say hello to Wanda and Reverend Marcus.

She walked to the stove to put some tea on. Junior ran over to the table to say hi to his other caretakers.

Junior happily said, "Hi, Wanda. Hi, Reverend."

Wanda held her arms out to hug Samuel Jr. Wanda hugged him and put Junior on her lap.

She then said to Junior, "Why, hello Little Samuel. How are you today?"

Samuel Jr. replied, "Fine. Guess what? Mommy has a gun."

The reverend intensely looked at Kora's son and said, "What did you say Samuel?"

Before Samuel could say anything, Kora walked over, took Samuel Jr.'s hand and said, "Shut up, Samuel!"

The reverend looked at Kora and said, "Kora, we all heard your son say you had a gun. That boy is too innocent to lie. So now the question is, why do you think you need a gun?"

Kora responded to the reverend by saying, "I don't have a gun..."

All of a sudden, Junior grabbed the bottom of his mother's blouse and exposed the handle of the reverend's pistol.

Junior laughed and said, "Here it is, Mommy."

The reverend recognized the handle on the gun and said, "Wait, is that my pistol you have?"

Kora realized that Wanda must have taken the reverend's pistol.

279

She covered the pistol handle with her hand and said, "No, no it is not. Now, come on Junior. We got to go."

The reverend stood up and said, "Kora, please give me the gun. Whatever it is that is bothering you, I will help you. You don't need a gun. "

While Kora looked at the reverend, she thought about her son seeing the pistol. She also thought about her husband's disapproval. After careful consideration, Kora decided that the gun was not worth all of the trouble that it was causing. She handed the gun to the reverend.

The reverend said, "Thank you, Kora. Now can you please tell me why you need a pistol?"

Kora said, "Alright, Reverend. Let me take Junior upstairs and I will come back and tell you."

She left the kitchen with Junior's hand in hers.

The reverend immediately looked at Wanda and said, "You have some explaining to do. Only two of us knew about this gun. So, you either told someone else, or you took it yourself. Which is it?"

Wanda confessed and said, "I took the pistol because I thought Kora needed it. I know it was wrong, but I wanted to help my friend protect herself."

The reverend then asked, "Protect her from whom?"

Wanda replied, "I will let her tell you that when she gets back."

Kora entered her family's room and found Samuel on the bed, asleep.

She woke him up and said, "I need you to watch Samuel Jr. for a few minutes while I go back into the kitchen to wrap up some things with Wanda and the reverend."

Samuel helped his son remove his clothes and put him to bed. Kora returned to the kitchen to face the reverend. Kora entered the kitchen and sat at the table with Wanda and the reverend.

She looked at the reverend and said, "I am sorry I accepted the gun. I know I made a mistake taking it. It has caused more turmoil in my life than it is worth. I thought it would give me peace of mind, but it has not. I have upset my husband and sent the wrong message to our son. I am glad that Samuel Jr. made me realize how foolish I was acting."

The reverend listened to Kora and replied, "Kora, why do you think you need a gun? What are you afraid of? You have nothing but friends here."

Kora took a deep breath and decided to confide in the reverend. She knew she should have told him a while ago about Maggie finding her, but she was ashamed.

In her embarrassed state she said, "Reverend, I have a very large problem. On my plantation, I ran away with another woman's husband. See, Samuel was married to Maggie. Samuel wanted to leave and Maggie did not. I wanted to run away also. So, Samuel and I left together. I thought I was leaving all my problems back on the plantation. Now, my past has caught up with me. Samuel's first wife Maggie is here and she has confronted me. She wants me dead. I thought I needed the pistol to protect myself. What should I do, Reverend? This woman wants me dead and she has every right to be upset with me."

Reverend Marcus thought for a moment.

He then said, "You are right, Kora. That is a big problem. Now that you know what you did was wrong, you need closure. You need to let Maggie know you are sorry."

Kora responded by saying, "I can't do that, Reverend. Maggie will kill me."

The reverend responded by saying, "I didn't say you had to be the one to tell her."

Kora then responded by saying, "I don't even know where to find her."

The reverend suggested, "Ask around. She shouldn't be hard to find."

Kora got up from the table and said, "OK, Reverend. I will try to find her and bring some closure to that part of my life. Right now I have an upset husband and confused son to deal with. Goodnight, you two."

Both the reverend and Wanda said, "Goodnight, Kora."

Kora returned to her family. When she entered the room Junior was asleep on the floor. Her husband was lying in the bed, in his thinking position, on his back with his hand under his head. Kora got undressed and climbed into bed. Once in bed, she rubbed Samuel's forehead from the front to the back of his thick, kinky hair.

She kissed Samuel and said, "I'm sorry for acting so foolish, Samuel. You were right. I never should have taken that gun."

Kora waited for Samuel to respond. He just lay in bed, motionless. Kora started rubbing Samuel's chest. Samuel stopped her by gently moving his wife's hand off of him.

Kora looked at Samuel and said, "Don't be move'n my hand off you, Samuel Freeman."

Samuel replied, "Kora please, I'm tired."

Kora sat up and removed her nightgown. She sat next to her husband with no clothes on.

With her breasts staring Samuel in his face, Kora said, "I know you ain't too tired for some make-up love'n."

Kora then straddled Samuel and softly kissed him.

She then said, "Yeah, you know you like it when I'm wrong."

While Kora said this, she was massaging Samuel's penis under the covers. She could feel her husband getting aroused. She knew that she was about to be forgiven. The two made love and fell asleep in each other's arms. All was forgiven and once again Samuel and Kora demonstrated how love can conquer any problem.

The next few days went by at a normal pace. Kora and her staff enjoyed their new working hours and Wanda and Debbie were becoming excellent teachers. Samuel enjoyed the peacefulness he found in his handyman chores. Samuel reported to Helen every morning to give a status report on the previous day's work and to obtain his assignments for the current day. One day, Helen mentioned to Samuel that the hotel needed a new front porch. Samuel agreed. Helen asked Samuel to come up with a plan to repair the porch without inconveniencing the customers. This was a difficult task because the hotel only had one entrance, in the front. The hotel had two very large doors for an entrance. Samuel decided to keep one door in use and repair the porch area in front of the other door. Once he completed the repair on the portion of porch in front of one unused door, he started to repair the other side. Samuel's repairs on the porch took several days. The porch was the only project he worked on all day every day. The day he completed the porch repairs, Samuel sat on the unoccupied section of the porch and admired his work as the dinner crowd entered the hotel. It was a cool, chilly evening, but Samuel had a jacket on and he was sipping hot tea that Kora had made for him. As he relaxed, he saw a familiar face entering the hotel. It was Donald.

When Donald noticed Samuel on the porch he walked over to him and said, "Hey man, where you been?"

Samuel replied, "Right here. How you been, man?"

Donald responded by saying, "I been good. Work'n hard, try'n ta stay out a trouble."

Samuel did not really feel like talking to Donald. He had no respect for Donald because he knew Donald had family in the south and he was up north living like a single man while his wife and children were still slaves. Samuel didn't understand how any man could call himself a man under those circumstances.

Samuel did ask Donald, "So, what brings you to the Bartram?"

Donald quickly replied, "Dinner plates. I need some of Kora's fine meals. See, I got this lovely lady back at the Last Stop Tavern. I want to surprise her with some real good food and flowers."

Samuel replied by saying, "Well, you in the right spot. Kora has the best meal in town."

Donald then said, "Man, you don't have to tell me twice. I better get inside and get my plates."

Samuel replied, "Alright man, I'll see you later."

Donald went inside and returned fifteen minutes later with two dinner plates wrapped up in paper bags. He also had a dozen roses that he had purchased inside the hotel lobby.

As Donald left, he looked at Samuel and said, "You know, you should come by the tavern some time. Maggie's singing has really brought the people in. I mean the tavern was jump'n before, but not like this."

Samuel looked up at Donald and said, "Did you say 'Maggie?'"

Donald replied, "Yeah man, Maggie. She this new gal in town."

Samuel then asked, "What she look like?"

Donald replied, "Short, dark-skinned with a big ass! You think you know her?"

Samuel replied, "I don't know. Maybe. I think I will come to the tavern to see if I do. When is the next show?"

Donald replied, "In about an hour."

Samuel then said, "Do you mind if I come with you now? I want to see if she is who I think she is before she goes on stage."

Donald replied, "Sure, man. Just remember she is with me."

Samuel left the porch and walked to the tavern with Donald. Samuel despised The Last Stop Tavern. It was smoky and he did not like the crowd or the prostitutes. He was anxious to see if this was his ex-wife Maggie singing at the tavern. He knew it probably was and he also knew he could talk to Maggie to bring some closure to the marriage and hopefully convince Maggie to leave Kora alone. The two men walked into the tavern. The tavern was just as Samuel remembered it. Smoky with loud, obnoxious people. As the men walked through the crowd to the stairs, Donald stopped and greeted several people. To Samuel it seemed like Donald knew everyone in the tavern and he had to stop and talk to everyone he knew. After several minutes of salutations to several people Donald finally made it to the stairs and walked up. Donald was about to knock on Maggie and Mandy's door when Samuel said, "Look, Donald. I'll stay back here and you go inside. Tell Maggie to come out of her room to meet a fan of hers."

Donald said, "OK, man. I'll do that for you, but remember, she is with me."

Samuel laughed to himself and replied, "Don't worry, man. I ain't after yo' woman."

Samuel walked back to the stairs and went halfway down them so he was out of sight.

Donald knocked on Maggie's door and Mandy answered. She greeted Donald by saying, "Hello, Donald. Come on in."

Donald walked in and walked to Maggie in the middle of the room. He handed her the flowers and put his bag on the table.

Maggie said, "Thank you for the flowers, Donald. I haven't seen you in a while, where you been?"

Donald replied, "Working."

Mandy interrupted the two and said, "I can put these lovely flowers in some water."

Mandy walked over to Maggie to get the flowers and left the room. Mandy left the room and headed for the stairs. She was going downstairs to get a vase that she had seen on one of the tables. Samuel heard her coming and he thought it was Maggie. He walked to the top of the steps and put himself in plain view of Mandy instead of Maggie. Mandy's jaw dropped when she saw Samuel.

She said, "Samuel, what you dewn here, Samuel?"

Samuel replied, "I came to talk to Maggie."

Mandy then asked, "About what?"

Samuel replied, "Relax, Mandy. I ain't trying to get her back. I just want to talk to her."

Mandy looked at Samuel for a moment and thought about what he said. She realized that Maggie loved her and that she should trust Maggie. She went downstairs without saying anything else to Samuel. Mandy stayed in the kitchen and waited for Maggie's show to start.

Back in the room, Maggie asked, "What else you got there, Donald. What's in the bag?"

Donald replied, "Dinner for the three of us."

Maggie walked over to Donald to show her gratitude and said, "Ahh, dinner, flowers, you sure know how to treat a girl."

She put her arms around him and kissed him.

Donald kissed her back and said, "We got time for this after yo' show tonight. Right now I'm hungry. Also, you have a fan outside that wants to meet you."

Maggie walked to the door and opened it. She saw her ex-husband standing in the hallway. She could not hide the joy that she felt as her face lit up when she saw Samuel. She quickly composed herself and closed the door.

She turned to Donald and said, "Donald, this is an ol' friend of mine. You mind leave'n us alone for a little while? We need to catch up."

Donald replied, "Hell yeah I mind. Shit, I'm hungry and y'all can catch up with me in the room."

Maggie was getting frustrated with Donald.

She said to him, "Donald! Get out! I will talk to you later."

Angrily, Donald left the room and Samuel was alone with Maggie for the first time in four years. As her door closed, Maggie stared at Samuel in silence. Suddenly, she had memories of making love to Samuel. She remembered Samuel helping her get over her alcoholism. She remembered Samuel's arrival and Charles's departure. She realized that, after everything she had been through, she still loved this man dearly.

Maggie composed herself and said, "What you dewn here, Samuel?"

Samuel replied, "I came to see you to tell you how sorry I am."

Maggie's hardened demeanor returned and she said, "Nigga, please. You don't owe me no apology. You made yo' choice."

Samuel then said, "Look Maggie, I left you because I had to leave. I could not have survived on that plantation too much longer. I knew I was reaching my breaking point and feared I would do something stupid like kill Charles."

Maggie looked at Samuel and said, "I'll be damn. She even got you talk'n like ha."

Samuel asked, "What? What are you talking about?"

Mocking Samuel, Maggie said, "*What? What are you talking about?* Nigga please! You sound whiter than yo' man-steal'n wife and she half white! What's yo' excuse?"

Samuel responded to Maggie by saying, "I went to school and learned how to read, write and count. We also speak proper English now. You should try it. The church has classes every evening."

Maggie grew more aggravated and said, "Motherfucker, you have lost your mind! I ain't go'n to no school'n!"

Samuel walked within six inches of Maggie.

He took her hands and said, "You have so much anger. So much hostility. You must have went through a lot after I left."

Maggie broke down and started crying.

While weeping, she said, "You have no idea what happened after you left. My life was a living hell. Charles made me his wife. He made me cook fo' him and give him love'n every night. At first, I was miserable. I wanted to die. Then Mandy and I grew very close. She has been there for me. She understands me. After a while, I stopped being afraid of leave'n. Then Ol' Man Eli told Mandy Harriet was come'n. We left wit' her and Amanda tol' Mandy where you may be. So, here we are. Now what, Samuel?"

Samuel asked Maggie, "Why did you come looking for us, Maggie?"

Maggie replied, "To kill Kora!"

Samuel pushed Maggie onto the bed with force and angrily said, "Now Maggie, you know I cain't allow that!"

Maggie removed her knife from her waist and slashed at Samuel. Samuel moved and grabbed her hand with the knife in it. He slammed Maggie's arm over her head and against the wall. Maggie's hand hit the wall with extreme force. Her hand opened and the knife fell out. Samuel secured his large hand on Maggie's petite neck. He applied pressure to cut off the air to her brain.

Samuel put his face right next to Maggie's and very firmly said, "If you ever think about hurting my family, I'll kill you and yo' girlfriend!"

Then, Samuel let Maggie go, took the knife and left the room. Donald and Mandy saw Samuel leave the tavern. They went upstairs and found Maggie lying on her bed, crying profusely. Donald immediately moved to Maggie's side and attempted to comfort her. Maggie just cried out for Mandy. Mandy came to her side. Donald stepped back, and watched as Mandy held Maggie.

He then asked, "What did Samuel do to you?"

Maggie knew that Donald had a gun. In her angry mindset, she wanted revenge.

She said to Donald, "Samuel tried to have his way with me! When I said no, he started choking me! I begged him to stop and he did, then he left."

Donald was infuriated. He thought that Samuel had used him to get to Maggie. He left the room and went to his house to get his pistol. He then headed for the Bartram.

Samuel made it back to the hotel and went into his family's room. He found Kora sitting on the bed reading to Samuel Jr.

Kora looked up and said, "You missed dinner. Where you been?"

Samuel replied, "I ran into Donald. He has been seeing Maggie. He took me to her and I made sure she will not ever mess with us again."

Kora responded by asking, "You did not hurt her did you?"

Samuel replied to his wife and said, "No, I just made sure she knows not to even think about mess'n with my family."

Just as Samuel finished his sentence, he heard his name being called from downstairs outside his window. Samuel looked out the window and saw Donald standing in the middle of the street calling his name. Samuel was looking forward to hurting Donald. He did not like Donald and he was also upset with Donald for contributing to his ex-wife's prostitution activities.

Kora also heard Donald and asked, "Samuel, why is that man calling your name?"

Samuel replied, "That is Donald. He is probably upset with me for putting my hands on Maggie."

Kora replied, "Samuel, you said you didn't hurt her."

Samuel replied, "I didn't, I just choked her so she would get my point. I let her go."

Then Samuel walked toward the door. Kora asked, "Where are you going?"

Samuel replied, "I am going to kick Donald's ass! That dumb-ass nigga thinks he is defending his woman. He had no idea she is my ex-wife!"

Kora demanded that Samuel not go by saying, "No! Samuel, I don't like all this violence! Just stay here with me."

Donald was still downstairs, yelling Samuel's name. Samuel opened the door and left. Junior tried to go with his father. Kora held him as Samuel closed the door. Donald's yelling attracted everyone's attention. When Samuel walked onto the front porch of the hotel, the Reverend Marcus Lovejoy and Wanda were sitting on the porch looking at Donald standing in the middle of the street.

When the reverend saw Samuel he said, "Samuel, I know you are not going to respond to this fool."

Samuel said, "Relax, Reverend. This will not take long."

Samuel walked off the porch toward Donald and Donald pulled out his pistol. Samuel saw the gun and froze. Then there was a loud gunshot and Donald fell to the dirt street dead. Samuel looked in the direction of the gunshot. It came from where Marcus and Wanda were sitting. He saw Reverend Marcus Lovejoy sitting in his chair with his smoking pistol still drawn. Wanda screamed and ran into the street to see if Donald was alive. Samuel stood a few feet off the porch, in shock. Wanda kneeled down and checked for a pulse.

She looked up and said, "He's dead, Marcus."

When Samuel heard Wanda announce Donald's death, he came back to reality. Samuel walked over to the reverend and took the pistol. Kora came running downstairs with Junior in her arms.

She asked, "What happened, Samuel?"

Samuel walked past her and went into the kitchen. He went out the back and temporarily hid the pistol within the firewood bin. When he returned, he noticed a crowd gathering. The police were nowhere in sight. Samuel and his family returned to their room to get away from all the chaos.

As soon as they walked into the room, Kora asked, "Are you OK, Samuel?"

Samuel replied, "I'm fine. Everything happened so fast, but I'm OK."

Then Kora asked, "What happened Samuel?"

Samuel replied, "Donald pulled a gun on me and the reverend shot him."

Kora then asked, "Where is the reverend now?"

Samuel replied, "I don't know. I took his pistol and hid it. When I returned, I came up here to check on you two. I am going back downstairs to check on the reverend now."

Samuel returned to the front porch only to find the reverend and Wanda gone. The police and undertaker were finally on the scene. Samuel looked in the kitchen for his savior and girlfriend. He did not see either one of them.

Samuel returned to his family's room and said, "I didn't see them. I hope they're alright."

Kora said, "They must have gone back to the church."

Samuel replied, "You're right. I'll go check on the reverend tomorrow."

In front of the hotel, the police were stopping everyone and asking them if they saw who had shot the victim. All of the witnesses were residents of South Philly. The majority of them attended The African Methodist Episcopal Church of Our Lord. Everyone had heard Donald calling Samuel to a fight. Everyone had seen Donald pull out his pistol. Everyone also saw the reverend shoot Samuel's would-be assailant. Yet no one said anything to the police.

Back at the Last Stop Tavern, Maggie was recovering from Samuel's aggressive warning. Mandy was still consoling Maggie.

As Maggie returned to her senses, Mandy asked, "Hey girl, you feel'n better?"

Maggie replied, "Yeah. I'm OK. I need a drink."

Mandy then said, "You know you gon' get that man hurt."

Maggie asked, "Girl, what you talk'n 'bout?"

Mandy replied, "I'm talk'n 'bout Donald. You sent him after Samuel. Samuel will hurt that man, you know he ain't no match fa Samuel."

Maggie smiled and said, "Don't underestimate Donald, baby. He can hold his own."

Mandy just looked at Maggie and said, "It's almost time fa you ta sing. You need to eat sumtin' first. All we got is Kora's dinners. You ain't eat'n that, is ya?"

Maggie replied, "Shiiiit, the hell I ain't. I'm starving and that little bitch can cook. We ain't waste'n all this good food."

Mandy then sarcastically said, "You better save a piece of meat to put on the black eye Samuel gon' give yo' man."

Maggie snapped back and said, "I have told you befo', he ain't my man! Besides, he'll be alright."

The two ladies stopped talking and enjoyed Kora's cooking.

The next morning, everyone at the Bartram Hotel awakened and proceeded with their normal routine. Samuel gathered firewood, Kora, Samuel Jr. and Debbie fed the hotel breakfast and no one had seen Wanda since the night before. When Samuel went to the firewood bin, he noticed that the pistol he had hidden was gone. With the gun gone and Marcus disappearing last night, Samuel figured that Marcus had it. The workers' break came and they all met in the kitchen to enjoy a meal and good company. After everyone sat down and began eating, Wanda came through the door. Wanda fixed herself a plate and took her seat at the table. She acted as if nothing was wrong and, as far as she was concerned, there wasn't anything wrong. Everyone stared at her when she sat down.

Wanda asked, "What the hell y'all look'n at?"

Debbie replied, "We look'n at you. Where you been, girl? We were get'n worried."

Wanda then said, "I told y'all I ain't miss'n no meals. I don't have to tell y'all where I'm at twenty-four seven, do I?"

Debbie snidely said, "Don't be get'n mad at us cuz you was wit' yo' man all night. I would think you would come home in a better mood."

Wanda angrily said, "I know you didn't just put my business in the street! That's why I just saw yo' man walk'n back to the church. He sure had a big smile on his face. So, when I'm away, I guess you think you can play."

Annoyed, Debbie replied, "Now you know I didn't want everyone to know my man was with me last night don't you? Hell, at least I was in my own bed!"

Kora then said, "Oh Debbie relax. We already knew Reverend Marcus was with you last night."

Confused, Debbie asked, "What are you talking about, Kora?"

Kora replied, "Thin walls, remember?"

Debbie sarcastically replied, "You're just glad you heard someone else beside yourself for once."

Kora quickly responded, "You just glad you FINALLY got some!"

Everyone laughed when Kora said that, even Debbie.

Samuel interrupted the ladies' conversation by saying, "Ladies, can we please stop talking about S-E-X in front of the C-H-I-L-D?"

Samuel Jr. looked at his father and sounded out the letters that his father had said out loud.

Junior said, "Sss ek xs. Daddy, what's sex?"

Everyone looked at the three year old that had just sounded out his first word. They were all thinking that they did not learn how to read until they were grown and here this three year old child was doing what they had just learned how to do.

Samuel replied to his son by saying, "You're too young to know."

Wanda said, "That boy is too damn smart. You need to watch him."

Kora responded and said, "No I don't, we need to keep him in the classroom with us. We ain't slaves no mo'. I want him to learn everything he can."

Debbie jovially returned to the previous subject by asking Wanda, "So Wanda, since my evening was heard by everyone, tell us, how was your night."

Wanda replied, "It was fine."

Debbie asked, "That's it? It was fine? Details girl, details."

Wanda seriously said, "Look y'all, I was just there to consult my man. He was very upset. We talked about what happened. He is contemplating going back to Boston."

Samuel responded to Wanda and said, "I was about to go see him."

Wanda replied, "He would like that."

Samuel got up from the table and put his jacket on. He walked to the church on that chilly late morning. When he reached the church, Samuel walked in and found both reverends in the pulpit praying. He polite waited for them to finish, then approached the two men. Samuel walked close to Reverend Marcus Lovejoy and hugged him.

He said, "Thank you, Reverend. Thank you."

Marcus replied, "No problem, Samuel. I know you would have done the same for me."

The two men broke their embrace and Samuel said, "I hear you're thinking about going back to Boston?"

Just as Samuel finished his sentence, there was a loud bang on the church's front door and several members of the Philadelphia Police Department came through the door.

The sergeant was in the front of his five white law enforcement clan members and he said, "You ain't go'n nowhere, nigger! Nowhere but to jail! Marcus Lovejoy, you're under arrest for the murder of Donald Harris."

Samuel, Marcus and his brother Edgar watch the police charge toward them. Marcus had his gun on him, but he decided not to use it for fear of endangering his brother and

Samuel. The police approached him so fast that he did not get a chance to lose the weapon that he had defended his friend with. When the sergeant put the handcuffs on Marcus, he found the pistol. The police took him into custody and he did not resist. Marcus willingly allowed the police to put him in a police wagon outside the front of the church. Marcus was hauled off to jail while Samuel and Edgar were left in the church without their leader.

Edgar headed to the jail to try to keep an eye on his older brother while Samuel quickly returned to the hotel. Samuel went straight into the kitchen and found Kora, Debbie and Samuel Jr. preparing lunch.

Samuel anxiously said, "Kora, Reverend Marcus has been arrested!"

Kora and Debbie stopped working and Debbie asked, "What was he charged with?"

Samuel replied, "Murder!"

Kora replied, "That's ridiculous, he didn't murder anyone."

Samuel responded by saying, "We all know what happened. What I want to know is who told the police?"

Debbie then said, "We need to get down to the jail to check on him."

Kora replied by saying, "We can't just close the kitchen."

Samuel then replied by saying, "Kora's right. We all have work to do. Reverend Edgar is at the jail now. We can all go when we get off."

Kora then asked, "Who's going to tell Wanda?"

Debbie replied, "I'll tell her."

By the time that Samuel had run back to the hotel, the police were arriving at the jail. They aggressively handled Marcus, but still he did not resist. He did not want to provoke them. The police pushed him into a room and locked him in it. The room was dark and Marcus could not see own feet on the ground. He was still handcuffed. Marcus found one of the walls, leaned against it and slowly sat on the floor.

Reverend Edgar showed up at the jail soon after his brother had arrived. He asked to see his brother and the police denied having him. Edgar was prepared for their response. He anticipated it. He quietly left and headed for the hotel. Almost an hour later, several policemen entered the dark room that Marcus was in. They had lanterns and nightsticks with them. When they lit up the room with their lanterns, Marcus could see the room clearly. The room was small with a table and two chairs. It had no windows and only one door. The police picked Marcus up off the floor and put him in a chair.

Then the sergeant asked, "Did you kill Donald Harris?"

Marcus did not answer.

One of the policemen punched the handcuffed reverend in the jaw and said, "The man asked you a question, boy! ANSWER HIM!"

The blow to Marcus's jaw almost knocked him out of his seat. Marcus caught his balance and lifted his head up. Once his head came up, he tasted his own blood in his mouth. At that moment, Marcus knew that he was going to get a very bad beating. The sergeant gave Marcus a moment to get himself together after the hard right cross to his jaw.

Once Marcus was upright in his chair, the sergeant put Marcus's gun on the table said, "Alright boy, let's try this again. Did you kill Donald Harris with this pistol?"

Once again, Marcus said nothing. Once again, the right cross connected with Marcus's jaw. Marcus remained in his seat and quickly sat up. He was determined not to let the police break him. This brutal ritual went on for almost an hour. Marcus took several blows to his jaw. After an hour of constant blows to his face, with no hands accessible to defend himself, Marcus's jaw was broken and several of his teeth were knocked out of his mouth. He was getting sick from swallowing his own blood. Yet still Marcus managed to stay in his seat and lift himself up.

The sergeant said, "You are one big dumb nigger! Now I'm gon' ask you one mo' time. Did you kill Donald Harris?"

There were several seconds of silence after the sergeant asked the last question. When Marcus did not answer, the Philadelphia Police sergeant looked at one of his men who was standing over Marcus. The sergeant nodded with his head to indicate to the other police officer that it was OK to strike the victim again. This time, the officer reached back with his hand open and smacked Marcus on the back of his neck with all his force, *SMACK!* Marcus could not recover from this blow. He immediately fell to the cold concrete floor, motionless. The men on the Philadelphia Police force were experts in torturing a suspect until he confessed. The majority of the time, their victims confessed after only being in the interrogation room for a few minutes. Marcus was in the room over an hour and he did not say one word. He did not give the police the satisfaction of screaming in pain either. When Marcus refused to talk, they wanted to teach him a lesson, not kill him. The last blow that struck him in the back of his neck was not meant to be a deadly strike. After Marcus fell to the ground, the police dragged him into a jail cell and left him on the cold hard dirty floor.

When Edgar left the jail, he went back to the church. He knew that his brother needed help. Edgar began writing a letter to the general consul of the African Methodist

Episcopal church. Their headquarters were in Boston and Edgar knew that he could not wait for a response. He still followed protocol and created the letter because he knew it was what Marcus would want him to do. The letter informed the general consul that Reverend Marcus Lovejoy had been arrested. Edgar also asked for permission to use the church tithes to start a legal defense fund for Marcus. As soon as Edgar finished the letter, he headed for the hotel to see Debbie and her friends.

Edgar arrived at the hotel around five. He walked past the awaiting customers and into the kitchen. When Debbie saw her man, she stopped working and gave him a big hug. Debbie was frying chicken and had flour all over her hands and apron. When the two broke their embrace, Edgar had flour on his suit and in his hair where had Debbie grabbed him.

When they stopped hugging, Debbie asked, "So, did you see him?"

Edgar replied, "No. They wouldn't let me see him. I'm thinking about ringing the bell when everyone gets off."

Kora replied by saying, "I think that is a good idea. We all need to come together for our reverend."

Edgar responded to Kora by saying, "OK, I'm going back to the church and I'll ring the bell at 6pm sharp. I also need to see Wanda. Can one of you get her for me, please?" Debbie went upstairs to get Wanda. Debbie had already given Wanda the bad news about Marcus's arrest. Wanda was taking it well, but she was obviously upset. Debbie found Wanda and the two of them returned to the hotel kitchen.

Once in the kitchen, Wanda said, "You wanted to see me, Reverend Edgar?"

Edgar replied, "Yes, Wanda. I know that my brother kept the church offerings in the church. I just don't know where. I need the offerings to hire a lawyer for Marcus."

Wanda knew that she had been sworn to secrecy about the location of the church offerings. She also knew that Edgar was Marcus's brother and may be his best chance to get out of jail. Without hesitation, Wanda said, "The offerings are in the first room on the right when you get upstairs. Go all the way to the closet in the back of the room. On the right wall of the closet there is a panel. Lift it up, the offerings are behind the wall."

Edgar replied, "Thank you, Wanda."

Wanda did not reply to Edgar. She just left the kitchen and returned to work. When Wanda left, Edgar headed for the front door. Debbie and Kora looked at each other as if they had something else to say. Edgar noticed the look and asked, "What is it, ladies?"

Kora motioned for Debbie to say something and Debbie said, "Alright, alright. Edgar, Helen doesn't like us having guests while we are working. I need to ask you to leave out the back entrance and, in the future, please use that entrance when you come calling on me."

All of Edgar's emotions about his older brother being arrested came rushing to the front of his mind and Marcus said with authority, "Fuck Helen!"

Debbie and Kora felt the same way. They looked at Edgar as he walked toward the back doors and exited. The two ladies continued cooking dinner and Samantha entered the kitchen. Samantha took over for Kora and Debbie when they left at six. Her main responsibilities were to complete preparation of the dinner menu, clean up the kitchen, finish serving the guests and clean up the dining area.

Edgar returned to the church. He followed Wanda's precise instructions and found the offering buckets and journal ledger with no problem. Marcus had converted a lot of the

302

silver and cooper coins to gold coins to conserve space. Edgar put several of the gold coins in his pockets, made the proper journal entry, and waited for six o'clock.

When six o'clock arrived, Kora and Debbie heard the church bell ringing. They stopped working and left the kitchen out the back as Helen requested. They did not wash up and were covered with the evidence that they worked in a kitchen. Their hair scarves had flour and on them, and they were still wearing their aprons with grease stains and flour on them. Debbie and Kora left the hotel out the back and Kora was holding Samuel Jr.'s hand tightly. Once the three exited the alley, they were on Bartram St. Kora looked up the street and witnessed an abundance of African-American laborers exiting merchant stores and businesses. The church bell was still ringing. Samuel and Wanda came out of the hotel alley and joined their friends and family. The educated former slaves gathered on the street and headed toward the ringing bell. They were all members of the church and knew that the bell was a call for an emergency meeting. The rumor had spread about Reverend Marcus shooting Donald to save Samuel. Everyone knew that if they heard the alarm, it meant that the reverend was in trouble.

The Reverend Edgar continued ringing the church bell even after he viewed the church members showing up and waiting at the church's front steps for further instruction. Months ago, the Reverend Marcus Lovejoy had implemented an emergency meeting plan. He instructed his congregation that if they ever heard the bell, they were to meet at the church steps and wait for further instructions. He also informed the members that only he or the next in charge could ring the bell. Finally, he informed the members that the bell would ring for exactly fifteen minutes. Edgar started ringing the bell at six o'clock. He noticed people gathering at the front steps and he continued ringing the bell until six fifteen.

Edgar stopped ringing the bell at six fifteen. He then walked up the steps and onto the front porch in front of the awaiting congregation. It was understood by all Philadelphians that there were two sets of laws. One for white Philadelphians and one for Negroes. The unwritten Negro law would punish any Negro that took another

303

human's life. The one thing that Reverend Marcus had on his side was that he had taken the life of another Negro. This meant that there was a chance that Reverend Marcus could get a fair trial. Once Edgar walked up the porch steps, a silence fell over the crowd. They waited to hear their leader's fate and their next course of action.

Edgar looked out onto the crowd and said, "Our worst fear has come to fruition. Your reverend, Reverend Marcus Lovejoy was arrested this afternoon around lunchtime. I went down to the jail to see him and the police denied having him. Now, we need to all go down to that police station and let them know Reverend Marcus has our support. We shall walk to the jail with lanterns in hand in a peaceful manner. We will stand outside of the jail in a nonviolent, nonthreatening way."

After informing the congregation of his plan, Edgar walked off of the porch and to the back of the crowd. Dawn was setting in and the streets were getting dark. When Edgar walked with his lantern in his hand through the crowd, each individual kept their eyes on him and, as he passed them, the former slaves turned one hundred and eighty degrees to keep their eyes on Edgar. Once Edgar reached the back of the congregation, he turned around to face them and they were all facing him. Edgar's walk through the crowd made the back of the group the front and Edgar started walking toward the jail with one hundred educated Negroes following him.

Inside the early evening hours, Reverend Edgar Lovejoy led his congregation to the Philadelphia Jail House. In the darkness, what everyone saw was approximately one hundred floating lights. Citizens of South Philadelphia gathered and followed to see what these lantern-carrying Negroes were doing.

Once Edgar reached the precinct, he walked up the front steps and into the station. The congregation waited outside peacefully as instructed. The same officer that had told Edgar that his brother wasn't in the jail a few hours ago was still at the front desk.

Edgar approached the front desk and said, "Excuse me, officer. I am here to see Marcus Lovejoy."

The officer replied, "I told you once, he is not here."

Edgar politely responded by saying, "Officer, take a look out the window."

The officer looked out the window and viewed the South Philadelphia African Methodist Episcopal Church of Our Lord members.

The officer looked at Edgar from the window and asked, "Boy, just what are you trying to pull?"

Edgar responded in his calm demeanor and said, "I am not trying to pull anything. I simply wish to see Marcus Lovejoy."

The officer replied, "I told you he wasn't here. You call'n me a liar, boy?"

Edgar replied, "No, sir. I am suggesting maybe he was brought in after I checked the first time and his paperwork hasn't been filed yet. Perhaps you can check your cells?"

The officer replied, "Wait here, boy."

The officer then went into the back and found the sergeant.

He said, "Sarge, there is an uppity Negro in the lobby looking for Marcus Lovejoy."

The sergeant asked, "Did you tell him we did not have him?"

The officer replied, "Yes and he returned with a crowd of Negroes carrying lanterns. They are outside now."

The sergeant looked out of a window and witnessed the crowd himself. He then said to the officer, "I'll handle this."

The Sergeant then walked to the lobby and up to Edgar and said, "You the one looking for Marcus Lovejoy?"

Edgar replied, "Yes sir."

To the officer's surprise, the Sergeant said, "Follow me."

The Sergeant then led Edgar to his brother's jail cell. Marcus's cell row had no windows. It was dark and reeked from the other inmates' human waste. Edgar put his handkerchief over his nose and mouth to help ease the smell.

He said to the sergeant, "Can I please have a little light, Sergeant?"

The sergeant motioned for the other officer to get a lantern. When the officer returned with the oil-burning metal and glass, Edgar saw his brother's condition for the first time. Marcus was still on the floor. He was conscious but delirious with pain. Edgar took the lantern and kneeled down to get a better look at his brother. Edgar was horrified by what he saw. Marcus's jaw was broken and out of alignment. He was missing several teeth. His face was swollen from the beating that he had received a few hours ago. He was lying in a pool of blood that was coming from his mouth. It took everything Edgar had to contain himself. Edgar took a deep breath and stood up.

He looked at the sergeant and said, "Sergeant, do you mind if we go somewhere and talk?"

The sergeant and other officer led Edgar out of the cellblock row and into the room that Marcus had been beaten in. The three men entered.

Edgar said, "Sergeant, I was hoping we could talk alone."

Again, the sergeant motioned for the other officer to leave and Edgar and the sergeant were alone in the room with the lantern providing the only light. Edgar was holding the lantern up and facing the sergeant.

While looking at the sergeant through the orange flickering wick light Edger said, "Sergeant, I need you to stop beating my brother and allow a doctor to see him."

The sergeant angrily replied, "Now look here boy, I have been very accommodating with you. Now, if you think just because you have a large crowd of nig..."

Before the sergeant could finish his sentence, Marcus pulled a handful of the golden coins out of his pocket. He moved the lantern close enough to his hand so that he could feel the heat from the wick. The wick flame flickered over Edgar's hand and exposed the several golden coins in front of the sergeant. The sergeant stopped talking instantly and observed the gold coins in Marcus's hand for a moment.

When he reached for Marcus's hand, Marcus pulled it back and said, "I want one of us to be allowed to feed him three times a day. I want you to put him in a cell with a bed, a window and some fresh air."

Marcus put all but one of the coins back in his pocket.

He moved his hand with the one coin in it toward the sergeant and said, "I'll give you one golden coin a week until my brother is free. Do we have a deal?"

The sergeant knew that it would not cost him anything to do what Marcus asked. All he had to do was instruct his men to leave Marcus alone and put him in a cell upstairs with a window and bed.

307

He replied, "Yeah, we have a deal."

Edgar smiled and gave the sergeant the coin.

Edgar then said, "One of us will be back tonight to feed Marcus."

The sergeant just nodded. Edgar went outside of the police station and led the A.M.E. disciples back to the church.

Once at the church again, Edgar walked up on the porch and said, "I want to thank all of you for your support. Marcus is fine and myself and selected members of our congregation will be feeding him three times a day. Thank all of you again and I will keep you posted on Marcus's trial date."

The crowd dispersed and everyone went home. Debbie, Wanda, Kora, Samuel and Samuel Jr. all stayed at the church to talk to Edgar.

Once alone, Wanda walked onto the porch with Edgar and asked, "How is he, Edgar?"

Edgar replied, "He is OK, but he has a broken jaw."

Wanda's eyes opened wide, she took a deep breath and put her hand over her mouth.

Edgar comforted her by saying, "Relax, Wanda. A broken jaw is not that serious. It is painful, but it will heal. We got to it in time to set it. I need you ladies to make Marcus some soup three times a day until his jaw heals. In fact, I need some tonight. I am going back with a doctor."

Everyone went back to the hotel. Edgar left to find a doctor for Negroes. An hour later, Edgar and another Negro gentleman were walking through the back door of the Bartram Hotel.

Edgar walked into the kitchen with his company and said, "Hey, ladies. Soup ready?

Wanda replied, "Yeap, and who is this with you, Edgar?"

Edgar responded to Wanda's question by saying, "This is Doctor Michael Jones."

Doctor Jones was a medium-sized brown skinned man. He was about five foot seven, one hundred and fifty pounds. His hair was black and cut in a neat, conservative afro. The doctor was well dressed. He was wearing a white cotton shirt with black wool slacks and Italian cut shoes.

Wanda asked the young Doctor, "Doctor Jones, where did you go to medical school?"

Doctor Jones replied with an English accent, "Harvard."

Kora responded by saying, "I didn't know they let Negroes in Harvard."

Doctor Jones replied to Kora by saying, "There aren't many of us. I was the only one in my class."

Debbie then asked the Doctor, "You sure do talk funny. Where you learn to talk like that?"

Doctor Jones simply replied, "I am from England."

Edgar quickly interrupted Debbie and Doctor Jones' conversation by saying, "Can we get to know each other later? I want Doctor Jones to see Marcus and I want to feed him."

Debbie responded by saying, "You're right, Edgar. Wanda, is the soup ready yet?" Wanda replied, "It sure is."

Wanda handed Edgar a cooking pot with a wooden handle and a metal top on it.

Edgar said, "Thank you Wanda."

He then left with Doctor Jones to go see Marcus. Once back at the jail, Edgar had no problem seeing Marcus with Doctor Jones. The police had been instructed to let Edgar see Marcus without giving him any trouble. Marcus was coherent now. He ate his soup through a straw, but he could not finish it because he was in too much pain to eat. Doctor Jones examined Marcus and agreed that his jaw was broken, but said he could not set it until the swelling went down. For the next several days, Edgar fed Marcus three times a day. Five days after Marcus's jaw was broken, the swelling was completely gone. Edgar informed Doctor Jones that the swelling was gone and Doctor Jones returned to the jail to set Marcus's jaw.

The police allowed Doctor Jones to enter Marcus's cell with Edgar watching from the outside.

Doctor Jones said to Marcus, "This is going to hurt, but it is the only way your jaw will heal properly."

Marcus bobbed his head up and down, indicating that he understood. Doctor Jones then opened his black leather bag and removed a razor. Marcus' eyes got very large and he put his hands up as if to stop Doctor Jones.

Doctor Jones said, "Relax, Marcus. I need this razor to shave your head."

Marcus relaxed and allowed Doctor Jones to shave his head.

Doctor Jones then said, "Now comes the painful part. I need to set your jaw. Lie down on your back."

Marcus lay down, closed his eyes and clenched his fists in the sheets on his bed. Doctor Jones put one hand on each side of Marcus's face.

He then said, "OK, I will count to three and set it."

Marcus started breathing very hard.

Doctor Jones said, "One, two, three."

On three, Doctor Jones pushed Marcus's jaw very hard and straightened it out.

Marcus moaned in pain very loudly.

Doctor Jones said to Marcus, "OK, the worst is over."

He reached for the medical tape that he had placed on the side of the bed. He kept one hand on Marcus's jaw to keep it in place. He wrapped the tape around Marcus's face and head to secure his jaw in place. He then placed two wooden splints on each side of Marcus's jaw and taped them securely also.

Doctor Jones then said, "Get some rest, my friend. We have to do this once a week. I'll be back to check on you in a day or two to see how you are healing."

Doctor Jones and Edgar started to leave.

Edgar said to his brother, "I will come back tonight to get you your evening soup."

The two men walked out of the jail and went their separate ways after Edgar gave Doctor Jones a gold coin. Edgar headed to the hotel to see Debbie. It had been a long day and he was looking forward to seeing his girlfriend. Once back at the hotel, Edgar walked in through the back door and into the kitchen. Debbie and Kora were starting dinner.

Edgar walked into the kitchen and said, "Hey ladies, how is my favorite girl today?"

Debbie smiled and said, "I'm fine."

She walked over and gave Edgar a quick kiss and then continued working. Edgar sat at the table and removed his jacket. He opened a newspaper and started reading it like he always did while he waited for Debbie to get off work.

This time, Kora interrupted him and said, "I know you are not just going to sit there and act like you don't have any explaining to do."

Edgar put the paper down and replied, "What are you talking about, Kora?"

Kora responded by saying, "Don't play with us, Edgar. Tell us about Doctor Jones."

Edgar replied, "Oh, him. Well, what do you all want to know?"

Debbie then said, "Well, for starters, where did you find a Negro Doctor?"

Edgar replied to Debbie by saying, "I didn't find him, he found us. He has attended worship service a few times. He usually sat in the back away from everyone. He liked Marcus's style of preaching. One day, he approached Marcus and myself and gave the

312

church a very nice tithe. He told us if we ever need anything to just ask him. So I asked him."

Kora then said, "You know what my next question is, right?"

Edgar replied, "No, Kora. He is not married, and do not try to fix him up either."

Kora responded to Edgar with her famous smirk on her face and said, "I wasn't thinking of such a thing."

Edgar responded by saying, "Yeah, right. Please try a little harder not to think about it. The Doctor wants to be left alone."

Kora and Debbie returned to work and completed their shift. Samantha came in at six o'clock to finish dinner and clean up. Debbie, Kora, Wanda, Samuel and Samuel Jr. walked to the church with Reverend Edgar to prepare for their classes. Over the next several months, Marcus's jaw did start to heal. Thanksgiving and Christmas came and went. Marcus received a court date of April 15th, 1854. The church did reply to Edgar's letter giving them permission to use the church offerings that they were already using. The church also informed Reverend Edgar that they would be sending a lawyer from Boston to represent Reverend Marcus.

Kora and Samuel were blessed with their second child in early February. Kora gave birth to a healthy baby girl named Carrie. The winter passed and the spring rains came. Spring flowers began to bloom. Marcus's jaw was strong enough to allow him to slowly speak again. Once Marcus started speaking again, the sergeant agreed to allow Marcus up to three guests a day on his approved visiting list. Wanda started serving Marcus soup in the South Philadelphia holding cells herself in January. Doctor Jones was hopeful that Marcus could start chewing solid food by March. One spring day in March, Kora and Samuel went with Wanda to see Marcus.

Marcus was very happy to see his old friends. His face lit up with joy when Kora, Samuel and Wanda came into his view outside of his cell. This was the first time Marcus was with Samuel since the day he was arrested.

He looked at Samuel, stuck his hand through the cell bars and said slowly, "It is good to see you, old friend."

Samuel replied, "It is good to see you also, Reverend."

Samuel studied the reverend for a moment. Marcus had lost a lot of weight. He was wearing clothes that fit before the police had broken his jaw. Now those same clothes were very baggy and sagged off Marcus's body. He looked frail and weak.

Trying to make small talk, Kora said, "I understand that the church is sending you an attorney very soon."

Marcus hesitated in pain and replied, "Yes, but I do not think you will be around to see him."

In surprise, Kora asked, "Why do you say that, Reverend?"
Marcus replied, "A day before I was arrested, I received a letter from the church about your family. The letter is in the church vault. Ask Edgar to find it for you. All answers to your questions are in the letter."

Kora replied, "OK, Reverend. I'll talk to Edgar as soon as we leave here."

The reverend slowly said, "I have to ask you to leave now. I want to eat with Wanda. It was good seeing the two of you again."

Kora and Samuel both said, "Goodbye, Reverend."

As they were leaving, the reverend said, "Oh, I understand congratulations are in order. Wanda told me you two have a healthy baby girl."

Kora turned around and said, "Yes, her name is Carrie. Goodbye, Reverend."

Kora and Samuel left and headed toward the church to see Reverend Edgar. They walked into the church and found Reverend Edgar preparing for his Sunday service. The reverend was happy to see his friends. He was working so hard that it had been a few days since he had spent time with anyone.

The reverend greeted his friends by saying, "Hello Samuel and Kora. How are you two today?"

Kora replied, "We are fine, Reverend. How are you?"

Edgar replied, "I am fine. Busy, but nothing I cannot handle. What do I owe the pleasure of your visit?"

Kora said, "We were visiting Reverend Marcus for the first time today. He said there is an important letter from the church board of directors about us and he wants you to find it and give it to us."

Without hesitation, Edgar headed toward the steps to go to the church vault.

He said, "OK, wait here and I'll look for the letter."

Edgar returned in fifteen minutes with a letter in his hand.

He said, "I believe this is the letter Marcus was referring to."

He handed the letter to Kora.

Kora opened it and read it out loud, "Dear Reverend Marcus, we have received your letter of recommendation to hire Kora Freeman as an educator for our upstart Negro school, Wilberforce Institute. We are anxious to meet this great educator you speak of and her fine family. Please be advised we will send a representative to your South Philadelphia church sometime in March when the weather is better. If your family meets our qualifications, we are prepared to offer them jobs on the land we have purchased for higher education."

The three of them stood in silence while Kora slowly put the letter down.

Kora then asked Edgar, "Edgar, what can you tell us about this Wilberforce school for Negroes?"

Edgar replied, "I know the church is planning on opening an institution for teaching Negroes in Wilberforce, Ohio very soon."

Kora said, "Ohio! That's what Reverend meant when he said we would be gone before his lawyer arrived. Why should we go to Ohio when we are teaching right here?"

Edgar responded by saying, "The school the church is opening in Ohio is a institution for higher learning. Also, they may have a blacksmith position for Samuel. Just wait to talk to the church representative. According to the letter, someone from the church should be here any day now looking for your family. I will keep an eye out for them. When they come, I will let you two know. Until then, all we can do is go through our normal, everyday activities. I do not think we should tell anyone about your departure."

Kora and Samuel agreed not to say anything and returned to the hotel to feed their children. Debbie was watching the kids for her friends. Samuel went into their bedroom while Kora went into Debbie and Wanda's room to get their children. Kora returned to their room carrying Carrie. Samuel Jr. walked next to his mother. Carrie was asleep in his mother's arms. Kora put their daughter in the bottom drawer of their dresser, the same drawer that Junior used to sleep in. Samuel started getting Junior ready for bed also. Once the kids were in and on their beds, Samuel and Kora relaxed and got ready for bed themselves.

Kora observed their children falling asleep and said, "You know, Samuel, we might get a house in Wilberforce if we are lucky."

Samuel was silent.

Kora then said, "Samuel something has been on my mind. I want to bring closure to Maggie. I know I cannot ask her to forgive me for taking you from her. We were wrong and we need to do something to help her. If we decide to leave, I am going to ask Edgar to invite her and Mandy to visit the church."

Samuel looked at his wife and said, "Let's just wait to hear the church offer."

Kora observed her husband and said, "You don't seem excited about the good news at all."

Samuel replied, "I just don't like getting my hopes up. Reverend Edgar said we should go on with our everyday routine and wait to hear from them. Let's do that."

Kora replied, "OK, Samuel."

The evening grew long and Samuel and his wife fell asleep in the room that their family had outgrown. In the morning, the family awakened and Samuel started on his handyman chores. Kora went into the kitchen with her children and started on breakfast with Debbie. The two finished breakfast and everyone met in the kitchen for lunch.

317

Once everyone was seated and eating, Wanda asked, "So Kora, when and where are you all moving to?"

Kora replied, "Ohio, maybe."

Wanda said, "That is so far. We will never see you again."

Samuel joined in by saying, "We do not know if we are moving yet. We really shouldn't be talking about it."

Kora responded, "Samuel's right. We haven't heard anything yet and we don't want to get everyone's hopes up."

Debbie added, "Well, when you two do hear something, I hope it is good news."

Kora replied, "Thank you, Debbie."

Everyone finished lunch and went back to work. Debbie and Kora made lunch and dinner. After dinner, everyone went to the church to teach classes. Even Samuel had started teaching a carpentry class. Everyone entered their respective classrooms.

After class was over, Reverend Edgar entered Kora's class and said, "Sister Freeman, you have a visitor."

Kora asked, "Where are they, Reverend?"

Edgar replied, "In the kitchen, and you need to get Samuel also."

Kora found Samuel talking to another student.

She waited for him to finish talking and said, "Samuel, we have a visitor in the kitchen."

Samuel, Kora and their children went downstairs into the kitchen. There was a man in the kitchen waiting for Kora and her family. Kora recognized the man. He had been in her class for the past week. A few minutes after Kora and her family walked into the kitchen, the student that Samuel had been talking to in the hall entered the kitchen.

Samuel looked at the student and said, "Daniel, this is not a good time. Can I talk to you later?"

Daniel replied, "Samuel, I have to apologize to you and your wife. I am Deacon Daniel Roberts. The other student that was in Kora's class is Deacon Luke Johns. We are both deacons on the A.M.E. church board. Our week with you two was our observation and your interview."

Samuel and Kora looked at each other in a moment of shock.

Then Kora asked, "So, how did we do?"

Deacon Roberts replied, "The fact that we are here shows how impressed we were with both of your classroom capabilities. If we were not impressed, we would have continued on our quest for higher level educators and you two would have never known we were here."

Samuel said, "Deacon Roberts, we do not hold any grudges for being deceived. We understand your delicate selection procedure. You have not told us, why should we go with you all the way to Ohio?"

Deacon Roberts replied, "Forgive me, Samuel. We are prepared to offer you and your family a small cottage on one acre of land. Samuel, we need a blacksmith. Kora, we think you would be a fine educator. As far as salary, we can pay Kora ten dollars a week. Samuel, we cannot put you on the church payroll, but you will be the only Negro

319

blacksmith in the town. There will be an abundance of Negro families with horses needing shoes. You can also do carpentry for the church. We need workers to continue building and expanding the school. We can pay you two dollars a day for your carpentry skills. We will also provide you with a wagon and two horses."

The more Deacon Roberts talked, the more excited Kora became. It was as if all of her prayers were answered. By the time Deacon Roberts finished talking, Kora was in tears. Samuel consulted his wife by hugging her.

Samuel Jr. asked, "Why are you crying, Mommy?"

Kora answered her son.

While sobbing she said, "I'm just so happy for us, baby."

Samuel then asked Deacon Roberts, "When do we leave for Ohio, Deacon?"

Deacon Roberts replied, "Tomorrow morning."

Kora asked, "Why so soon?"

Deacon Roberts replied, "Well we still have other educators to meet and we have a long wagon ride back to Ohio."

Kora then said, "We need to get packed and we have to say goodbye to everyone."

Deacon Roberts asked, "Then I take it you are accepting our offer?"

Kora looked at Samuel and he nodded his head indicating that he was ready to accept the church's offer.

Kora then replied to the Deacon, "Yes, Deacon Roberts! Yes, we accept your offer."

Deacon Roberts then replied, "Good. Now, if you don't mind, Samuel and I have to go pick out a wagon and some horses for your family."

Kora replied, "Oh no Deacon, I don't mind at all. You two go right ahead. I'll start packing."

Samuel and Deacon Roberts left the church in search of a good wagon and some fine horses.

As soon as they left, Kora turned to Reverend Edgar and said, "Reverend Edgar, I need a favor."

Reverend Edgar said, "Sure, Kora. Anything for you."

Kora said, "I know a young lady that desperately needs to be saved. She is living a very dangerous lifestyle. Right now, she is a singer and whore at The Last Stop Tavern. You will have to wait for us to leave because she will not come to the church if she thinks I am still here. Tell her Samuel and I left and tell her we are very sorry for everything."

Edgar asked, "What's her name, Kora?"

Kora replied, "It's Maggie."

Edgar replied, "OK, Kora. I will find her as soon as you all leave."

Kora thanked Edgar and headed home with her children.

After Deacon Roberts and Samuel left, Deacon Roberts took Samuel to look at a wagon that he had his eye on. It was late and Deacon Roberts had anticipated Samuel accepting the church offer. He had a wagon and two horses picked out for Samuel already. Samuel liked the wagon and horses and the Deacon paid for the merchandise with his church allowance. Samuel hooked his new horses up to his new wagon and rode back to the hotel to help Kora pack. When Samuel entered his room, everyone was in there talking, asking questions and helping Kora pack.

Samuel looked around the room and observed all of his friends in their room to say goodbye and spend a few more precious moments with his family. Samuel observed everyone in his room and noticed a stranger. He noticed a white man with black hair in the room with everyone else. No one was talking to the outsider. The white man noticed Samuel in the doorway and approached him.

He walked up and asked, "Hi, are you Samuel?"

Samuel replied, "Yes. Who are you?"

The stranger said, "My name is not important. We need to go somewhere to talk, it's important."

The stranger walked past Samuel and out into the hall. He turned and looked at Samuel as if he expected Samuel to follow him. Samuel did and the two men walked downstairs. The stranger continued to walk through the empty lobby and exited through the front door. Samuel hesitantly followed and the two men ended up on the front porch. Once on the porch, the man stopped. Samuel looked at him, waiting for him to start talking.

The stranger said, "Samuel, I am a cop. I am not your ordinary cop. I am an ex-slave. I am half white. My plantation master is also my father. My mother is Negro. I was born with a white complexion. When my father realized I was not going to get darker he took me in his home and raised me as a son he acknowledged. He sent me to white schools and when I graduated from Temple University I became a police officer in Philadelphia. No one knows I have a Negro mother. I want to keep it that way. If you tell anyone, I will deny it. No one will believe you."

Samuel interrupted the stranger and asked, "Man, why are you telling me all this?"

The man raised his voice and said, "Don't interrupt me again! I'm trying to help you. Just listen. I remember looking out the window of our house. I remember looking at the slaves working hard. I remember seeing my mother working hard. I always felt bad because I couldn't help her. I had the good life and she had it very hard. She died while I was away at school. I am going to give you some valuable information because I am half black and I feel the need to tell you how the police found out Reverend Marcus shot Donald. Helen told the police."

Samuel studied the stranger while he was talking. He listened diligently.
After the stranger was finished, Samuel said, "That makes sense. Helen never liked Reverend Marcus. She thinks he turned us against her."

Samuel looked at the stranger and said, "Thank you."

The man left and Samuel went back inside. He went upstairs and everyone was still in their room talking, laughing and reminiscing. Samuel joined in the party. After about an hour everyone left. The Freemans' possessions were packed and they were ready to leave.

After everyone left, Samuel asked Kora, "Did you tell Helen we are leaving yet?"

Kora replied, "No, I forgot all about Helen."

Samuel said, "Don't tell her."

Kora asked, "Why not?"

Samuel replied, "I just found out it was Helen that told the police about Reverend Marcus shooting Donald."

Kora then replied, "I'm not surprised. She is still upset with us for organizing a work stoppage. She thinks Reverend Marcus Lovejoy was our leader. You're right, we shouldn't tell Helen. I will tell the girls. They need to know."

Samuel replied, "Yeah, tell the girls. We need to get some sleep. We have a long journey ahead of us tomorrow."

Samuel and Kora put their children to sleep in their small room one last time. They went to bed and made love in the room one more time. They knew others could hear them and that was their final farewell. In the morning, they loaded up the wagon and met up with Deacon Roberts and Deacon Johns. The two wagons left South Philadelphia heading west toward Ohio. With tears in her eyes, Kora turned around one last time and took one last look at the Bartram Hotel. The sun coming up provided light for the road to their new life.

THE END

Message from the author, I would like to thank you for your interest in Love Slaves. I hope you enjoyed the book. You can email me at LoveSlaves1850@gmail.com for any questions or comments. I have also registered a Face Book page for posting questions or comments. The Face Book page can be found on FaceBook.com under the name Love Slaves. I uploaded the Love Slaves book cover for the profile picture. That's how you know you have the right page. If you have a problem finding the face book page, email me and I will attempt to send the friend request to you.

Thanks again for your support.